LEIBNIZ'S 'NEW SYSTEM' AND ASSOCIATED CONTEMPORARY TEXTS

Leibniz's 'New System' and Associated Contemporary Texts

Translated and edited by

R. S. WOOLHOUSE
RICHARD FRANCKS

CLARENDON PRESS · OXFORD

OXFORD
UNIVERSITY PRESS

Great Clarendon Street, Oxford OX2 6DP

Oxford University Press is a department of the University of Oxford.
It furthers the University's objective of excellence in research, scholarship,
and education by publishing worldwide in

Oxford New York

Auckland Cape Town Dar es Salaam Hong Kong Karachi
Kuala Lumpur Madrid Melbourne Mexico City Nairobi
New Delhi Shanghai Taipei Toronto

With offices in

Argentina Austria Brazil Chile Czech Republic France Greece
Guatemala Hungary Italy Japan Poland Singapore
South Korea Switzerland Thailand Turkey Ukraine Vietnam

Oxford is a registered trade mark of Oxford University Press
in the UK and in certain other countries

Published in the United States
by Oxford University Press Inc., New York

© R. S. Woolhouse and Richard Franks 1997

The moral rights of the authors have been asserted

Database right Oxford University Press (maker)

First published 1997
First published in paperback 2006

British Library Cataloguing in Publication Data

Data available

Library of Congress Cataloging in Publication Data

Data available

Printed in Great Britain
on acid-free paper by
Biddles Ltd,
King's Lynn, Norfolk

ISBN 0–19–824846–6   978–0–19–824846–0
ISBN 0–19–824845–8 (Pbk.)   978–0–19–824845–3 (Pbk.)

1 3 5 7 9 10 8 6 4 2

ACKNOWLEDGEMENTS

We are very grateful to the following colleagues and scholars for their help on many matters of translation and scholarship: Marilyn Adams, R. M. Adams, Bernard Barr, Jonathan Bennett, James Binns, Stuart Brown, Mathilde Cheix, Stephen Dumont, J. V. Field, Gordon Finlayson, Paddy FitzPatrick, David Fowler, Denise Fowler, Roger French, Tom Graham, Sheila Gregory, Glenn Hartz, Laura Hawksworth, Marie-Anne Hintze, Michael Hoskins, Nicole Jouve-Ward, Eberhard Knobloch, Mark Kulstad, Amanda Lillie, Niall D. Martin, Christopher Megone, G. H. R. Parkinson, Christian Piller, A. W. Price, Donald Rutherford, Robert Sleigh, Jr., Tom Sorell, Clair Souter, and D. T. Whiteside.

NOTES ON CONVENTIONS

In the translations which follow, square brackets enclose our editorial additions (often section or paragraph numbers—though the breaks themselves are as in the original). Curly brackets—often in letters—enclose material which, though in a draft, was not finally included in the letter as sent.

There are three types of superscript cues: arabic numbers, lowercase letters, and capital letters. Cues of the first type are frequent, and signal editorial footnotes. Those of the second, of which there are few, are internal, and signal an author's own notes to his text; these appear at the end of the relevant text. Cues of the third type, which appear in texts F1, PB1, PB3, J9 (all by authors other than Leibniz), signal comments which Leibniz himself made at that point in his reading of the text. These appear as separate texts.

In the interests of uniformity and where little or nothing seemed to hang on it we have not always been faithful to capitalization or italicization (removing the latter from proper names, and often using quotation marks instead). Spelling of proper names has typically been stabilized and modernized—even though this has meant losing the pleasant variety of spellings of 'Leibniz'—'Leibnitz', 'Leibnits', 'Leibnit', 'Leibnis'.

Leibniz sometimes misquotes or is misquoted by his co-discussants. Divergences such as might affect the sense have been noted; others have sometimes been corrected, and sometimes left without comment.

It would appear that the date on which journals were actually available did not always coincide with the 'publication date' printed on them. (As Fontenelle (FC1, pp. 231–2) reported in 1704, the *Histoire des ouvrages des savants* was at that time only up to 1702.) So dates of articles may sometimes seem not to square with those of related letters and events.

Translations of letters are often of copies in the possession of the sender, and so not necessarily of the letters as sent. Where letters had both Old and New Style dates, we have given only the former.

SUMMARY OF CONTENTS

CONTENTS

ABBREVIATIONS

A   Deutsche Akademie der Wissenschaften (ed.), *Leibniz Sämtliche Schriften und Briefe* (Darmstadt and Leipzig, 1923–) (references are to series and volume).

AG   Roger Ariew and Daniel Garber (eds. & trans.), *G. W. Leibniz: Philosophical Essays* (Indianapolis, 1989).

Aiton   E. J. Aiton, *Leibniz: A Biography* (Bristol and Boston, 1985).

AT   Charles Adam and Paul Tannery (eds.), *Œuvres de Descartes*, 13 vols. (Paris, 1897–1913; repr. 1957–8) (references are to volume and page).

B   References by item number of the works listed in 'Articles by Leibniz, or containing references to him, in French periodicals, 1670–1716', Appendix in Barber.

Barber   W. H. Barber, *Leibniz in France from Arnauld to Voltaire: A Study in French Reactions to Leibnizianism, 1670–1760* (Oxford, 1955).

Cordemoy Gerauld de Cordemoy, *Le Discernement de l'âme et du corps* (1666), as repr. in Pierre Clair and François Girbal (eds.), *Gerauld de Cordemoy (1626–1684): Œuvres philosophiques* (Paris, 1968).

Cout   Louis Couturat, *Opuscules et fragments inédits de Leibniz* (Paris, 1903; repr. Hildesheim, 1961).

CSM   John Cottingham, Robert Stoothoff, and Dugald Murdoch (trans. and eds.), *The Philosophical Works of Descartes*, 2 vols. (Cambridge, 1985) (references are to volume and page).

D   Ludovicus Dutens, *G. G. Leibnitii . . . Opera Omnia. Nunc primum collecta . . .*, 6 vols. (Geneva, 1768) (references are to volume and page).

Desmaizeaux	Pierre Desmaizeaux, *Recueil de diverses pièces sur la philosophie* . . . , 2 vols. (1st edn., Amsterdam, 1720; 2nd edn., 1740).
E	J. E. Erdmann (ed.), *G. G. Leibnitii Opera Philosophiae Quae Extant*, 2 vols. (Berlin, 1840) (references are to volume and page).
FC1	Louis Alexandre Foucher de Careil, *Lettres et opuscules inédits* (Paris, 1854).
FC2	Louis Alexandre Foucher de Careil, *Nouvelles Lettres et opuscules inédits* (Paris, 1857).
Feder	J. G. H. Feder, *Commercii Epistolici Leibnitiana* (Hanover, 1805).
G	C. I. Gerhardt (ed.), *Philosophischen Schriften*, 7 vols. (Berlin 1875–90) (references are to volume and page).
GM	C. I. Gerhardt (ed.), *Mathematischen Schriften*, 7 vols. (Berlin and Halle, 1849–55) (references are to volume and page).
Grua	Gaston Grua (ed.), *G. W. Leibniz: Textes inédits* (Paris, 1948).
Klopp	Otto Klopp, *Die Werke von Leibniz*, 11 vols. (Hanover, 1864–84).
Latta	Robert Latta (trans. and ed.), *Leibniz: The Monadology and Other Philosophical Writings* (London, 1898).
LB	Eduard Bodemann, *Der Briefwechsel des Gottfried Wilhelm Leibniz* (Hanover, 1895; repr. Hildesheim, 1966).
LH	Eduard Bodemann, *Die Leibniz-Handschriften* (Hanover, 1889; repr. Hildesheim, 1966).
LLP	G. H. R. Parkinson (trans. and ed.), *Leibniz: Logical Papers—A Selection* (Oxford, 1966).
Loemker	Leroy L. Loemker (trans. and ed.), *Leibniz: Philosophical Papers and Letters* (2nd edn., Dordrecht, 1969).
Œuvres	*Œuvres diverses de Pierre Bayle*, 4 vols. (Rotterdam, 1727–31).
Parkinson and Morris	G. H. R. Parkinson and Mary Morris (trans. and eds.), *Leibniz: Philosophical Writings* (London, 1973).

R   References by item number of the works listed in
             Ravier.
Ravier   Emile Ravier, *Bibliographie des œuvres de Leibniz*
             (Paris, 1937).
RB   Peter Remnant and Jonathan Bennett (trans. and
             eds.), G. W. *Leibniz: New Essays on Human Under-
             standing* (Cambridge, 1981).
UL   C. Urbain and E. Levesque (eds.), *Correspondance
             de Bossuet*, 15 vols. (new edn., Paris, 1909) (refer-
             ences are to volume and page).
Watson   Richard A. Watson, *The Breakdown of Cartesian
             Metaphysics* (Atlantic Highlands, NJ, 1987).

I

Introduction

Until 1710, with the publication of his book-length *Essais de théodicée*, the ideas of the German philosopher Gottfried Wilhelm Leibniz (1646–1716) were publicly available only through his articles in learned journals such as the Latin-language *Acta eruditorum* (Leipzig, from 1682) and the French-language *Journal des savants* (Paris, from 1666),[1] *Nouvelles de la République des lettres* (Amsterdam, from 1684), *Histoire des ouvrages des savants* (Rotterdam, from 1687), and *Mémoires pour l'histoire des sciences et des beaux arts* (Trévoux, from 1701).[2] These did not always have a large European-wide audience: Barber points out that 'Leibniz seems to have assumed that an article in the *Acta* alone [which he himself helped found] was inadequate as a means of reaching the French public; his first article in the *Nouvelles de la République des lettres* is a translation of one in the *Acta*'.[3]

Up till the mid-1680s these articles show a Leibniz interested mainly in mathematics, technology, and chemistry. From that time on they begin also to reveal a Leibniz who is a dogged, ingenious critic of the physics and metaphysics which René Descartes had set up some years earlier on the basis of his notion of extended substance. The criticisms Leibniz makes hint at a radical alternative to the Cartesian metaphysics of substance. But these ideas do not make their appearance in print in anything like a developed form

---

[1] From 1684 the weekly parts of the *Journal des savants*, the official organ of the French Academy of Sciences, were gathered together into one volume (with its own volume number and pagination), and published in Amsterdam the following year.

[2] A Jesuit journal, often known as *Mémoires de Trévoux*. From 1701 to 1705 there was also a Protestant edition, 'Séconde Edition augmentée de diverses Remarques et de plusieurs Articles nouveaux', published in Amsterdam (see Gustav Dumas, *Histoire du journal de Trévoux* (Paris, 1936)).

[3] Barber, p. 29, n. 3; see pp. 29–32 for more details on these points. It is of interest to note that Leibniz wrote differently for these different journals. 'In those of Leipzig I accommodate what I say to some extent to the language of the School; in the others [Paris, Holland] I accommodate myself rather to the style of the Cartesians' (Leibniz to Remond, 26 Aug. 1714 (G 3.624)).

until about ten years later, in a short article, 'De Primae Philosophiae Emendatione, et de Notione Substantia', in the *Acta eruditorum* for 1694, and, most importantly, in a longer one, 'Système nouveau de la nature et de la communication des substances, aussi bien que de l'union qu'il y a entre l'âme et le corps', in the *Journal des savants* for 1695.

In fact, and bearing out his oft-quoted comment that 'he who knows only what I have published does not know me',[4] Leibniz's ideas were often explained or worked out and formulated in private letters; so something of them was known to some of his many correspondents throughout Europe and to the members of the intellectual circles in which they moved. The mid-1680s figures as an important time here too, for it was during this period that Leibniz composed his 'Discours de métaphysique' (1686), about which he entered into a lengthy correspondence (1686–7) with Antoine Arnauld (1612–94). The references which the published 'Système nouveau' make to this period show what an important stage it was on the road which eventually led to Leibniz's formulating his ideas for public appraisal.

Not long after its public presentation in the *Journal des savants* article of 1695, Leibniz's 'New System of the Nature of Substances' became the increasingly famous 'system of pre-established harmony between substances';[5] and, as he had hoped,[6] he was drawn into further discussion and development of his metaphysical ideas with a variety of protagonists, both in public and in private. The purpose of this volume is to present an English translation of the text of the 'Système nouveau' of 1695 and of the articles and letters which followed from its publication.

In the 'Système nouveau' Leibniz reveals (or, sometimes, merely hints at) his thoughts about the unsatisfactory nature of the Cartesian understanding of material substance as merely extended matter, about the importance of the notion of force for both physics and metaphysics, and about the connected need for the rehabilitation of the substantial forms or souls of the scholastics as principles of substantial unity. He distinguishes various types of soul, from the fully rational mind with its close relation to God down to those 'which are sunk in matter'; and he hints at the presence of these imperishable souls through the whole of matter. In the second part of the article he turns from this account of the nature of substances

---

[4] D 6. 65.   [5] See Ch. 6, n. 20.   [6] See NSI, § 1.

to one of their 'communication', specifically the union or connection between the body and the mind. Here, finding fault with
the system of occasional causes as put forward by Cartesians such
as Malebranche, he proposes at some length, and as a 'hypothesis
which is certainly possible', what he first referred to as the 'theory
of concomitance', and what before long became known as the
'system of pre-established harmony' between body and mind.

In fact, as it stands, Leibniz's 'New System' is still something of a
sketch, produced 'in order to test the water'.[7] It is, as he wrote in
the draft of a letter to Bossuet, essentially little more than an
explanation of the union between the mind and the body.[8] If 'the
public receives these meditations well', he wrote to Foucher, 'I will
be encouraged to add to them some rather unusual thoughts [about
fate and contingency; and about substantial form]'.[9] Moreover,
whether the public would, or would not, receive his ideas well was
a matter of real concern to him; he published the 'New System'
under the cloak of anonymity, because 'thoughts of this nature are
unpopular with at least nine-tenths of readers'.[10] Now the public
Leibniz chose to test out his ideas on was that constituted by the
readers of the *Journal des savants*. It is of some significance that
Leibniz should have chosen this Paris journal as his platform.

In his twenties, Leibniz, under the patronage of Baron von
Boineburg of Frankfurt, was employed as a legal adviser to the
Elector of Mainz. In 1672 von Boineburg sent him on diplomatic
business to Paris, and here, until 1676, Leibniz spent four of his
most intellectually stimulating and formative years, meeting important figures in the intellectual world such as Antoine Arnauld,
Christian Huygens, and Nicolas Malebranche. The central hub of
European intellectual life, Paris had recently seen, in 1666, the
foundation of the Académie Royale des Sciences. Leibniz cherished
the hope of remaining in Paris permanently, either as the intellectual
representative of the Elector of Mainz, or with some paid post in
the Academy. In the end, however, he had to return to Germany to
the post of Court Councillor to the Duke of Brunswick in Hanover.

In Germany Leibniz had not only access to, but also some
responsibility for, the fine libraries in Hanover and nearby Wolfenbüttel. Furthermore, his philosophical interests could to an extent

[7] Letter to Bossuet, 3 July 1694; see Ch. 2, app. C.
[8] See also letter to des Billettes, 4 Dec. 1696 (G 7. 452) (Ch. 3, app. C.).
[9] Leibniz to Foucher, 15 July 1695 (G 1. 423 f.).
[10] See also Leibniz's letter of late 1695 to Basnage de Beauval (Ch. 4, app. A).

be shared—as with Duke Johann Friedrich and Countess Sophie, the wife of Johann Friedrich's successor, Duke Ernst August. He had hopes, moreover, of persuading Johann Friedrich to create his own Academy of Sciences in Hanover. But Hanover was hardly the centre of intellectual gravity which Paris was; and, apart from longer or shorter periods in Berlin, Vienna, and Italy, Leibniz's participation in the intellectual world was dependent on visitors to Hanover, on his private correspondence, and on the exchanges provoked by his publications in the more widely read journals.

The concern of this volume, then, is the wave of intellectual activity which broke around Leibniz with the 1695 publication in a French journal of the 'New System'. Chapter 2 is concerned with the 'New System' itself and, following an account of some of the events leading up to its publication, it presents the text and one of its early drafts. The first public response was made in the same year by Simon Foucher, someone who from earlier personal correspondence had some familiarity with Leibniz's ideas, and via whom Leibniz submitted the text of the 'New System' to the *Journal des savants*. Chapter 3 contains his response, together with Leibniz's notes on it and his published reaction—what is now known as 'The First Explanation of the New System' (1696). 'Second' and 'Third Explanations' were published in other journals that same year, following a letter that Leibniz had written to Henri Basnage de Beauval, who had made some comments on his ideas (Chapter 4).

Perhaps the most famous, both then and now, of the discussions which the publication of Leibniz's original *Journal des savants* article provoked was that with Pierre Bayle (Chapter 5). The first public manifestation of this was a lengthy footnote in Bayle's *Historical and Critical Dictionary* of 1696. Leibniz's published 'Explanation of Bayle's Difficulties' (1698) was followed by another long note in Bayle's second edition of 1702, to which Leibniz again replied.

Chapter 6 contains the texts pertaining to a rather less well-known interchange, one which has at its centre an adversely critical discussion of Leibniz's 'New System' account of a pre-established harmony between body and mind published in the second edition of François Lamy's *The Knowledge of the Self* (1699). Lamy's inclination (already expressed, as Leibniz had been aware, in the first edition of his book) was for a so-called occasionalist approach to mind/body union and, at least partly because of the difficulties he thought Leibniz's system had for free will, he saw no reason to give that up. In both unpublished and published comments Leibniz raised objections to Lamy's occasionalism, and defended the 'way of pre-established harmony' against Lamy's strictures.

At various times during the early 1700s Leibniz discussed philosophy, sometimes *viva voce* and sometimes by letter, with Isaac Jaquelot, court chaplain to the French colony in Berlin. Though at first he had not done so, Jaquelot eventually (as explained in the introduction to Chapter 7) read the original 'New System' article, and he too felt it held problems for free will. These problems, which Leibniz never accepted as such, were outlined in his criticisms of Leibniz's pre-established harmony in the appendix to his *Conformity of Faith and Reason* (1704).

The exchanges concerning his 'New System' which took place between Leibniz and Damaris Masham, daughter of the English philosopher Francis Cudworth, were confined wholly to private correspondence in 1703 and 1704 (see Chapter 8). Their correspondence began when Leibniz learnt of Masham's intention to send him a copy of her father's book *The True Intellectual System of the Universe*. Prompted by Leibniz's modest reference to the discussion of his own ideas in Bayle's *Dictionary*, Masham read both what Bayle had said in the first edition about the 'New System' and Leibniz's own account in his initial *Journal des savants* article of 1695. She too, as she brings out in their subsequent correspondence, wonders how Leibniz's system leaves room for free will.[11]

Chapter 9 consists of translations of texts (mainly published) which arose out of a critique which Pierre Desmaizeaux wrote of the 'New System'. Though he had sent a copy of this to Pierre Bayle as early as 1700, it was not until 1711 that he sent part of it to Leibniz. Both it and Leibniz's prompt reply were eventually published some years later, in 1716.

[11] Leibniz's correspondence with Masham, which at first concerned her questions about *his* system, later focused on a certain aspect of her father's system—namely, his advocacy in the *True Intellectual System* of so-called plastic natures to account for the formation of animals, a formation which, it was held, could not have happened by the laws of mechanics alone. Following some dispute in the journals on this matter between Jean le Clerc and Pierre Bayle, le Clerc asked Leibniz for his opinion. Though his article 'Reflections on Vital Principles and Plastic Natures' in the *Histoire des ouvrages des savants* of May 1705, was advertised as being by 'the author of the "system of pre-established harmony"', and though it throws light on the ideas of the 'New System', this whole controversy and Leibniz's part in it are perhaps marginal to the focus of this book, and we have not included it.

About eight years after the publication of the 'Système nouveau' a Jesuit, René Joseph de Tournemine, reflected on its account of the relation between body and mind in an article he published in his own journal, *Mémoires de Trévoux* (see Chapter 10). The correspondence, or harmony, which it proposed was not, he thought, sufficient to establish an essential connection between the two. In a reply, published five years later, Leibniz concedes this point, a concession which Tournemine, responding that same year, found crucial.

Leibniz's exchange with Tournemine in 1708 is clearly part of the wave of activity initiated by the publication of the 'Système nouveau' a dozen years earlier. It should be noted, however, that as this wave flattened out, another began to mount, one which broke in 1710 with the publication of Leibniz's *Essais de théodicée*, a book which excited much interest and praise—Nicolas Remond called it 'the Venus de Medici of the intellectual world'.[12] Where the one wave ends and the other begins is not always determinate (the *Theodicy* itself refers back to the 'New System'[13]), and towards the end of the period between 1695 and 1710 Leibniz and his correspondents increasingly look forward to the *Theodicy* as much as back to the 'New System'.

[12] Remond to Leibniz, 2 Sept. 1714 (G 3. 626). This classical Greek statue (then, as now, in the Uffizi in Florence) was much admired in the seventeenth and eighteenth centuries (see Francis Haskell and Nicholas Penny, *Taste and the Antique: The Lure of Classical Sculpture 1500–1900* (New Haven and London, 1981)).

[13] G 6. 39–45, 289 f. But even after the publication of the *Theodicy* Leibniz was thinking of collecting together various of his earlier pieces, of which the 'New System' and its various progeny would undoubtedly have been some (Leibniz to Remond, 26 Aug. 1714 (G 3. 624)).

2

The 'New System of the Nature of Substances'

INTRODUCTION

Leibniz's 'New System of the Nature of Substances and their Communication, and of the Union which Exists between the Soul and the Body' was published in the *Journal des savants* of 27 June and 4 July 1695. He first thought of the system, he says in introducing it, some years earlier, when he told 'various learned men', including 'one of the greatest theologians and philosophers of our time',[1] of it. One thing he has in mind here is his composition of the 'Discourse on Metaphysics' in 1686, and the subsequent discussion of it with Antoine Arnauld (1612–94), to whom he had sent a summary. The other 'learned men' include Simon Foucher, whom Leibniz elsewhere mentions in this connection.[2]

Leibniz goes on to say that he now ventures to offer his views because some people had wanted to see them clarified. Jacques-Bénigne Bossuet (1627–1704), Bishop of Meaux and adviser to Louis XIV, was certainly one of these. Leibniz had been in correspondence with him since 1683, in connection with his (Leibniz's) attempts to effect a reconciliation between the Lutheran and Catholic churches. In the course of this Bossuet had, in 1692, prompted Leibniz to tell him something of his philosophical views.[3] Leibniz had to express regret that as yet he had no systematic account to present to Bossuet's judgement, but, in a few hundred words, he outlined something of his theory of substance and corporeal matter, particularly in so far as it related to Descartes's theory.[4] Bossuet was immediately interested and encouraging, and soon complained that he had still not had a full account.[5] In response Leibniz sent an

[1] NS1, § 1. [2] See app. A.
[3] Bossuet to Leibniz, 28 Mar. 1692 (UL 5. 89; A 1. 7, N. 144).
[4] Leibniz to Bossuet, 18 Apr. 1692 (UL 5. 130–1; A 1. 7, N. 144).
[5] Bossuet to Leibniz, 30 May 1692 (UL 5. 184–5; A 1. 7, N. 162); 27 July 1692 (UL 5. 216; A 1. 8, N. 92).

article (now lost, it seems) on the nature of matter, an article which replies to an objection which someone had put to him.[6] Again Bossuet was favourably impressed[7] — so much so that, remarking that it is not easy to make such ideas acceptable to those accustomed to Gassendi and Descartes, Leibniz noted that Bossuet's opinion seemed to be not far from his own.[8] In 1694 Bossuet was still begging Leibniz to write a full account of his doctrines in which, he believed, 'there would be many excellent things which would be of relevance to theology'.[9] Three months later Leibniz replied that 'with your usual penetration you rightly say how useful a properly established dynamics would be for theology':[10] it would explain the operation of created things, the nature of the union between body and mind, and make clear what is necessary, in addition to extension, for an understanding of material substance.

Leibniz went on to tell Bossuet that 'with a view to submitting my ideas to the public judgement I am working now to put down in writing what I think is the only intelligible explanation of the union of the soul with the body'. He had, he said, 'had this explanation for several years, and it is only a corollary of the notion that I have worked out of substance in general'. With this letter Leibniz sent an enlarged, French version[11] of an article which he had published, with the title 'On the Improvement of Metaphysics and the Notion of Substance', under the initials 'G. G. L.' (= Godfroi Guillaume Leibniz) in March 1694 in the Acta eruditorum.[12]

In fact, Leibniz almost sent Bossuet a version of the 'New System' itself. On 3 July he drafted a letter to him which was evidently to enclose a text of the 'New System', to be submitted, if Bossuet approved, to Cousin, the editor of the Journal des savants.[13] This letter and its enclosures were apparently not sent, however, and, indeed, four days later Leibniz seems to have had it in mind to send

[6] Leibniz to Bossuet, 17 Oct. 1692 (UL 5. 253; A 1. 8, N. 104).
[7] Bossuet to Leibniz, 27 Dec. 1692 (UL 5. 290; A 1. 8, N. 119).
[8] Leibniz to Bossuet, 19 Mar. 1693 (UL 5. 336–7; A 1. 9, N. 72).
[9] Bossuet to Leibniz, 12 Apr. 1694 (UL 6. 219; A 1. 10, N. 80).
[10] Leibniz to Bossuet, 2 July 1694 (see app. A).
[11] See app. B.
[12] R 133.
[13] Leibniz to Bossuet, 3 July 1694 (see app. C.). The difference of stated dates notwithstanding, that part of the '2 July' letter (see nn. 10, 66) which implicitly refers to the 'New System' was perhaps added after the 3 July composition of this abandoned letter (see editorial notes at A 1. 10, pp. 133, 137).

the 'New System' direct to Cousin himself, for he drafted a letter to this effect.[14]

In the event, Leibniz did not send this letter either; and he left the matter of publication till the next year, when, in April, he turned to Foucher as intermediary between himself and the *Journal des savants*,[15] where, only a couple of months later, the 'New System' was eventually published.

The draft of the 'New System' which Leibniz temporarily had it in mind to send to Bossuet was, he records in a postscript to his unsent letter of 3 July, in an unsatisfactory state, and really required a fair copy to be made. Perhaps this explains why it was not sent there and then. But why should Leibniz have then delayed for nine months? The answer perhaps is that he was unhappy not just with the appearance but, more seriously, with the content of his text, and set about a radical rewriting. At any rate, the five extant manuscript drafts of the 'New System' are of two distinct sorts.[16]

The first of the five, described by Bodemann as 'heavily corrected', is printed by Gerhardt, and we translate it below (NS2). Perhaps it represents the state of things as they were in July 1694 when Leibniz was thinking of sending the 'New System' to Bossuet.[17] As may be observed, essentially no more than its first paragraph survived into the published *Journal des savants* version.

The second, third, and fourth drafts are successive and extensive reworkings of this first one, and, from the very start, are much closer to the final printed version. So much is this so that Bodemann states that the fourth is what is printed by Dutens in his early edition of 1768, and L. J. Russell held that it (or, presumably, a copy) is what Leibniz sent to the *Journal des savants*.[18] The last of

---

[14] See editorial note at A 1. 10, p. 133.

[15] For details of this, see introduction to Ch. 3.

[16] As listed and described by Bodemann (LH, IV, II, 1a, 1b, 1c, 1d, 1e (pp. 61–2)).

[17] See Stuart Brown, 'Leibniz's *New System* Strategy', in R. S. Woolhouse (ed.), *Leibniz's 'New System'* (Rome, 1996). (We are indebted to Stuart Brown for helpful details concerning the publication of the 'New System'.) Perhaps, indeed, it is the very MS which Leibniz almost sent to Bossuet; Bodemann's description of it as 'heavily corrected' certainly squares with Leibniz's 3 July proposed postscript to Bossuet that he had 'thought of additions when everything had been copied'.

[18] As noted on the transcripts which L. J. Russell made of 1b, 1c, and 1d. (We are grateful for this information to Donald Rutherford of Emory University, Atlanta, Ga., where the Woodruff Library holds microfilms of these transcripts. Bodemann and Russell cannot be quite right, for, from the very start and as observed by Rutherford (in a personal communication), while the fourth draft,

the five 'New System' manuscripts is an amended copy of the fourth. It too is printed by Gerhardt, and some of its amendments, which appear to post-date the *Journal des savants* version, are recorded in our notes to NS1 below.

NS1. LEIBNIZ: 'New System of the Nature of Substances and their Communication, and of the Union which Exists between the Soul and the Body. By M. D. L.' (1695)[19]

[1] I thought of this system several years ago and communicated some of it to various learned men, and in particular to one of the greatest theologians and philosophers of our time, who, having heard about them from a person of the highest rank, had found some of my opinions quite paradoxical.[20] But after receiving my explanations, he withdrew what he had said in the most generous and admirable way possible; and, having accepted some of my points, he withdrew his censure of the others with which he did not yet agree. Since then I have continued my meditations whenever I have had the opportunity, so as to give the public only well-considered opinions; and I have also tried to answer objections raised against my essays on dynamics, which have some connection with this.[21] And now, because some notable people wanted to see my views clarified,[22] I have ventured to offer these meditations,

like the first three, begins 'Il y a déjà plusieurs années', both the *Journal des savants* version and that printed by Dutens begin 'Il y a plusieurs années'. (As to the conjecture—Rutherford, in private correspondence—that Dutens based his text on that of the *Journal des savants*, it should be noted (see nn. 45, 52) that there are differences.)

[19] 'Système nouveau de la nature et de la communication des substances, aussi bien que de l'union qu'il y a entre l'âme et le corps. Par M. D. L. [= Monsieur de Leibniz]', *Journal des savants*, no. 23 (27 June 1695), pp. 294–300; no. 24 (4 July 1695), pp. 301–6 (Amsterdam edn. vol. 23, pp. 444–62) (B 37; R 141). Where these would importantly affect the translation or the sense, we have noted differences between the original and the versions printed by Dutens (D 2. 49–56) and Erdmann (E 1. 124–8), and what appears to be a post-publication revision (= 1e; see n. 16) printed at G 4. 477–87.

[20] 1e explicitly identifies him as Antoine Arnauld.

[21] For Leibniz's own account of this, see his proposed letter to Bossuet, 2 July 1694—app. A below. See also the correspondence with Pellisson described by Aiton, pp. 190–1.

[22] 1e implicitly identifies Bossuet as one of these (see n. 56).

although they are by no means popular in style, nor such as can be appreciated by all types of mind.[23] I am doing this mainly in order to benefit from the judgements of people who are enlightened in these matters, for it would be too troublesome to seek out and consult individually all those who might be willing to give me advice—which I shall always be glad to receive, provided it shows a love of the truth, rather than a passion for preconceived opinions.

[2] Although I am one of those people who have done a lot of work on mathematics, ever since my youth I have continued to meditate upon philosophy, for it always seemed to me that there was a way of establishing something solid in it by clear demonstrations. I had gone far into the country of the scholastics, when mathematics and modern authors drew me out again, while I was still quite young. Their beautiful way of explaining nature mechanically charmed me, and I rightly scorned the method of those who make use only of forms and faculties, from which we learn nothing. But afterwards, having tried to go more deeply into the principles of mechanics themselves in order to explain the laws of nature which are known through experience, I realized that the consideration of mere *extended mass* is insufficient, and that use must also be made of the notion of *force*, which is perfectly intelligible, though it belongs to the sphere of metaphysics. I realized also that the opinion of those who transform or demote animals into mere machines, although it seems possible, is implausible, and indeed contrary to the order of things.

[3] At first, when I had freed myself from the yoke of Aristotle, I was in favour of atoms and the void, because this view best satisfies the imagination. But thinking again about this, after much meditation I saw that it is impossible to find *the principles of a real unity* in matter alone, or in what is only passive, since this is nothing but a collection or aggregation of parts *ad infinitum*. Now a multiplicity can derive its reality only from *true unities* which come from elsewhere, and which are quite different from points,[24] from which it is obvious that something continuous cannot be composed. So, in order to get to these *real unities* I had to have recourse to a formal atom, since a material thing cannot simultaneously be material and

---

[23] Possibly a reference to Pascal (cf. Ch. 4, n. 33 and esp. Ch. 5, n. 68).
[24] For 'points', 1e reads 'mathematical points, which are only the extremities of extended things, and mere modifications'.

perfectly indivisible, or possessed of a genuine unity.[25] So it was necessary to recall and, as it were, to rehabilitate *substantial forms*, which are so much decried these days—but in a way which would make them intelligible, and which would separate the use which should be made of them from their previous misuse. I found, then, that the nature of substantial forms consists in force, and that from this there follows something analogous to feeling and desire; and that they must therefore be understood along the lines of our notion of *souls*. But just as the soul ought not to be used to explain in detail the workings of an animal's body, I decided that similarly these forms must not be used to solve particular problems of nature, although they are necessary for grounding true general principles. Aristotle calls them *first entelechies*.[26] I call them, perhaps more intelligibly, *primary forces*, which contain not only *actuality*, or the mere fulfilment of a possibility, but also an originating *activity*.

[4] I saw that these forms and souls had to be indivisible, like our minds, and indeed I remembered that this was the opinion of St Thomas about the souls of animals.[27] But this truth reintroduced all the great difficulties about the origin and duration of souls and forms. For, since every *substance*[28] which has a genuine unity can begin or end only by a miracle, it follows that they can come into being only by creation and end only by annihilation. So I had to recognize that (with the exception of souls which God still intends to create specially) the constitutive forms of substances must have been created with the world and must always continue to exist. Thus the scholastics, such as Albertus Magnus and John Bacon, had glimpsed part of the truth about the origin of these forms.[29] And this idea should not seem extraordinary, for we are only attributing to forms the duration which the Gassendists accord to their atoms.[30]

[5] Nevertheless, I held that we must not mix up with these the

---

[25] For 'a formal atom . . . genuine unity', 1e reads 'what might be called a *real and animated point*, or to an atom of substance, which must contain some kind of form or activity in order to make a complete being'.

[26] *De anima*, II, 412a. 27–8.

[27] Perhaps a reference to *Summa Theologica* 1a. 76. 8.

[28] For 'substance', 1e reads '*simple substance*'.

[29] Albert the Great (*c.*1200–80), German Dominican and teacher of Thomas Aquinas; John of Baconthorpe (d. 1346), English Carmelite. (Latta, p. 302, n. 24, cites relevant passages.) See also Leibniz to Arnauld, 9 Oct. 1687 (G 2. 116).

[30] In his commentary on Epicurus, Pierre Gassendi (1592–1655) described atoms as everlasting, but created by God (see *Syntagma philosophicum*, pt. 2, sect. 1, bk. 3, ch. 8).

mind,[31] or rational soul, which is of a superior order and has incomparably more perfection than those forms which are sunk in matter.[32] In comparison with those, minds or rational souls are like little gods, made in the image of God, and having within them a ray of the divine light. That is why God governs minds as a prince governs his subjects, or as a father looks after his children; whereas he deals with other substances as an engineer handles his machines. Thus minds have special laws which raise them above the mechanical operations of matter,[33] and we might say that everything else is made only for them, for even those mechanical operations are arranged for the happiness of the good and the punishment of the wicked.

[6] To return to ordinary forms or *material souls*,[34] however, the duration which must now be attributed to them, rather than to atoms, as before, might give rise to the idea that they pass from body to body; this would be *metempsychosis*, rather like the transmission of motion and of species as certain philosophers have maintained it. But this fancy is very far from how things are: there is no such passing. And here the *transformations* noted by MM. Swammerdam, Malpighi, and Leeuwenhoek, who are among the best observers of our day, have helped me, and have led me to accept more readily that no animal or other organized substance begins when we think it does, and that its apparent generation is only a development, or a kind of augmentation.[35] And I have noticed that the author of *The Search after Truth*, M. Regis, M. Hartsoeker, and other able men have not been far from this opinion.[36]

[31] For 'mix up ... the *mind*', 1e reads 'mix up with these, or confuse with other forms or souls, the *mind*'.

[32] For 'matter', 1e reads 'matter, which in my view are to be found everywhere'.

[33] For 'matter' 1e reads 'matter, which it carries out in accordance with the order God has imposed on it'.

[34] For '*material souls*', 1e reads '*primitive [brute] souls*'.

[35] John Swammerdam (1637–80), Dutch microscopist (see also Ch. 5, n. 127); Marcello Malpighi (1628–94), Italian anatomist and embryologist; Anton van Leeuwenhoek (1632–1723), Dutch microscopist and embryologist who met Leibniz in Holland in 1676, and rather later corresponded with him (see R 339, 345, 473, 740).

[36] Nicolas Malebranche's *La Recherche de la vérité* did not bear his name until its 5th edn. in 1700. (Leibniz's reference is to 2. 1. 7. 3.) Like Malebranche, Pierre-Sylvain Regis (1632–1707, author of *Cours entier de philosophie ou système général d'après les principes de Descartes* (1691)), and Nicolas Hartsoeker (1656–1725, Dutch physicist who corresponded with Leibniz (G 3. 483 ff.)) subscribed to

[7] But there still remained the even bigger question as to what becomes of these souls or forms on the death of the animal or the destruction of the individual organized substance.[37] This question is all the more difficult, because it seems hardly reasonable that souls should remain, useless, in a chaos of confused matter. This led me to decide in the end that there is only one view that can reasonably be taken, which is that not only is the soul conserved, but so also is the animal itself and its organic mechanism; although the destruction of its cruder parts has made it so small as to be as little perceptible to our senses as it was before its birth. And indeed, no one can exactly tell the true time of death, which for a long time may be taken for a mere suspension of observable actions and which ultimately is nothing more than that in the case of simple animals: witness the *resuscitation* of flies which have been drowned and then buried in powdered chalk, and several similar instances[38] which show clearly that there would be many more resuscitations, even in more extreme cases, if men were in a position to repair the mechanism. It seems it was of something of this kind that the great Democritus spoke, complete atomist though he was, even though Pliny laughs at what he said.[39] It is natural, then, that an animal, since it has always been living and organized (as some people of great insight are beginning to recognize), should always remain so. And so, since there is therefore no first birth or entirely new generation of an animal, it follows that it will have no final extinction or complete death in the strict metaphysical sense; and that consequently, instead of the transmigration of souls, there is nothing but a transformation of one and the same animal, according as its organs (*organes*) are differently packed up, and more or less developed.

[8] Meanwhile rational souls follow much higher laws, and are exempt from everything which could make them lose their status as citizens of the society of minds; God has provided for them so well that no changes in matter can ever make them lose the moral

'preformationism', according to which the parts of, e.g., a fly are already present in miniature in the maggot, and merely expand or inflate as the organism develops. 'Epigenesism' (e.g. Harvey), on the other hand, postulates a genuine metamorphosis or transformation of one form into the other.

[37] Aristotle's *De anima* (411b) had stimulated discussion of the question of what happens to its soul when an insect is divided (see R. K. French, *Robert Whytt, the Soul, and Medicine* (London, 1969), pp. 101–2, 119 ff.)

[38] See Leibniz to Arnauld, 9 Oct. 1687 (G 2. 123) for some light on this.

[39] See Ch. 9, n. 56.

qualities of their personality. And we can say that everything tends to the perfection, not only of the universe in general, but also of these created beings in particular; for they are destined for such a degree of happiness that the universe becomes involved in it, in virtue of the divine goodness, which is communicated to each one to the extent that the sovereign wisdom can allow.

[9] As for the ordinary run of animals[40] and other corporeal substances, which up till now have been thought to suffer total extinction and whose changes depend on mechanical rules rather than on moral laws, I was pleased to see that the ancient author of the book *Diet* (which is attributed to Hippocrates[41]) had glimpsed something of the truth, when he expressly said that animals are not born and do not die, and that the things which we suppose to come into being and to perish merely appear and disappear. This was also the opinion of Parmenides and of Melissus according to Aristotle.[42] (For these ancients are sounder than we think.)

[10] I am as ready as anyone to do justice to the moderns; nevertheless I think they have carried reform too far, among other things in conflating natural things with artificial ones, through not having sufficiently grand ideas of the majesty of nature. They take the difference between nature's machines and ours to be only that between great and small. This recently led a very able man, the author of *Conversations on the Plurality of Worlds*,[43][44] to say that on close inspection nature appears less wonderful than we had thought, it being only something like a craftsman's window display. I think that this gives an inappropriate and[45] unworthy idea of nature, and that it is only my system which shows the true, and immense distance there is between the least productions and mechanisms of divine wisdom and the greatest masterpieces

[40] For 'the ordinary run of animals (*cours ordinaire des animaux*)' 1e reads (according—erroneously?—to Gerhardt) 'ordinary animal bodies (*corps ordinaire des animaux*)'.

[41] The book is not now attributed to Hippocrates. For discussion of this passage see D 1. 4–8.

[42] *De caelo*, III. 2, 298b14.

[43] 1e omits 'the author . . . *Worlds*'.

[44] Bernard de Fontenelle (1656–1756), scientist and writer, later Secretary to the Paris Academy of Sciences (and correspondent of Leibniz). Leibniz may be referring to the famous passage in the First Evening of his *Entretiens sur la pluralité des mondes* (Paris, 1686), where Fontenelle says that 'it is now thought that the universe is only a large-scale version of a watch'. Fontenelle, however, held that this made the world no less admirable, and denied that 'a thing is dishonoured . . . as soon as it can be understood'.

[45] D and E omit 'inappropriate and'.

produced by the skill of a limited mind—a difference which is not merely one of degree, but one of kind. It needs to be recognized, then, that nature's machines have a truly infinite number of organic parts (*organes*), and are so well provided for and proof against all accidents that it is not possible to destroy them. A natural machine is still a machine even in its smallest parts; and, what is more, it always remains the same machine it was, being merely transformed by being packed up in different ways; sometimes extended, sometimes contracted and as it were concentrated, when we think that it is destroyed.

[11] Furthermore, by means of the soul or form, there is in us a true unity which corresponds to what we call 'I'; this can have no place in artificial machines or in a simple mass of matter, however organized it may be. Such masses can only be thought of as like an army or a flock, or like a pond full of fish, or like a watch composed of springs and wheels. Yet if there were no true substantial unities there would be nothing substantial or real in such a collection. It was this that forced M. Cordemoy to abandon Descartes and adopt Democritus's doctrine of atoms in order to find a true unity.[46] But *atoms of matter* are contrary to reason, quite apart from being still composed of parts, since the invincible attachment of one part to another (even if it could rationally be understood or imagined) would certainly not take away the difference between them. It is only *atoms of substance*, that is to say real unities absolutely devoid of parts, that can be the sources of actions, and the absolute first principles of the composition of things, and as it were the ultimate elements in the analysis of substances.[47] They might be called *metaphysical points*; they have *something of the nature of life* and a kind of *perception*, and *mathematical points* are their *point of view* for expressing the universe. But when a corporeal substance is contracted, all its organs together make what to us is only a *physical point*. Thus the indivisibility of physical points is only apparent. Mathematical points really are indivisible, but they are only modalities. It is only metaphysical or substantial points (constituted by forms or souls) which are both indivisible and real, and without them there would be nothing real, since without true unities there would be no multiplicity.

[46] Gerauld de Cordemoy (d. 1684), French occasionalist, distinguished between indivisible material 'bodies', or atoms, and 'matter', a divisible collection of such atoms (Cordemoy, p. 99).

[47] For 'substances', 1e reads 'substantial things'.

(*The remainder of this article will be published in next week's journal.*)

[12] Having decided these things, I thought I had reached port, but when I set myself to think about the union of the soul with the body I was as it were carried back into the open sea. For I could find no way of explaining how the body can make something pass over into the soul or vice versa, or how one created substance can communicate with another. As far as we can see from his writings, M. Descartes gave up the game at this point, but his disciples, seeing that the popular opinion is incomprehensible, said that we are aware of the properties of bodies because God produces thoughts in the soul on the occasion of the motions of matter; and when in its turn our soul wishes to move the body, they said that it is God who moves the body for it. And as the communication of motion also seemed incomprehensible to them, they held that God gives motion to one body on the occasion of the motion of another. This is what they call the *System of Occasional Causes*, which has been made very fashionable by the excellent reflections of the author of the *The Search after Truth*.[48]

[13] It must be admitted that they have gone a long way with this problem in telling us what cannot happen; but their account of what actually does happen does not appear to have solved it. It is quite true that in the strict metaphysical sense, one created substance has no real influence upon another, and that all things, with all their reality, are continually produced by the power of God. But to solve problems it is not enough to make use of a general cause and to introduce what is called a *deus ex machina*. For to do this, without giving any other explanation in terms of the order of secondary causes, is really to have recourse to a miracle. In philosophy we must try to show the way in which things are carried out by the divine wisdom by explaining them in accordance with the notion of the subject we are dealing with.

[14] Being thus obliged to admit that it is impossible that the soul or any other true substance should receive anything from outside, except through divine omnipotence, I was led gradually to an idea which surprised me, but which seems inevitable, and which in fact has very great advantages and very considerable attractions. This is that we should say that God first created the soul, or any other real unity, in such a way that everything in it arises from its own nature,

[48] See, e.g., Malebranche's *Search*, 6. 2. 3.

with a perfect *spontaneity* as regards itself, and yet with a perfect *conformity* to things outside it. And thus, since our inner sensations (that is, those which are in the soul itself and not in the brain or in the subtle parts of the body) are only a sequence of phenomena relating to external things, or are really appearances or systematic dreams, as it were, these internal perceptions in the soul itself must arise from its own original constitution, that is to say from its representational nature (its ability to express external things which are in relation with its organs), which it has had since its creation, and which constitutes its individual character. And this means that since each of these substances accurately represents the whole universe in its own way and from a particular point of view, and since its perceptions or expressions of external things occur in the soul at just the right time in virtue of its own laws, as in a world apart, as if there existed nothing but God and that soul (to use the expression of a certain lofty-minded person, famous for her sanc-tity[49]), there will be a perfect agreement between all these sub-stances, which produces the same effect as would be observed if they communicated with one another by means of a transmission of species or qualities, such as most ordinary philosophers suppose. Furthermore, the organized mass in which the point of view of the soul lies is more immediately expressed by it, and is in turn ready, just when the soul desires it, to act of itself according to the laws of the bodily mechanism, without either one interfering with the laws of the other, the animal spirits and the blood having exactly at the right moment the motions which correspond to the passions and perceptions of the soul. It is this mutual relationship, arranged in advance in each substance in the universe, which produces what we call their communication, and which alone constitutes *the union of soul and body.* And in this way we can understand how the soul has its seat in the body by an immediate presence, which is as close as could be, since the soul is in the body in the way in which unity is in that resultant of unities which is multiplicity.

[15] This hypothesis is certainly possible. For why could not God give to a substance at the outset a nature or internal force which could produce in it in an orderly way (as in a *spiritual or formal automaton; but a free one*, in the case of a substance which is

---

[49] St Teresa of Avila (1515–82), *Life*, ch. 13: 'remember that in the entire world there is only God and the soul' (*The Complete Works of Saint Teresa of Jesus*, trans. and ed. E. Alison Peers (London, 1946), i. 77). (See also Leibniz to Morell, 10 Dec. 1696 (Grua, p. 103).)

endowed with a share of reason) everything that is going to happen to it, that is to say, all the appearances or expressions it is going to have, and all without the help of any created thing? This is the more likely since the nature of a substance necessarily requires and essentially involves some progress or change, without which it would have no force to act. And as the nature of the soul is to represent the universe in a very exact way (though with more or less distinctness), the succession of representations which the soul produces for itself will naturally correspond to the succession of changes in the universe itself: just as on the other hand the body has also been adapted to the soul for the occasions when we think of the soul as acting externally. What is all the more reasonable about this is that bodies are made only for minds which are capable of entering into association with God, and of celebrating his glory. Thus as soon as we see that this *Theory of Agreements* is possible, we see also that it is the most reasonable, and that it gives a wonderful sense of the harmony of the universe and the perfection of the works of God.

[16] It also has the great advantage that instead of saying that we are free only in appearance and in a way which is sufficient for practical purposes, as several clever people have held,[50] we must rather say that we are determined only in appearance, and that, in strict metaphysical language, we are perfectly independent of the influence of all other created things. This again puts into a marvellous light the immortality of our soul and the perfectly unbroken conservation of our individuality, which is perfectly well-regulated by its own nature and sheltered from all external accidents, however it may appear to the contrary. Never has any system made our elevated position more clear. Every mind is like a world apart, sufficient to itself, independent of every other created thing, involves the infinite, and expresses the universe, and so it is as lasting, as continuous in its existence and as absolute as the universe of created things itself. Thus we should conclude that each mind should always play its part in the way most fitted to contribute to the perfection of the society of all minds which constitutes their moral union in the City of God. There is also here a new and surprisingly clear proof of the existence of God. For this perfect agreement of so many substances which have no com-

[50] Perhaps Hobbes; see Leibniz's discussion of his 'Questions Concerning Liberty, Necessity, and Chance' in the *Theodicy* (G 6. 391).

munication with one another could come only from their common cause.

[17] Besides all these advantages which this theory has in its favour, we may say that it is something more than a theory, since it hardly seems possible to explain things in any other intelligible way, and because several serious difficulties which have perplexed men's minds up till now seem to disappear of themselves when we fully understand it. Our ordinary ways of speaking may also be easily preserved. For we may say that the substance whose state explains a change in an intelligible way (so that we may conclude that it is this substance to which the others have in this respect been adapted from the beginning, in accordance with the order of the decrees of God) is the one which, so far as this change goes, we should therefore think of as *acting* upon the others. So the action of one substance upon another is not an emission or a transplantation of an entity as is commonly thought,[51] and it can be reasonably understood only in the way I have just described. It is true that we can easily understand in connection with matter both the emission and the receiving of parts, by means of which we quite properly explain all the phenomena of physics mechanically. But a material mass is not a substance, and so it is clear that action as regards an actual substance can only be as I have described.

[18] These considerations, however metaphysical they may seem, are nevertheless marvellously useful in physics for grounding the laws of motion, as my dynamics will be able to show. For we can say that when bodies collide, each one is affected only by its own elasticity, caused by[52] the motion which is already in it. And as for absolute motion, nothing can determine it mathematically, since everything ends in relations: the result being that there is always a perfect equivalence of theories, as in astronomy; so that, whatever number of bodies we take, we may arbitrarily assign either rest or some degree of velocity to whichever we like, without it being possible for us to be refuted by the phenomena of motion, whether in a straight line, a circle, or composite. It is still reasonable however, in conformity with the notion of activity which we have established here, to attribute genuine motions to bodies in accordance with what explains the phenomena in the most intelligible way.

[51] See Eileen O'Neill, '*Influxus Physicus*', in Steven Nadler (ed.), *Causation in Early Modern Philosophy* (University Park, Pa., 1993), pp. 27–55.
[52] For 'caused by (*causé du*)' D. and E. read 'the cause of (*cause du*)'.

NS2. LEIBNIZ: Draft of 'New System for Explaining the Nature of Substances and the Communication between them, as well as the Union of the Soul with the Body' (1694?)[53]

[1] I thought of this system several years ago and communicated some of it to various learned men, *but* in particular to one of the greatest theologians and philosophers of our time, who, having heard about them *through correspondence with* a person of the highest rank had found some of my opinions quite *strange*. But after receiving my explanations, he withdrew what he had said in the most generous and admirable way possible; and, having approved some of my points, he withdrew his censure of the others with which he did not yet agree.[54] Since then I have continued my meditations whenever I had opportunity, so as to give the public only well-considered opinions; and I have also tried to answer *those who have raised objections* against my essays on dynamics, which have some connection with this.[55] And now, because some notable people wanted *me to work to set about laying out my views, which they think can help to reconcile faith with reason on some important matters,*[56] I have ventured to offer these meditations in *order to benefit from the most enlightened judgements,* for it would be too troublesome to seek out and consult individually all those who might be willing to give me advice—which I shall always be glad to receive, *whether publicly or individually, provided that they are meant kindly.*

[2] Some will be surprised that I claim to rehabilitate to some extent the school philosophy, so disparaged in the opinion of many people, and that I undertake to provide the wherewithal to explain Aristotle, St Thomas, and the scholastics intelligibly on several matters where it seems that they have been abandoned, and because of that it will perhaps be imagined that I am one of those who want to explain the phenomena of nature by qualities and faculties, by

---

[53] 'Système nouveau pour expliquer la nature des substances et leur communication entre elles, aussi bien que l'union de l'âme avec le corps' (as printed from MSS LH IV, II, 1a, at G 4. 471–7). Except for the italicized words and phrases the first paragraph is the same as that of the published 'New System'; thereafter this draft was not taken over into NS1.

[54] See n. 20.   [55] See n. 21.

[56] See Bossuet to Leibniz, 12 Apr. 1694 (UL 6. 219; A 1. 10, N. 80).

archees[57] or some other such term. That obliges me, then, to make clear from the start that in my view everything in nature happens mechanically, and that to give an accurate and complete reason for some particular phenomenon (such as heaviness or elasticity, for example) it is sufficient to appeal only to shape and motion. But the principles of mechanics and the laws of motion themselves derive, in my view, from something higher, which depends more on metaphysics than on geometry, and which the imagination can never reach, although the mind can conceive it very well. So I find that in nature it is necessary to employ not only the notion of extension but also that of force, which makes matter capable of acting and of resisting. By 'force' or 'potency' I do not mean a power or a mere faculty, which is only a bare possibility (*une possibilité prochaine*) for action and which, being itself dead as it were, never produces an action without being excited from outside; instead I mean something midway between power and action, something which involves an effort, an act, an entelechy—for force passes into action by itself so long as nothing prevents it. That is why I consider it to be what constitutes substance, since it is the principle of action, which is its characteristic feature. So I find that the efficient cause of physical actions lies in the province of metaphysics. In this I am very far from those who recognize in nature only what is material or extended, and who thereby make themselves suspect, with some reason, in the eyes of people of piety. I even hold that the consideration of goodness, or of final causes, although to some extent it involves morality, is still usefully employed in the explanations of natural things, since the author of nature acts by the principle of order and of perfection, and with a wisdom which could not be surpassed. I have shown elsewhere,[58] by the example of the general law of the radiation of light, how the principle of the final cause is often enough to uncover the secrets of nature, pending the immediate efficient cause which is more difficult to discover. (Although I agree that what M. Huygens has told us about the production of light and of refraction seems far more likely than anything else we have been told so far.[59])

[57] The alchemist Theophrastus Paracelsus (1493–1541) and, later, Jean Baptiste van Helmont (1577–1644) made use of *archees* (from the Latin *archeus* and the Greek *archē* for 'principle') or spiritual principles in giving physical explanations.
[58] 'Unicum Opticae, Catoptricae et Dioptricae Principium, Autore G. G. L.', *Acta eruditorum*, June 1682 (R 85).
[59] Christian Huygens, *Traité de la lumière* (Leiden, 1690).

[3] But to come to the account that we promised, I begin with the distinction that must be drawn between a substance and a collection, or an aggregate of several substances. When I say 'me', I speak of a single substance; but an army, a herd of animals, a pond full of fish (even if it is frozen solid with all its fish) will always be a collection of several substances. That is why, leaving aside souls or other such principles of unity, we will never find a corporeal mass or portion of matter which is a true substance. It will always be a collection, since matter is actually divided *ad infinitum*, in such a way that the least particle encloses a truly infinite world of created things, and perhaps of animals. This difficulty forced the late M. Cordemoy to abandon Descartes and resort to atoms, thinking to find in them a genuine unity. But besides the fact that an atom is contrary to reason and to order, it already has actual parts of which it is composed, and it makes no difference whether they are separated or not. However, since it must necessarily be that true unities can be found in corporeal nature, for otherwise there could be neither multiplicity nor collections, it is necessary that what constitutes corporeal substance is something which corresponds to what in us is called 'me', which is indivisible and yet active: for being indivisible and without parts it will not be a being by aggregation, but being active it will be something substantial. There is reason to think that there is something similar in animals, which makes them capable of sensation and which is called their soul, which St Thomas believed would also be indivisible. In fact it seems that in every kind of organic species, there must be something which corresponds to the soul, and which philosophers have called a substantial form, which Aristotle calls a first entelechy, and which, perhaps more intelligibly, I call a primitive force, in order to distinguish it from the secondary, which is called the moving force, and which is a limitation, accident, or variation of this primitive force. But even if we do not want to say anything definite about animals, plants, or any other species in particular, we must still recognize in general that everything has to be full of such species, which contain in themselves a principle of true unity which is analogous to the soul, and which is joined to some kind of organized body. Otherwise we would find nothing substantial in matter, and bodies would only be phenomena or like very orderly dreams. The ancients too, Plato above all, recognized perfectly well that by itself, that is to say without this indivisible principle that we have

just described, matter would be nothing real or determinate, for there would be no corporeal substance.

[4] As for the beginning and end of these forms, souls, or substantial principles, it must be said that they could only ever have their origin in creation, and their end in annihilation expressly brought about by the supreme power of God. Philosophers have been very puzzled, for they have looked for the impossible in looking for their origin. (It is true that even among the scholastics, Albert le Grand, Jean Bachon,[60] and others appear to have glimpsed a part of the truth.) These forms, then, do not naturally begin or end; and why should they not share the privilege of atoms, which according to the Gassendists are always conserved? This privilege should be granted to everything which is truly a substance, for true unity is absolutely indissoluble. That being so, we have to suppose that these substances were created in the beginning, with the world. But if God in his omnipotence is not still creating souls, I can foresee that those who judge hastily will immediately declare war on me over this, and will say that by granting them pre-existence I am bringing in metempsychosis, or the transmigration of souls, by giving them pre-existence. I reply that the transmigration of souls is an absurdity. Substantial principles do not fly about outside substances. The soul is never naturally without a body. So instead of believing in the transmigration of souls, we should believe in the transformation of one and the same animal. It appears that strictly there is neither generation nor death, but only unfoldings and enfoldings, augmentations and diminutions of already formed animals which continually subsist in life, although with different levels of awareness. The late M. Swammerdam hinted at this generation of animals, and M. Leeuwenhoek's observations confirm it.[61] It seems that the Revd. Father Malebranche, and perhaps even M. Regis, who describes such views, are not far removed from it.[62] But if we reject the initial birth of an animal, it is natural also to dismiss final extinction, or death as understood in philosophical rigour. The author of book 1 of *Diet* (which is attributed to Hippocrates[63]) was of this view; he holds that what are called life and death are only appearance or disappearance, to a greater or lesser extent. Parmenides and Melissus say the same according to Aristotle.[64] And as the subtlety of organic bodies can be infinite (as

[60] See n. 29.   [61] See n. 35.   [62] See n. 36.
[63] See n. 41.   [64] See n. 42.

can be seen from seeds which are contained one in another, and which contain a continual replication of organized and animated bodies), it is easy to see that even fire, which is the most subtle and the most violent of agents, will not destroy an animal, since at the very most it can only reduce it to a smallness on which that element can no longer act. However, I do not want all that to be applied to the rational soul, which is of a superior order, and in regard to which God has particular laws which make it exempt from mechanical operations of matter. With creatures which are without reason God acts simply as creator and master, but with souls which can know and love him he acts as father and as leader. The intellectual world (which is nothing else than the republic of the universe, or the city of God) is not subject to the inferior laws of the corporeal realm, and the whole system of bodies appears to have been made only for the intellectual world. (I will add that it appears that the sensibility and pain of animals is of a completely different nature from our own, and, since they have no reflection, does not make them capable of being unhappy. This answers those who imagine that if animals had souls, God's justice would be compromised with regard to them.)

[5] But in order to understand the nature of substance better, we have to realize that the perfect notion of each substance, although indivisible, involves the infinite, and always expresses all its past and all its future, in such a way that God or he who knows it completely, can see it all in the present. However, the present dispositions (however inclining they may be) are never necessitating, and do not take away the contingency of the future. Indeed it is greatly increased, for each substance by itself expresses in itself the whole universe; it mirrors perfectly, from its own position or point of view, even though this combining of an infinite number of things in each one prevents it from having a distinct understanding of them. It is in the universe as it is in our bodies, of which Hippocrates said that everything there meshes together.[65] It follows from this that, in metaphysical rigour, one created substance strictly never acts on another; everything comes from the individual depths of each one, since each on its own represents the whole universe in its own way. This comes about only through participation, albeit to a limited extent, in the divine perfections; for it is the expressing of

---

[65] See D1, § 6.

a common cause which produces the matching effects. This independence or spontaneity of substances goes further than we think. For I hold that even by the laws of motion, a body is never affected by the impact of another except by virtue of its own elasticity, which comes from a motion which already exists within it. But that is much more absolutely true of the indivisible substantial principle, on which, strictly speaking, no other created thing can ever act, although we attribute such action to the body whose situation is best able to explain it. So the system of occasional causes, which has God produce changes in a substance on the occasion of another substance, is (unless it is explained in the same way) quite unnecessary. It seems to me that the hypothesis of spontaneity is enough, without always having to make the divine power intervene, as a *deus ex machina*, in an inexplicable and miraculous manner. It is very true that everything is continually produced by the power of God; but when one comes to explain the actions of created things, one can suppose that each substance was created in the first place once and for all in such a way that everything happens to it, in virtue of its own laws or inclinations, in a way which accords perfectly with what happens in all the others, just as if the one transmitted something to the other in their encounters—of which there is nevertheless no need, and indeed no possibility. I call this the system of correspondence. I see nothing which prevents God from creating from the outset such perfect substances, which are as independent of all others (and nevertheless as well adjusted to them) as I have said, without any of them ever doing violence to another. Before the decree of creation God knew possible beings perfectly, with the whole sequence of their contingent happenings comprised in the perfect notion of each possible thing, and he chose those whose existence he foresaw would be most consistent with his wisdom. Thus good things come from him, and bad things come from the original imperfection of created things. Minds are perfectly free, and a substance depends only on God and itself. And it is through this that we have at last the solution to the great problem of the union of the soul with the body or with an organized mass. The body transmits nothing to the soul, nor the soul to the body, and neither is there any need to say that God does it for them. The soul was created from the outset in such a way that all that the body can provide appears in the soul, in virtue of the representative nature which was given to it with its being, for production at the relevant time. It is produced in the course of time by the train of the soul's thoughts and, so to speak, as if by its dreams (or rather internal phenomena) which are regular, and so true that they can be accurately predicted. All of this is quite independent of outside things which might make them arise in the soul, and nevertheless conformable to the rest of the universe, but particularly to the organs of the body which gives it its point of view in the world. And this is what their union consists in. Anything else that is claimed over and above this is unnecessary, and I dare add that it is not possible, for I believe that what we have said here is something more than just a theory.

Appendix A. LEIBNIZ: Letter to Bossuet, Hanover, 2 July 1694[66]

... With your usual penetration you rightly say, Monseigneur, how useful a properly established dynamics would be for theology. For, not to mention the operation of created things and the union between the soul and the body, it can show something more than what is ordinarily known about the nature of material substance, and what we have to recognize in it in addition to extension. I have some thoughts about this which I find useful both for clarifying the theory of corporeal actions and for calculating actual motions in practice. But because of all my distractions I have not yet been able to put these together into one work. I have discussed some of them with M. Arnauld[67] in connection with some points on which we had exchanged letters. Later, I published in the *Acta* of Leipzig (March 1686)[68] a brief demonstration of the Cartesians' error with regard to their principle of the conservation of the quantity of

[66] From the French at UL 6. 336–42 (see also A 1. 10, N. 90). See UL 6. 342, n. 39, and A 1. 10, p. 137, for the date of initial composition of this letter. Since this date is of course not necessarily that of dispatch, it does not rule out a later partial rewriting (see n. 13).
[67] UL perhaps identifies this as the letter of 23 Mar. 1690 (G 2. 134–8) but, because of his next sentence, Leibniz must be referring to their earlier correspondence.
[68] 'G. G. L. Brevis Demonstratio erroris memorabilis Cartesii ...', *Acta eruditorum*, Mar. 1686, pp. 161–3 (R 93) (and also as 'Démonstration courte d'une erreur considérable de M. Descartes ...', *Nouvelles de la République des lettres*, Sept. 1686, pp. 996–9 (B 10; R 97)).

movement, in place of which I claim that what is conserved is the quantity of force, for which I give a formula which is different from that for the quantity of motion. M. the Abbé Catelan replied in the *Nouvelles de la République des lettres* (September 1686, p. 999),[69] but without having understood me, as I eventually realized, and as I remarked in the *Nouvelles* for September in the following year.[70] The Reverend Father Malebranche (whose account of the rules of motion I had mentioned in my response to M. Catelan (February 87, p. 131)[71] certainly did not reject everything I said (8 April 87, p. 448),[72] and I tried to justify what he still disagreed with in the *Nouvelles de la République des lettres* (9 July 1687, p. 745).[73] I used a rather interesting kind of proof, by which one can judge, even without appeal to experience, whether a hypothesis is satisfactory; and I found that the Cartesian hypothesis, as well as that of the author of *The Search after Truth*, is self-inconsistent, in the light of an interpretation that one has to give of it. I say nothing of other people who have tried to defend the Cartesian principle in the *Acta* of Leipzig, to which I have written my reply.[74]

The late M. Pellisson, having very much liked what I mentioned of my dynamics, got me to send him a sample to be passed on to your Fellows of the Royal Academy of Sciences, in order to find out their opinion. But he could not manage it, even though M. the Abbé Bignon and the late M. Thévenot were involved. This is why M. Pellisson agreed that I should turn to public opinion by publishing in the *Journal des savants* a general rule for the composition of movements.[75] A long time earlier I had written about my hypo-

[69] 'Courte remarque de M. l'Abbé D. C.' (B 11).

[70] 'Réponse de M. L. à la remarque de M. l'Abbé D. C. . . . où il prétend soutenir une loi de la nature avancée par M. Descartes', *Nouvelles de la République des lettres*, Sept. 1687, pp. 952–6 (B 16; R 100).

[71] 'Réplique de M. L. à M. l'Abbé D. C. . . . Touchant ce qu'a dit M. Descartes que Dieu conserve toujours . . . la même quantité de mouvement', *Nouvelles de la République des lettres*, Feb. 1687, pp. 131–8 (B 12; R 98).

[72] 'Extrait d'une lettre du P. M. à l'Abbé D. C.', *Nouvelles de la République des lettres*, Apr. 1687, p. 448 (B 13).

[73] 'Extrait d'une lettre de M. L. sur un principe général, utile à l'explication des loix de la nature . . . pour servir de réplique à la réponse du R. P. M', *Nouvelles de la République des lettres*, July 1687, pp. 744–53 (B 15; R 99).

[74] Leibniz replied to Denis Papin's 'Mechanicorum de viribus motricibus sententia, asserta a Dn. Papino adversus cl. G. G. L. objectiones', *Acta eruditorum*, Jan. 1691, pp. 6–13, with his 'G. G. L. De Legibus Naturæ et Vera æstimatione virium motricium contra Cartesianos', *Acta eruditorum*, Sept. 1691, pp. 439–47 (R 112).

[75] The 'sample' Leibniz sent to Pellisson is his 'Essai de dynamique' (GM 6. 215–31). The article on the composition of movements is his 'Règle générale de la

thesis to M. the Abbé Foucher, Canon of Dijon, about my theory, and about why I did not agree with the system of occasional causes.[76] An Italian professor to whom I had said something in conversation, found it much to his liking and later wrote to me about it, and I replied to him.[77] A friend of mine in Rome asked me why I did not take the nature of body to be extension, and I sent him a reply which seemed to me to be accessible and capable of being understood without any need to have already immersed oneself in speculations, so I had it printed in the *Journal des savants* (18 June 1691).[78] A Cartesian replied to it (16 July 1691).[79] I discovered this rather late, but I did eventually discover it when M. the Abbé Foucher drew my attention to it.[80] I then replied to it (5 January 1693),[81] and M. Pellisson[82] thought my reply was very clear. M. l'Enfant, minister to the French exiles in Berlin, sent me his objections about something he had seen in the Paris journal, and I tried to satisfy him.[83] I was told that M. Bayle planned to present some ideas about the nature of body, and was going to discuss my view;[84] but that has not happened. Finally, on the invitation of a friend in Leipzig, I put into the *Acta* for this year the little discourse

composition des mouvements. Par M. de Leibniz', *Journal des savants*, 7 Sept. 1693 (B 32; R 129). For details of the whole episode see Aiton, pp. 190–1; Pierre Costabel, *Leibniz and Dynamics* (London, 1973), pp. 31–9.

[76] Perhaps a letter of 1686 (see Ch. 3, app. A).

[77] A 1. 10, p. 142, identifies him as Michel Angelo Fardella.

[78] The friend is Antonio Alberti Amable de Tourreil, and Leibniz's reply was sent in April 1691 (G 7. 446–9; see also A 1. 10, p. 142, line 22). The reply was printed as 'Extrait d'une lettre de M. de Leibniz, sur la question, Si l'essence du corps consiste dans l'étendue', *Journal des savants*, 18 June 1691 (B 19; R 109). For details of its publication see Aiton, p. 190.

[79] 'Extrait d'une lettre de M. Nanu à M. Rigo sur celle de M. Leibniz . . .', *Journal des savants*, 16 July 1691 (B 20).

[80] Foucher to Leibniz, Aug. 1692 (G 1. 408); Leibniz to Foucher, 17 Oct. 1692 (G 1. 410).

[81] 'Extrait d'une lettre de M. de Leibniz . . .', *Journal des savants*, 5 Jan. 1693 (B 27; R 122).

[82] Leibniz sent the reply via Paul Pellisson-Fontanier (Leibniz to Pellisson, 18 Oct. 1692 (A 1. 8, p. 181)), who thought it 'highly ingenious and very well expressed' (Pellisson to Leibniz, 15 Nov. 1692 (A 1. 8, p. 183)).

[83] Jacques l'Enfant (1661–1728, chaplain to Queen Sophie Charlotte) to Leibniz, 30 June 1693 (see note to A 1. 10, p. 142, line 12). What l'Enfant had seen in the Paris journal (*Journal des savants*, 12 May 1692) was a review of *De la Tolerance des religions: lettres de M. de Leibniz et réponses de M. Pellisson* (Paris, 1692). Leibniz 'tried to satisfy' l'Enfant in further correspondence that year (see note at A 1. 10, p. 142).

[84] Leibniz was told this by Basnage de Beauval in an undated letter (Jan. 1693, according to A 1. 10, p. 142) and one of 15 Jan. 1694 (G 3. 92, 108).

I enclose here, about the nature of substance, and about the use of the notion of force in regard to it.[85] So you see, not yet having had the time to put together my thoughts, I have contented myself with presenting some small samples of them, and to replying to friends and others who have proposed objections to them. And so one gradually advances, responding to the demands of the moment.

With a view to submitting my ideas to the public judgement, I am working now to put down in writing[86] what I think is the only intelligible explanation of the union of the soul with the body, with no recourse to an extraordinary concourse of God, and no special intervention of the first cause in the ordinary workings of secondary ones. I have had this explanation for several years, and it is only a corollary of the notion that I have worked out of substance in general. If you think it appropriate, Monseigneur, the two enclosed pieces could be put into the *Journal des savants*, in order to give some indication of my plan.[87] The kindness you have shown in asking about my thoughts has emboldened me to send them to you. I think I have at least made some progress with regard to the notion we should have of substance in general, and of corporeal substance in particular. Since I find nothing so intelligible as force, I believe that is what we must turn to in order to defend the real presence, which I hold does not fit at all well with the view which takes the essence of body to be nothing but bare extension. For what Descartes said about the Sacrament relates only to the conservation of accidents, and although the Reverend Father Malebranche has promised us a reconciliation of multi-presence with the notion of extension pure and simple, I do not recall having seen it yet.[88]

[85] See Otto Mencke (the then editor of *Acta eruditorum*), to Leibniz, 2 Dec. 1693 (A 1. 9, N. 427, p. 637). The article is 'G. G. L. De Primae Philosophiae Emendatione, et de Notione Substantiae', *Acta eruditorum*, Mar. 1694 (R 133). The version which Leibniz sent to Bossuet was in French, and, together with a reply which Leibniz made to some objections by l'Enfant, is translated here in app. B.

[86] i.e. NS1.

[87] The 'two enclosed pieces' are Leibniz's 'Reflections on the Advancement of True Metaphysics' and his 'Reply to Objections' (see n. 85). According to the editors of the Akademie edn. (A 1. 10, notes to p. 142, line 12, and p. 143, line 12), the objections and reply originally formed part of the correspondence between Leibniz and l'Enfant (see n. 83).

[88] For Descartes on transubstantiation see his 'Reply to the Points which may cause Difficulty to Theologians', in *Replies* to the *Fourth Set of Objections* to the *Meditations*. In *Search* (3. 2. 8) Malebranche does not in fact promise one, but says only that he could give one.

Appendix B. LEIBNIZ: 'Reflections on the Advancement of
True Metaphysics and Particularly on the Nature of Substance
Explained by Force' (1694)[89]

I notice that most people who take pleasure in the science of
mathematics have no taste for metaphysical meditations; they find
enlightenment in the one, and darkness in the other. The main
cause of this seems to be that general notions, which are thought to
be the best known, have become ambiguous and obscure because of
people's negligence and the inconsistent way in which they explain
themselves. And ordinary definitions, far from explaining the
nature of things, do not even explain the meanings of words. This
problem has spread to other disciplines, which are subordinate in
various ways to this first and architectonic science; thus, instead of
clear definitions, we have been given petty distinctions, and instead
of universal axioms, we have only local rules, which meet with
almost as many exceptions as they have instances. Yet at the same
time people are obliged to use metaphysical terms all the time, and
they convince themselves that they understand words that they
have grown used to using. People are always talking about substance, accident, cause, action, relation or ratio, and numerous
other terms, whose true meanings have, however, not yet been
made clear; for those true meanings are rich in excellent truths,
whereas those we have given to them are barren. That is why we
should not be surprised that this primary science, which is called
'first philosophy', and which Aristotle called the 'sought after',[90] is
still to be found.

Plato is often concerned, in his dialogues, to investigate the
richness of these notions; and Aristotle does the same thing in the
so-called metaphysical books; but they do not seem to have made
much progress in it. The later Platonists spoke in a mysterious way,
which they carried to absurdity; and the scholastic Aristotelians
were more interested in raising questions than in answering them.
They should have had a Gellius, the Roman magistrate whom
Cicero reports[91] as having offered his services to the philosophers of
Athens, where he held office, in the belief that their arguments

[89] From the French at UL 6. 523–8.
[90] See *Metaphysics* A. 2, 983a21; B. 1, 995a24; B. 2, 996b3.
[91] *De legibus*, bk. 1, ch. 20.

could be settled like lawsuits. In our own day, several excellent men have extended their interests into metaphysics, but their success has so far not been very great. It must be admitted, though, that M. Descartes did something of importance here: he revived Plato's efforts to free the mind from its enslavement to the senses, and he made good use of the doubts of the Academicians. But having been too hasty in his assertions, and not having distinguished certainty from uncertainty sufficiently well, he didn't achieve his aim. He had a mistaken idea of the nature of body, which he saw, without proof, as being pure extension, and he couldn't see any way of explaining the union of the soul with the body. This was through not understanding the nature of substance in general; he made a kind of leap into examining difficult questions without having explained their component parts. The dubious nature of his *Meditations* couldn't be seen more clearly than it is in a little work in which he tried, at the request of Father Mersenne, to condense them into the form of demonstrations. The work is included among his *Replies to Objections*.[92]

There have been other able men who have had some profound thoughts; but they have lacked clarity, which is, however, more necessary here even than in mathematics. In mathematics truths carry their proofs along with them, and it is the fact that we can always examine those proofs that has made them so certain. This is why metaphysics, lacking such proofs, needs a new way of treating things which will take the place of calculation; it will serve as a thread in the labyrinth, and yet will retain an accessibility comparable to that which is found in the most popular speech.

The importance of these investigations will be seen in what we have to say about the notion of substance. The idea I have of it is so rich, that there follow from it most of the most important truths about God, the soul, and the nature of body, which are generally either unknown or unproved. To give some flavour of it, I will say here that the consideration of *force*, to which I have assigned a special science which might be called 'Dynamics', is of great help in understanding the nature of substance. This active force is different from a 'faculty' of the schools, in that a faculty is only a proximate possibility of action, which in itself is dead, so to speak, and inactive unless it is excited by something from outside. But active force involves an 'entelechy', or an activity; it is half-way between a

---

[92] *Replies to Second Set of Objections*, AT 7. 155–70; CSM 2. 110–20.

faculty and an action, and contains in itself a certain effort, or *conatus*. It is led by itself to action without any need of assistance, provided nothing prevents it. All this can be clarified by the example of a hanging heavy body, or a bent bow; for although it is true that weight and elastic force must be explained mechanically by the movement of etherial matter, it is nevertheless also true that the ultimate reason for the movement of matter is the force given at creation, which is there in every body, but which is as it were constrained by the mutual interactions of bodies. I hold that this power of action is there in every substance, and that in fact it always produces some actual activity, and that body itself could never be perfectly at rest—which is quite contrary to the idea of those who see body solely as extension. It will also be seen from these meditations that a substance never receives its force from another created substance; what comes from there is only the constraint or determination which gives rise to secondary force, or what is called *moving force*, which must not be confused with what some authors call *impetus*, which they measure by the quantity of movement, and make proportional to speed, when bodies are equal. By contrast, moving force, which is absolute and vital, that is, that which is always conserved, is proportional to the possible effects which can arise from it. This is where the Cartesians went wrong, in thinking that the same quantity of movement is conserved in meetings between bodies. And I see that M. Huygens is of my opinion in this, according to what he gave us, some time ago, in the *Histoire des ouvrages des savants*, where he said that the same elevating force is always conserved.[93]

Finally, a most important point which will be clarified by these meditations is communication between substances, and the union of the soul with the body. I hope that this great problem will be thereby resolved in such a clear manner that that in itself will serve as a proof to show that we have found the key to part of these matters. I do not think there is any way of giving an alternative explanation without reference to an extraordinary concourse of the first cause in the ordinary workings of secondary causes. But I will talk more of this another time, if the public does not reject this, which is meant only to test the water. In fact I communicated something of it some years ago to several capable judges; I will

[93] 'Remarques de M. Huygens sur la lettre précédente [from l'Hôpital] ...', *Histoire des ouvrages des savants*, June 1690, art. 2, pp. 449–52.

simply add here my reply to some difficulties which one very able man made to my way of explaining the nature of body by means of the notion of force.

'Reply of the Same to Objections Against the Explanation of the Nature of Substance by Force'

M. [l'Enfant]'s words are so civil and fair that his objections are to be received with pleasure as much as profit. If everyone wrote in the same way, we would go a long way. It seems that he is not taken by the opinions which are in vogue. I would be wrong to think that he would easily turn to mine; and I do not flatter myself so far as to hope entirely to satisfy him as to his objections. However my duty requires that I do what I can in that direction.

1. I prefer to say that the notion of force is prior to that of extension, because extension signifies a mass or aggregate of several substances, whereas force must exist even in a subject which is a single substance only; and unity is prior to multiplicity. It can even be said that force is constitutive of substance, just as action, which is the exercise of force, is its distinguishing mark. For actions pertain only to substances, and pertain always to all substances.

2. As regards the idea of force, I cannot do any more than give its definition, as I already have. The properties that can be deduced from it will enable it to be better understood. Its idea is not amongst those that can be grasped by the imagination, and we should not look there for anything which can capture it. Having put extension and its modifications or changes aside, there is nothing in nature more intelligible than force.

3. My axiom is not simply 'quod effectus integer respondeat causae plenae', but 'quod effectus integer sit aequalis causae plenae'.[94] And I do not use it to explain primitive force (which needs no explanation), but to explain the phenomena of secondary force. It provides me with equations in mechanics, just as the common axiom that the whole is equal to its parts taken together, provides us with them in geometry. The primitive force of bodies is indefinite in itself, but it results in secondary force, which is like a determination of primitive force, and arises from the combinations and collisions of bodies.

4. I am far from claiming that the controversy of the real presence

[94] 'that the whole effect corresponds to the complete cause' and 'that the whole effect is equal to the complete cause'.

is ended by what I have proposed; but it at least seems to me that such presence is incompatible with the opinion of those who make the essence of body to consist in extension. The natural impenetrability of bodies comes only from their resistance, which must be subject to the will of God; and this resistance of bodies is nothing other than the passive power of matter.

5. What I have replied to the first difficulty will apply again here. And since everything that can be understood in substances reduces to their actions and passions, and to the way they are arranged to produce those effects, I do not see that it is possible to find in substances anything more basic than the principle of all of that— that is, than force. It is also perfectly clear that force of action in bodies is something distinct and independent of anything else that one can understand in them. Everything else is as though dead without it, and incapable of producing any change. A *faculty*, about which there was a lot of noise in the schools, is nothing but a mere possibility of action; but the force of action is an entelechy or even a positive action. And that is what is needed. Possibility alone produces nothing, unless it is put into action; but force produces everything. It produces action by itself, and needs no assistance; it is enough that it is not prevented.

To all of this can be added what there is on this topic in the *Journal des savants* for 18 June 1691, 16 July 1691, and 5 January 1693.[95]

Appendix C. LEIBNIZ: Letter to Bossuet, Hanover, dated 3 July 1694[96]

... I am sending you these philosophical meditations, which I submit to your judgement, which is among the most enlightened and also among the fairest. If you do not find them entirely worthless, Monseigneur, I believe that M. le President Cousin would accept them, coming from you, and would put them in his

[95] 'Extrait d'une lettre de M. de Leibniz, sur la question, Si l'essence du corps consiste dans l'étendue', *Journal des savants*, 18 June 1691 (B 19; R 109); 'Extrait d'une lettre de M. Nanu ... sur celle de M. Leibniz, qui se trouve dans le *Journal* ... du lundi 18 juin 1691', *Journal des savants*, 16 July 1691 (B 20); 'Extrait d'une lettre de M. de Leibniz pour soutenir ce qu'il y a de lui dans le *Journal* ... du 18 juin 1691', *Journal des savants*, 5 Jan. 1693 (B 27; R 122).
[96] UL 6. 346–8; A 1. 10, N. 88. In the opinion of the editors of the Akademie edn. this letter was never sent (A 1. 10, p. 133).

Journal des savants. But in order to test the water I would not want my name to be given, for thoughts of this nature are unpopular with at least nine-tenths of readers, and would be unpopular even if they were the soundest in the world. The small number of people who can appreciate them and who are kind enough to enquire as to the author can easily find it out from the circumstances. Part of the foundations of my dynamics is contained in them. You will yourself be surprised at my undertaking to rehabilitate something of the received philosophy. But you will see, Monseigneur, that it is not without due consideration or in a manner which rejects recent advances. In fact, I often find that when the ancients have been properly explained there is no need to overturn received dogmas. But I have thought that I might be allowed to build something new on their foundations. And that is how I think I have solved the great problem of the origination of forms or souls, by showing that we must say of them what the Gassendists say of their atoms, namely that they were created with the world, or at least that they can begin or end only by a miracle—by creation or annihilation, that is to say. This must be said of any substance which has true unity. But, although it thus seems to me that souls or forms embodied in matter have always been present in their animal (an animal which is merely transformed by what are called generation and death), I have a completely different view about minds, or about our soul, which is a mind, and which must be exempted from the revolutions of matter. God governs minds by special laws, or rather all the rest of the universe is made only for the love of minds. I also think I have solved the great problem of the union of the soul and the body. My explanation will be taken as a hypothesis, but I take it to have been proved. But I would have had to go too far back to have given the proof. . . .

3

Leibniz and Simon Foucher

INTRODUCTION

Abbé Simon Foucher (1644–96), an honorary Canon of Dijon, Burgundy, spent most of his life in Paris, where Leibniz met him during the four years (1672–6) he spent there. His intellectual activities were devoted to reviving Academic scepticism — the philosophy of Plato's Academy in its later years. He published criticisms of Malebranche from the point of view of the Academy,[1] and expositions of Academic philosophy.[2]

He and Leibniz exchanged letters until 1695, extracts of which (including F1 and F3 below) were published between 1692 and 1696 in the *Journal des savants*.[3] Their correspondence is warm and friendly, and Leibniz plainly both felt at ease with Foucher and valued his criticisms.

In late 1685 Foucher sent Leibniz his *Reply* (1676) to Robert Desgabet's *Critique* (1675) of Foucher's *Critique de [Malebranche's] la recherche de la verité* (1675).[4] Commenting on parts of this, and reacting to Foucher's wish to have some philosophy from him, Leibniz in effect outlined his future 'New System'.[5] Foucher showed these 'learned reflections', which he looked on as 'treasures that I shall preserve dearly', to friends. He told Leibniz he would make a full reply when he had had their reactions: 'It will not be disagreeable to you,' he promised.[6] Similarly, some four months later, he wrote that 'if your long letter is printed some day, I shall reply in a

---

[1] *Critique de la recherche de la verité* (1675); *Réponse pour la critique à la préface du second volume de la recherche de la verité* (1676).
[2] *Dissertation ... contenant l'apologie des académiciens* (1687); *Dissertation ... contenant l'histoire des académiciens* (1693).
[3] B 23, 29, 31, 38, 41; R 117, 128, 147. For their full correspondence see G 1. 363–427; also A 2. 1, pp. 120, 183, 205, 255.
[4] G 1. 379–80; A 2. 1, N. 255.
[5] See app. A.
[6] Foucher to Leibniz, Paris, 28 Dec. 1686 (G 1. 385–8).

manner that won't be disagreeable to you'.[7] That same year, 1687, or the next, an undated letter from Leibniz again gave a lengthy account of the ideas he was to publish in the 'New System'.[8]

Some time later, in a letter of 26 May 1689, Foucher made some reply to Leibniz's ideas:

Your hypothesis of the concomitance of causes needs to be more fully explained. As a system it has some very good points, and above all it involves great insight and intelligence. But it does not seem to be entirely without its problems. God is the cause of all finite forms and of all powers, but created things have their own particular activity, which makes determinate the general impression which God continually gives them, by which they are carried toward their goal.[9]

Leibniz eventually began seriously to think of providing this fuller explanation. In July 1694 he almost sent a text of the 'New System' to Bossuet, with a request for help in getting it published in the *Journal des savants*; and then, a few days later, almost sent it directly to Cousin, the journal's editor.[10]

Whatever his reasons for stepping back at that point, he actually did put in train something further about the matter nine months later, this time with Foucher. Telling his erstwhile correspondent that his health had not been too good for some time, he wrote that this

makes me think of publishing some of my ideas, among others my system about the communication of substances and the union of soul and body, on which I once sent you something. I think it is the only one that can provide an intelligible explanation without needing to have recourse to the omnipotence of God. I would be very happy if some discerning people were able to make comments which might cast some light on it—and I particularly look forward to some from you. Perhaps M. Arnauld's objections and my reply to him could also be added. Perhaps too the Reverend Father Malebranche will not refuse you his opinion on it.[11]

In reply, Foucher told Leibniz that he was delighted at his announcement that he was going to publish his system of concomitance.

Anything that comes from someone as able as you are, sir, cannot but be very useful to the public. You did write me something about it around ten

[7] Foucher to Leibniz, Paris, 5 May 1687 (G 1. 388–90).
[8] Leibniz to Foucher, 1687/8? (see app. B).
[9] Translated from a transcript (kindly provided by Niall D. Martin) of the original MS.
[10] See introduction to Ch. 2.
[11] Leibniz to Foucher, 6 Apr. 1695 (G 1. 420).

years ago, but the matter needs some clarification, and I look forward to this with pleasure; let us hope that you will not delay in fulfilling your promise.[12]

Leibniz fulfilled his promise within weeks, in late May or early June, when he evidently sent a text of the 'New System' to Foucher in Paris for publication in the *Journal des savants*.[13] Shortly after publication, in the late June and early July issues of the journal, he again wrote to Foucher, this time with a short summary of his views:

You will have seen that my system is founded on the idea of real unities which are indestructible and *sui juris*.[14] Each of them expresses the whole universe in its own particular way by means of the laws of its own nature, without receiving any influence from outside apart from that of God, who ensures that it subsists, once he has created it, by a continual renewal. If M. Lantin were alive, I believe that he would take a particular delight in these considerations, judging from a letter that he wrote me about 24 years ago in which he said that my thoughts on dynamics, *de conatu*, could also clarify matters of metaphysics.[15]

It was not long before Foucher made the reply which Leibniz's letter in May had hoped for. The 'Reply of M. S. F. to M. de L. B. Z. on his New System of the Communication between Substances' (F1 below) came out in the *Journal des savants* in September, only two months after the 'New System' itself.[16]

---

[12] Foucher to Leibniz, Paris, 28 Apr. 1695 (G 1. 422).

[13] A letter to l'Hôpital (13 May 1695) reports that 'In order to get some of my thoughts off my hands I will send to Paris my way of explaining the communication of substances and the union of the soul with the body' (GM 2. 283). (It also, perhaps trying to enlist l'Hôpital's help, says how pleased Leibniz would be to have some response from Malebranche.) In a later letter, to Nicaise (24 Sept. 1695), Leibniz reports that 'I have sent a piece of philosophy to M. l'Abbé Foucher. In accordance with my intentions he has put it in the *Journal des savants*' (G 2. 555). For more on Leibniz's use of Foucher as a contact with the *Journal des savants* see Stuart Brown, 'Leibniz's *New System* Strategy' (esp. nn. 7, 8), in R. S. Woolhouse (ed.), *Leibniz's 'New System'* (Rome, 1996).

[14] Literally 'of one's own right', i.e. beings in their own right.

[15] Leibniz to Foucher, 5 July 1695 (G 1. 423). Jean Baptiste Lantin (a friend of both Foucher and Leibniz) was presumably referring to Leibniz's *Theoria motus abstracti* . . . (1671) (R 14). Another person to whom Leibniz sent an account of the 'New System' shortly after its publication was Gilles Filleau des Billettes (1634–1724) of the Paris Academy of Sciences and a friend of Leibniz from his Paris days—see app. C.

[16] Telling Nicaise in Sept. 1695 (see n. 13 above) that, having seen to the publication of the 'New System' in the *Journal des savants*, Foucher had also published a response already, Leibniz commented that this had meant having a printed reply to his letter before a written one.

Having first written some informal notes on this (F2 below),
Leibniz composed and dispatched a formal reply within a matter of
days. Believing Foucher to be away from Paris, he sent this to the
Marquis de l'Hôpital,[17] asking him to pass it on for publication to
Cousin, the editor of the *Journal des savants*. L'Hôpital had been a
correspondent of Leibniz for a number of years, and had already
sent him favourable comments about the 'New System'.[18]

It had seemed to Foucher, so he had said in his 'Reply', that
Leibniz's system of concomitance 'is hardly any better' than the
occasionalist one of Malebranche and the Cartesians, and Leibniz
tells l'Hôpital that it will be clear from his counter-reply to Foucher
just how it does improve on Malebranche's. Malebranche himself,
Leibniz says, perhaps will recognize that what he says is right, for
his view is more of a development than a rejection of Malebranche's.[19] Writing in December from his estate at Ouques, l'Hôpital acknowledged receipt of the letter, and said that when he
returned to Paris, the next month, he would give it to Cousin.[20] In
March the next year, 1696, he reported that he had done this, and,
noting that it was some time since Leibniz had sent it, said that
Cousin would publish it without delay.[21] It (F3 below) appeared in
April 1696, the very month Foucher died. Not knowing this,
Leibniz was anxious about a reply. 'Is M. the Abbé Foucher dead or
alive? He has said nothing about my reply in the journal. When he
wrote against my new philosophical thoughts, he believed they
were no more than hypotheses; but on consideration he found that
they were demonstrations.'[22]

[17] Leibniz to l'Hôpital, 20 Sept. 1695 (see app. E). L'Hôpital (1661–1704) was
a mathematician and honorary member of the Paris Academy of Sciences.
    [18] See app. D.
    [19] Leibniz to l'Hôpital, 20 Sept. 1695 (see app. E).
    [20] L'Hôpital to Leibniz, 1 Dec. 1695 (see app. E).
    [21] L'Hôpital to Leibniz, Paris, 19 Mar. 1696 (GM 2. 311–12).
    [22] Leibniz to Nicaise, Hanover, 15 Feb. 1697 (G 2. 563).

F1. FOUCHER: 'Reply of M. S. F. to
M. de L. B. Z. on his New System of the
Communication between Substances, Proposed in
the Journals of 27 June and 4 July 1695'
(12 September 1695)[23]

[1] Although your system is not new to me, sir, and although I told you something of my opinion of it in replying to a letter you wrote me on the subject more than ten years ago,[24] [A] I will nevertheless tell you again here what I think of it, since you ask me to do so again.

[2] The first part[25] is intended only to show that in all substances there are unities which constitute their reality, and which, since they distinguish them from others, form (to speak in scholastic terms) their *individuation*. That is your first point on the subject of matter and extension. I agree with you that it is right to look for unities which underlie the structure and reality of extension.[26] Otherwise, as you quite rightly say, an infinitely divisible extension is only an imaginary composite, the foundations (*principes*) of which do not exist, since without unities there is no genuine multiplicity. However, I am amazed that you do not go any further, because the essential foundations (*principes*) of extension could never really exist.[B] In reality, points without parts could not exist in the universe, and two points joined together do not produce extension. It is impossible that there should exist any length without breadth, or any surface without depth. And it is useless to bring in physical points, because such points

---

[23] 'Réponse de M. S. F. à M. de L. B. Z. sur son nouveau système de la communication des substances, proposé dans les journaux du 27 juin & du 4 juillet 1695', *Journal des savants*, no. 36 (12 Sept. 1695), pp. 422–6 (Amsterdam edn., vol. 23, pp. 639–45) (B 38). The article is reprinted at G 1. 424–7 and, with a couple of minor changes, at G 4. 487–90, under the title 'Objections de M. Foucher, Chanoine de Dijon, contre le nouveau système de la communication des substances, dans une lettre à l'auteur de ce système 12 septemb. 1695'. Along with this second version Gerhardt prints some unpublished notes by Leibniz, headed 'Remarques sur les objections de M. Foucher' (G 4. 490–3). These notes, signalled in our text by A, B, etc. are given below in F2.
[24] The reference is to Leibniz's 1686 letter (G 1. 380–5)—see app. A. Though he here claims to have replied to this, and always spoke of doing so (Foucher to Leibniz, 28 Dec. 1686 (G 1. 385–8); Foucher to Leibniz, 5 May 1687 (G 1. 388–90)), Leibniz—see F3, § 1 below—appears not to have received a reply.
[25] i.e. NS1, §§ 1–11.
[26] i.e. at NS1, § 3.

are extended, and involve all the difficulties we wanted to avoid. But
I will not dwell any longer on this subject, which we have already
discussed, you and I, in the journals of 16 March 1693, and 3
August of the same year.[27]

[3] You also bring in unities of a different kind, which are strictly
speaking unities of composition or of relation, and which concern
the perfecting or the completing of a whole which, being organic,
performs certain functions. For example, a clock is one, an animal
is one; and you want to give the name *substantial forms* to these
natural unities of animals and of plants, so that it will be these
unities which constitute their individuation, by distinguishing them
from every other composite. It seems to me that you are right to
give animals a principle of individuation different from that which
they are usually given, which relates only to their external accidents. This principle must indeed be internal, as regards both the
soul and the body; but however the organs of the animal may be
arranged, the animal will not thereby be made sentient, for, after
all, all this concerns only the organic mechanical structure, and I do
not see that it gives you any reason for introducing a principle of
consciousness into animals, substantially different from that in
man.[c] After all, it is not without reason that the Cartesians hold
that if we allow a principle of consciousness in animals, capable of
distinguishing between good and bad, it will then be necessary also
to allow them reason, discernment, and judgement. And so, if I may
say so, sir, this does not resolve the difficulty either.

[4] Coming now to your *concomitance*, which is the second and
most important part of your system.[28] I can agree that God, the
great constructor of the universe, can assemble the organic parts of
the body of a man so well that they would be capable of producing
all the movements which the soul joined to that body might want to
produce in the course of its lifetime, without the soul's having the
power to change those movements or to modify them in any way;
and that correspondingly God can so structure the soul (whether or
not this will be a new kind of machine) that all the thoughts
and modifications which correspond to those movements come

[27] 'Extrait d'une lettre de M. Foucher chanoine de Dijon, pour répondre à M. de
Leibniz sur quelques axiomes de philosophie', *Journal des savants*, 16 Mar. 1693
(B 29); 'Réponse de M. de Leibniz à l'extrait de la lettre de M. Foucher chanoine
de Dijon, inserée dans le journal du 16 mars 1693', *Journal des savants*, 3 Aug.
1693 (B 31; R 128).
[28] i.e. NS1, §§ 12–18.

successively into being, just when the body performs its actions (*fonctions*). And I will also agree that this is no more impossible than it would be to make two clocks which are so well synchronized, and which operate so uniformly, that just when clock A strikes midday, clock B does the same, so that one would think that the two clocks were driven by the same weight, or the same spring.[29] But after all, what could be the point of this great contrivance with substances, if not to make us believe that they act on one another, even though this is not so?[D] In fact, it seems to me that this system is hardly any better than that of the Cartesians. We reject theirs because it pointlessly supposes that God, having regard to the movements which he himself produces in the body, also produces in the soul the thoughts which correspond to them—as if it were not more worthy of him to produce the thoughts and modifications of the soul straight away, without there being any bodies to guide him,[E] and so to speak to tell him what to do. If we are right in that, then is it not reasonable to ask you why God is not content to produce all the thoughts and modifications of the soul (whether he does it immediately or by means of some contrivance, as you wish) without there being any useless bodies which the mind can never either move or know? After all, even if there were no movement in these bodies, the soul might still think that there was; just as those who are asleep think they are moving their limbs, and walking, when all the time their limbs are at rest, and not moving at all. In the same way, even while awake, souls would be convinced that their bodies moved according to their wills, even though in reality these vain useless lumps were inactive, and remained in continual torpor. [5] In truth, sir, is it not clear that these opinions are concocted specially for the purpose, and that all these systems are only invented after the event, to defend certain preconceived principles? Thus the Cartesians, having assumed that there was nothing in common between spiritual and corporeal substances, cannot explain how the one operates on the other, and so are reduced to saying what they say. But you, sir, who could have disentangled

[29] Latta (p. 320) points out that in F3 Leibniz passes over this now-famous simile of the two clocks, but takes it up in B1 and in the Second and Third Explanations (Ch. 4, nn. 2, 3). There is a problem of translation connected with it, in that sometimes (as in B1) what are mentioned are 'pendules', rather than, as here, 'horloges'. In seventeenth-century English a 'pendulum' can be part of a clock and also a clock. Similarly, *un pendule* in French is a swinging bob and *une pendule* a clock. It is sometimes quite indeterminate which is meant.

yourself from that in other various ways, astonish me by burdening yourself with their problems. For who does not understand that when an extra weight is added to one side of a balance which is in equilibrium and at rest, there is an immediate movement, and one side makes the other go up, in spite of its efforts to go down? You realize that material beings are capable of effort and of movement, and it follows very naturally that the greater effort must overcome the weaker. But then, you also recognize that spiritual beings can make efforts;[F] and since there is no effort which does not presuppose some resistance, this resistance must turn out to be either stronger or weaker. If it is stronger, it overcomes; if weaker, it gives way. Now, it is not impossible that when the mind tries to move the body, it finds that the body makes an opposing effort which resists it sometimes more and sometimes less—in which latter case the body would give in to it. It is in this way that St Augustine sets out to explain the action of minds on bodies in his books on music.[30]

[6] I know that there are many more questions to ask before we have answered all those that can be raised, right back to first principles: that shows how true it is that we must observe the rules of the Academicians,[31] the second of which forbids us to call into question things which we can clearly see that we cannot decide, as are nearly all those of which we have been speaking. It is not that these questions are absolutely unanswerable, but that they are answerable only in a certain order, which requires that philosophers should first reach agreement on the infallible criterion of truth, and apply themselves to giving demonstrations from first principles. In the meantime, we can separate off what we understand clearly and adequately from other points or topics in which some obscurity is involved. . . .

---

[30] Augustine (354–430), *De musica*, bk. 6, ch. 1, sect. 9.
[31] Foucher gives five laws of Academic philosophy: e.g. 'Keep separate what one knows from what one doesn't know' (the fourth), and 'Do not raise questions which you can clearly see you can't answer' (*L'Apologie*, pp. 5–8, 44–5), and three axioms, such as that 'the truth of things is not to be found in the senses' (Watson, p. 20).

F2. LEIBNIZ: 'Remarks on M. Foucher's Objections' (1695)[32]

A. 'more than ten years ago': Because before the publication of the *'New System'*, the rule of Horace was observed: 'nonumque prematur in annum'.[33]

B. 'it is right . . . never really exist': It appears that the author of the objection has not understood my opinion very well. Extension or space, and the surfaces, lines, and points which can be conceived of within it, are only systems of relations (*rapports d'ordre*), or relations of co-existence (*des ordres de co-existence*), as regards both the actual existent and the possible existent which could be put in the place of what there is. So they have no constitutive principle at all, any more than number has. A divided number, for example ½, can be divided again, into two quarters or four eighths, etc., and so on to infinity; we cannot arrive at the smallest fraction, and think of the number as a totality formed by putting together such ultimate elements. And it is the same with a line, which can be divided just like that number. Thus, properly speaking, the number ½ in the abstract is a simple relation, in no way formed by a composition of other fractions, even though among numbered things there is equality between two quarters and one half. And the same can be said of an *abstract* line; for there is composition only in *concrete* things, or *masses*, the relations between which are marked by such abstract lines. And this is also the way that mathematical points come about; they too are mere modalities, i.e. extremities. And as everything about an abstract line is indefinite, they have regard only to what is possible, as do the fractions of a number; we are not concerned with divisions which are actually made, and which mark out these points in a different way. But in actual substantial things, the whole is a result, or assembly, of simple substances, or indeed of a multiplicity of real unities. It is this confusion of the ideal and the actual which has quite obscured, and made a labyrinth of, 'the composition of the continuum'.[34] Those

---

[32] Unpublished 'Remarques sur les Objections de M. Foucher', as printed by Gerhardt (G 4. 490–3).

[33] See Horace, *Ars poetica*, 388.

[34] This is an allusion to the title of a book, *Labyrinthus, sive de compositione continui* (Antwerp, 1631), by Liber Fromond (1587–1653), who raised some problems for Descartes's account of matter as infinitely divisible extension.

for whom lines are made up out of points have quite mistakenly
looked for primary elements in ideal things, or in relations; and
those who realized that relations like number, or space (which
comprises the system or relations of possible coexistent things),
could never be formed by the putting together of points, have for
the most part then gone wrong by saying that substantial realities
have no basic elements, as if they have no primary unities, and there
are no simple substances. However, number and line are not
imaginary things, even though they are indeed not made up in that
way, because they are relations which involve eternal truths, in
accordance with which the phenomena of nature are structured. In
this way we can say that ½ and ¼, taken in the abstract, are
independent of one another, or rather, the complete relation ½ is
prior (in nature (*dans le signe de la raison*), as the scholastics say[35])
to the partial relation ¼, since as regards the order of ideas it is by
subdivision of a half that we arrive at a quarter; and similarly with
the line, where the whole is prior to the part, because the part is
only possible, or ideal. But in real things, where we are concerned
only with divisions which are actually made, the whole is only a
result, or assemblage, like a flock of sheep. In fact, the number of
simple substances which make up a mass, however small that mass
may be, is infinite, since in addition to the soul which constitutes
the real unity of an animal, the body of a sheep (for example) is
actually subdivided: that is to say, it too is an assemblage of
invisible animals or plants, which themselves are also compounded,
in addition to also having that which makes up their own real
unity. And even though this goes on to infinity, it is obvious that, all
in all, everything comes down to these unities, all the rest, or the
resultants, being only well-founded phenomena.

C. 'I do not see . . . from that in man': I do this because we do not
consider animals to engage in the kind of reflection which constitutes
reason, and which, by providing knowledge of necessary truths or of
science, makes the soul capable of being a self. Animals can
distinguish good from bad, since they have perception; but they are
certainly not capable of moral good and bad, which presuppose
reason and consciousness.

D. 'what could be the point . . . not so?': This great contrivance

---

[35] For 'dans le signe de la raison' or—as the scholastics would also have said—
in signo rationis, see Ch. 5, n. 49.

which brings it about that each substance acts in conformity with
every other is necessary because all these substances are the effect
of a sovereign wisdom; and there is no other possible way (at least
in the natural order, and without miracles) to obtain their inter-
dependence, and for them to be changed by one another, or in
accordance with one another. It remains true, however, that they
do operate on each other, provided that we understand this correctly: interaction between created substances consists only in this
dependence which some have on others in consequence of the
original constitution which God gave them. But if we imagine an
influence of one over another, that is an error we have fallen into by
bad reasoning. And God is not obliged to make a system about
which we could not make mistakes, just as he was not obliged to
avoid the system of the moving earth in order to save us from the
error into which nearly all astronomers fell before Copernicus.

E. 'as if it were not . . . to guide him': God produced straightaway
not all thoughts (for thoughts need to succeed one another), but a
nature which produces them in sequence. And that is exactly my
point: all the body does is to act in conformity with them. But
bodies were necessary to produce not only our unities or souls, but
also those of the other corporeal substances, animals and plants,
which are in our bodies and in those which surround us.

F. 'material beings are capable . . . can make efforts': You want to
conclude from this that they can act on one another. But their
efforts are contained within themselves (*chez eux*), and do not pass
from one into another, because they are only tendencies to change
in accordance with the particular laws of each one.

F3. LEIBNIZ: '[First] Explanation of the New
System of the Communication between
Substances, in Reply to what was said of it in the
Journal for 12 September 1695' (April 1696)[36]

[1] I remember several years ago, sir, thinking that I was doing
what you wanted by sending you my theory of philosophy, even

---

[36] 'Éclaircissement du nouveau système de la communication des substances,
pour servir de réponse à ce que en a eté dit dans le journal du 12 septembre 1695',

though as I indicated to you at the time I had not yet decided to publish it.[37] I asked your opinion of it in return; but I do not remember receiving any objections from you. If I had, I am so compliant that I would not have made you raise the same objections twice. Nevertheless, they are not too late, even after publication; for I am not one of those for whom commitment takes the place of reason, as you will find when you are able to bring forward some precise and pressing argument against my opinions. But this apparently was not your intention here; you wanted to speak as a clever Academic,[38] and by so doing to enable us to get to understand things more deeply.

[2] I wanted to explain here, not the foundations (*principes*) of extension, but those of what is actually extended, of corporeal mass; and these foundations, according to me, are real unities, that is to say, substances with a genuine unity. In my view the unity of a clock, which you mention,[39] is completely different from that of an animal; for an animal may be a substance with a genuine unity, like what we call 'I' in ourselves, while a clock is nothing but an aggregate. I do not locate the principle of the animal's consciousness in the arrangement of its organs, which I quite agree concerns only the corporeal mass. I mention these things so as to avoid misunderstandings, and to show that what you say about them is not at all contrary to what I have maintained. It also seems that you do not disagree with me when I demand genuine unities, and so am led to rehabilitate substantial forms. But when you seem to say that the soul of animals must be rational, if we give it feeling, you draw a conclusion for which I see no grounds.

[3] With admirable candour you acknowledge that my theory of harmony or concomitance is possible, but you are still rather unhappy with it. No doubt that is because you think it is purely arbitrary, through not having realized that it follows from my views about unities; but everything is connected to that. Thus you ask, sir, what could be the point of all this contrivance which I attribute to the author of nature.[40] As if we could attribute too much contrivance

Journal des savants, no. 14 (2 Apr. 1696), pp. 166–8; no. 15 (9 Apr. 1696), pp. 169–71 (Amsterdam edn., vol. 24, pp. 248–56) (R 147; B 41). This piece is often known as 'The First Explanation of the New System'.

[37] Leibniz to Foucher, 1686 (see app. A).
[38] See introduction.
[39] The references to Foucher in this section are to F1, § 3.
[40] The references to Foucher in this and the next section are to F1, § 4.

to him, and as if this exact correspondence between substances, through their own laws that each received at the beginning, were not something wonderfully beautiful in itself, and worthy of its author. You also ask what advantage I find in it. I could refer to what I have already said about this; however, I reply, first, that when something cannot not be, there is no need to ask what the point of it is, before we accept it. What is the point of the incommensurability of the side with the diagonal? I reply in the second place that the point of this correspondence is to explain the communication between substances, and the union of the soul with the body, through laws of nature laid down in advance, and so without recourse either to a *transmission* of species, which is unintelligible, or to a further *intervention* by God, which seems inappropriate. For we must realize that as there are natural laws in matter, so there are also natural laws *in souls or forms*. And the operation of those laws is as I have just described.

[4] Again, I am asked why God does not think it enough to produce all the thoughts and 'modifications of the soul', without these 'useless' bodies, which the soul, it is said, could neither 'move nor know'. The answer is easy. It is that God wanted there to be more substances rather than fewer, and he thought it best that these 'modifications of the soul' should correspond to something outside. No substance is 'useless'; they all co-operate in fulfilment of God's plans. I am also far from willing to admit that the soul 'does not know' bodies, even though this knowledge arises without any influence of the one on the other. I am even willing to say that the soul 'moves' the body: just as, provided we understand them properly, a Copernican speaks truly of the rising of the sun, a Platonist of the reality of matter, and a Cartesian of the reality of sensible qualities, so I hold that it is quite true to say that substances act on each other—provided we understand that one is the cause of changes in the other in consequence of the laws of harmony. The objection about the 'torpor' of bodies, which could be at rest while the soul believed them to be in motion, cannot hold, because of this same unfailing correspondence which the divine wisdom has established. I have no knowledge of these 'vain, useless, and inactive lumps' which you mention. There is activity everywhere; I have established this more firmly than the received philosophy, for I hold there is no body without motion, no substance without effort.

(*The remainder of this explanation will open next week's journal.*)

[5] I do not understand the objection that is contained in these words: 'In truth, sir, is it not clear that these opinions are concocted specially for the purpose, and that all these systems are only invented after the event, to defend certain preconceived principles'.[41] All theories are 'concocted for the purpose', and all systems are invented 'after the event', in order to save the phenomena or appearances.[42] But I do not see what the preconceived principles are that I am supposed to want to defend. If the idea is that I am led to my theory by a priori reasons, or by certain principles, as is indeed the case, then this is a commendation of the theory rather than an objection to it. It is usually enough that a theory should be proved a posteriori by its fitting the phenomena; but when there are also other reasons for it, and these are a priori, then so much the better. But perhaps the idea is that, having fashioned for myself a new opinion, I was glad to make use of it, more to pride myself on being original than because I had found it useful. I do not think, sir, that you have such a bad opinion of me as to attribute these thoughts to me. For you know I love truth, and that, if I were so fond of novelties, I would be keener to put them forward than I am, even those whose soundness is recognized. [6] But in order that those who know me less should not give your words a meaning which we wouldn't want, it is enough to say, that in my view it is impossible to give any other explanation of 'emanating activity (*l'action emanente*)'[43] which conforms with natural laws, and that I thought that the usefulness of my theory would be obvious in view of the difficulty which some of the wisest philosophers of our time have found in the communication between minds and bodies, and even between corporeal substances themselves: and I do not know but that you yourself haven't found some difficulty in it. It is true that, according to me, there is effort in all substances; but this force

---

[41] F1, § 5.

[42] According to an ancient tradition, Plato set the mathematicians in his Academy the problem of 'what uniform and orderly motions must be hypothesized to save the phenomenal motions of the wandering stars' (Simplicius, *Commentary on Aristotle's De Caelo*, quoted and trans. Gregory Vlastos, *Plato's Universe* (Oxford, 1975), pp. 59–60); see ibid., pp. 111–12 for a discussion of the Platonic provenance of this phrase.

[43] Parkinson and Morris, p. 128 (and Latta, p. 326), translate this as 'transeunt activity' which they explain as 'activity which passes from the agent to some other; distinct from "immanent activity"' (p. 255).

is, strictly, only in the substance itself, and what follows from it in other substances is only in virtue of a 'pre-established harmony' (if I may use the expression), and not by a real influence or by the transmission of some species or quality. As I have explained what activity and passivity are, the nature of *effort* and of *resistance* can also easily be inferred. You say, sir, that you 'know that there are many more questions to ask before we have answered those that we have raised'.[44] But perhaps you will find that I have already asked them; and I am not sure that your Academics have themselves applied what is good in their method more rigorously and effectively than I have. I strongly approve of aiming to demonstrate truths from first principles. It is more useful than people think, and I have often put this precept into practice. So I applaud what you say about this, and I hope that your example will make our philosophers think of it as they ought. [7] I will add a further reflection, which seems to me helpful in making the true nature and use of my system better understood. You know that M. Descartes believed in the conservation of the same quantity of motion in bodies. It has been shown that he was wrong about this; but I have made clear that it is still true that there is conservation of the same moving force, which he mistook for the quantity of motion. However, the changes which take place in the body as a consequence of modifications of the soul caused him some difficulty, because they seemed to break this law. He therefore thought he had found a solution, which is certainly ingenious, by saying that we must distinguish between motion and direction; and that the soul can neither increase nor decrease the *moving force*, but does change *the direction or determination* of the course of the animal spirits: and this is how voluntary motions take place. Even so, he made no attempt to explain *how* the soul changes the course of bodies, which seems just as incomprehensible as its giving motion to bodies—at least so long as we do not have recourse to my pre-established harmony. But what we have to realize is that there is *another law of nature*, which I have discovered and demonstrated, and which M. Descartes did not know: *there is conservation* not only of the same quantity of moving force, but also *of the same quantity of direction towards whichever side one chooses*. That is to say, draw any straight line you please, and take whichever and however many bodies you like; you will find, considering all these

44 F1, § 6.

bodies together, and without omitting any of those which act upon any one of those you have taken, that there will always be the same quantity of progress in a given direction in all lines parallel to your straight line. Note that the total amount of progress is to be calculated by subtracting the amount of progress of the bodies which go in the opposite direction from the amount of progress of those which go in the chosen direction. Since this law is as excellent and as general as the other, it as little deserves to be broken; and this is what my system achieves, for it conserves both force and direction. In a word, it preserves all the natural laws of bodies, despite the changes which take place in body as a consequence of changes in the soul.

Appendix A. LEIBNIZ: Letter to Foucher, 1686[45]

... It seems to me that you are also right ... to question whether the body can act on the mind, and vice versa. I have an interesting theory about this which seems to me unavoidable, and which is very different from that of the author of the *Search*. I believe that every individual substance expresses the whole universe in its own way, and that each of its states is a consequence (although often a free consequence) of its preceding one, as if there were only God and that substance in the world. But since all substances are continually produced by the sovereign Being, and express the same universe or the same phenomena, they correspond exactly. This makes us say that one acts upon the other, because one expresses more distinctly than the other the cause or the reason for its changes, much as we (with good reason) attribute movement to a ship rather than to the sea as a whole. I also infer from this that if bodies are substances, they cannot consist solely of extension. But that makes no difference to the explanations of particular natural phenomena, which should always be explained mathematically and mechanically, provided that we realize that the principles of mechanics do not depend on mere extension. I am therefore in favour neither of the usual theory of a real influence of one created substance on another, nor of the theory of occasional causes, that God produced thoughts in the soul on the occasion of movements in the body, and so changed the course that the soul would otherwise have taken by a kind of completely useless perpetual miracle.

[45] From the French at G 1. 380–5.

Instead, I maintain a concomitance or agreement between what happens in the two different substances, because God created the soul from the outset in such a way that all these things happen to it, or originate from its own resources, without there being any need for it thereafter to accommodate itself to the body, or the body to the soul. With each one following its own laws, the one acting freely, the other without choice, they meet together in the same phenomena. All of that fits quite well with what you say in your reply to Dom Robert ... that man is the proper object of his awareness. It can nevertheless be added that God is, too, for he alone acts on us immediately in virtue of our continual dependence. So one can say that God alone, or what is in him, is our immediate object outside ourselves (if the term 'object' can be applied to God).

As for the sixth supposition, it isn't necessary that what we understand of things outside ourselves should resemble them perfectly, but only that it should express them; in the way that an ellipse expresses a circle seen from an angle, so that each point on the circle corresponds to one on the ellipse and vice versa, in accordance with a certain law of correspondence. For, as I have already said, each individual substance expresses the universe in its own way, rather like the way the same town is differently expressed according to different points of view. Each effect expresses its cause, and the cause of each substance is the decision which God took to create it. But that decision involved relations to the whole universe, because God had everything in view when coming to a decision about each part, for the wiser one is, the more one's plans are interconnected.

As for the question of whether there is extension outside of us, or whether it is only a phenomenon, as is colour, you are right to say that it is not easy. The notion of extension is not as clear as people imagine. We have to decide whether space is something real, whether matter contains something more than extension, whether matter itself is a substance and how, and although it would take too long to give my opinion on all that, I hold nevertheless that these things can be decided. . . .

Appendix B. LEIBNIZ: Letter to Foucher, ?1687/8[46]

. . . [W]e must not only reject what is poorly established, but also try to establish, bit by bit, solid truths. I once wrote an essay giving

[46] From the French at G 1. 390.

demonstrations, *de continente et contento*, in which I demonstrated by symbols (somewhat like algebra or numbers) some propositions (of which the rules of the syllogism and some mathematical propositions are only corollaries).[47] I could give many more of them, demonstrated hypothetically from a few assumptions by simple substitution of equivalent characters, not only with regard to size, but also quality, form, and relation. The most important would be about cause, effect, change, action, and time, where I find that the truth is very different from what is believed. For although a substance can reasonably be called a physical and often a moral cause of what happens in another substance, nevertheless, speaking with metaphysical rigour, each substance (together with the concurrence of God) is the real immediate cause of what happens to it, in such a way that, strictly speaking, there is no violent change. And it can even be said that a body is only ever pushed by the force which is in itself. This is also confirmed by experience, (for it is by its elastic force that it moves away from another body in restoring itself after having been compressed. And although elastic force derives from the motion of a fluid, nevertheless this fluid, when it acts, is in the body when it exercises its elasticity). But it also follows that in every substance which is a genuine substance and not simply a machine or an aggregate of several substances, there is some 'I' which corresponds to what we call the soul in ourselves, and which is ingenerable and incorruptible, and cannot begin except by creation. And if animals are not simple machines, there is reason to think that their generation, as well as their apparent corruption, is only a transformation of the same animal, which is sometimes more and sometimes less visible. This was long ago the view of the author of the book *Diet*, which is attributed to Hippocrates. Nevertheless, I hold that minds, such as our own, are created in time and are

[47] G. H. R. Parkinson has suggested to us that Leibniz is quite possibly referring to one of a series of papers on symbolic logic which he wrote in April 1679 (Cout, pp. 42–92), specifically perhaps to 'Regulae ex quibus de bonitate consequentiarum formisque et modis syllogismorum categoricorum judicari potest, per numeros' (Cout, pp. 77–84) (trans. in LLP, pp. 24–32, as 'Rules from which a Decision can be Made, by Means of Numbers, about the Validity of Inferences and about the Forms and Moods of Categorical Syllogisms'). The paper doesn't expressly mention 'container' and 'content' (*de continente et contento*), but it does say that the rules are derived from 'a higher principle' (LLP, p. 25)—i.e. that every true universal proposition is such that 'the predicate is ... contained in the subject' (Cout, p. 51; as at LLP, p. 19). Parkinson suggests that propositions such as the axiom that the whole is greater than the part are what Leibniz means by 'some mathematical propositions'.

exempt from these revolutions after death, for they have a very particular relation to the sovereign being, a relation, I say, which they need to preserve. {With regard to them this God is not only a cause, but also a lord; this is what both religion and reason teach us.} If bodies were only simple machines, or if there were only extension or matter in bodies, it is demonstrable that all bodies would only be phenomena. Plato saw this quite clearly, in my view. And it seems to me that I can detect something of the same kind in your thought (page 59 of your discourse on the opinion of St Augustine concerning the Academicians).[48] {I can also prove that extension, shape, and movement involve something imaginary or apparent, and although we conceive them more clearly than colour or heat, nevertheless, when one takes analysis as far as I have, one finds that these notions also contain something confused, and that, unless we suppose that there are some substances which consist in something else, they will be just as imaginary as sensible qualities, or as well-ordered dreams. For from motion in itself we cannot ascertain to which subject it belongs; and I hold it to be demonstrable that there is no precise shape in bodies. Plato saw something of all this, but he could not rid himself of his doubts, because in his day geometry and analysis were not advanced. Aristotle also understood the necessity of attributing something other than extension to bodies. But he did not understand the mystery of the duration of substances, and he believed in real generation and corruption, which for him turned all these ideas upside down. The Pythagoreans obscured the truth with their metempsychosis; instead of thinking of the transformation of the same animal, they believed, or at least proclaimed, the passage of the soul of one animal into another, which is not to say anything.} But these sorts of consideration are not suitable to be seen by everyone, and the usual run of people will never understand them unless their minds are first prepared. . . .

Appendix C. LEIBNIZ: Letter to des Billettes, 4 December 1696[49]

. . . My system, of which you were curious to have news, sir, is not a complete body of philosophy, and I certainly don't claim to give an account of everything that others have claimed to explain. One

[48] *Dissertation . . . contenant l'apologie des académiciens* (1683).
[49] From the French at G 7. 451–2.

has to take small steps to walk safely. I begin from principles, and hope to be able to answer most doubts of the kind which troubled the late M. Bernier. I believe that everything in nature in fact happens mechanically and can be explained by efficient causes, but also that at the same time everything happens morally, so to speak, and can be explained by final causes. And these two kingdoms, the moral realm of minds and souls and the mechanical realm of bodies, are interwoven and agree perfectly by means of the creator of things, who is simultaneously both the first efficient cause and the last final cause. I claim, then, that just as there is no void among bodies, so there is none among souls — that is to say, there are souls everywhere, and souls that once exist can never perish. Bodies are multiplicities, and souls are unities, but unities which express or represent a multiplicity in themselves. Each soul is a mirror of the entire world, from its own point of view. But minds are souls of the first order or of the highest class, which represent not only the world but also God in the world. So not only are they immortal, but also they always retain their moral qualities as citizens of the republic of the universe, in which nothing is lacking, since it is God who governs it. My explanation of the union of the soul and the body can be found in number 38 of this year's *Journal des savants*.[50]

Appendix D. LEIBNIZ: Letter to l'Hôpital, 12 July 1695[51]

... I shall be delighted to have your opinion on the thoughts recently published in your journal for June and July. It is mathematicians who should be asked for an opinion, and not the ordinary run of philosophers. Metaphysical ideas cannot fail to seem strange to minds which are not accustomed to thinking. I hope they won't drive themselves mad with it. I am firmly of the opinion of Reverend Father Malebranche in thinking that it is only God who acts immediately on substances by a real influence. But leaving aside the dependence we have in regard to God, which means that we are conserved by a continual creation; leaving that aside, I say, and speaking only of secondary causes or the ordinary course of nature, I hold that without having need of any new operation by God, we can be satisfied, in order to explain things, with what God gave them at the outset. So, according to me, every substance {already expresses in advance and} produces for itself, internally, in order,

---

[50] i.e. F3 above.   [51] From the French at GM 2. 294.

everything that will ever happen to it. God decided to sustain it only in conformity with {these basic outlines, or} the basic nature of the thing, the consequences of which are the unfolding of the future. M. Arnauld thought at first sight that this would be an attack on grace and would favour the Pelagians, but having received my explanation, he cleared me of that charge.[52] I think I can say, though, that nothing could be more favourable to our liberty than the view I have just put forward. The key to my doctrine on this subject consists in the consideration of (*que* [sic] = ? *de*) that which is genuinely a real unity, a monad. . . .

L'HÔPITAL: Letter to Leibniz, Paris, 3 September 1695[53]

. . . Talking of novelties, what you published in the *Journal des savants* has something of the air of one. Your theory that in creating a mind God gives it at the outset all the operations and functions of which it is capable, and that everything that follows is only an unfolding, seems to me to be exactly parallel to the theory that we have in nature, and with which many able men now agree, namely that in the first grain of wheat, for example, there were contained in miniature all the ears and grains of corn which there have been since, and which there will be till the end of time. The Reverend Father Malebranche, whom I told that you were hoping to have his opinion, asked me to assure you that for his part he has a very special regard for you, and that with regard to your metaphysical ideas they do not seem to him sufficiently explained. He said it is very difficult to philosophize by letter about these matters, which are in themselves so abstract. It has to be said that demonstrations of this kind are not as evident as those in mathematics, for it seems to me that one usually remains attached to the view that one held at the start. Between ourselves, I don't believe that Father Malebranche wants to abandon his system (*sistence*, [sic]) of occasional causes. . . .

---

[52] R. C. Sleigh, Jr., says of this passage: 'In general I have found Leibniz's accounts of his exchanges with Arnauld accurate and entirely fair. In the present case, I have no idea what passage in the letters from Arnauld Leibniz had in mind' (*Leibniz and Arnauld* (New Haven and London, 1990), p. 216).

[53] From the French at GM 2. 296.

Appendix E. LEIBNIZ: Letter to l'Hôpital, Hanover, 20 September 1695[54]

... Having seen in the *Journal des savants* that M. the Abbé Foucher, Canon of Dijon, has made some comments on my philosophical theory, I take the liberty of sending my reply to you, begging you to send it to M. the President Cousin, who perhaps would be good enough to put it in his journal if he finds it suitable. If I did not think that M. the Abbé Foucher is now in Burgundy, I would have addressed it to him. If there is any service I am able to render you as a means of expressing my devotion, I should be honoured to receive your instructions. . . .

You will see also, sir, from my reply to M. the Abbé Foucher, how my theory is different from that of the Reverend Father Malebranche, and that of the Cartesians, who are of his opinion: I believe that the actions of souls not only cannot change the quantity of moving force of bodies (with which M. Descartes was in agreement) but that they cannot even change the laws of its direction (as he believed they could). So the changes which take place in the one as a consequence of those in the other could do so only by a pre-established harmony, and they are always entirely in conformity with the natural laws of each substance by itself. Perhaps even the Reverend Father Malebranche himself will see that what I say makes sense, once he has considered what I have to say about it. It could perhaps be said that it is not so much a rejection as a development of his doctrine, and that it is to him that I owe my basic principles on this subject. We agree that the mind and the body have no influence on each other, and that all the perfections of things are always produced by the operation of God. I add only that what God produces in A, in conformity with what he produces in B, is also precisely in conformity with the relevant laws that he has established for A—a topic that had not been thought about enough. However if perhaps he has some reason for saying nothing about this, I would not want to press him, however much I want to hear his opinion. For I know what precautions one sometimes has to take; although in the end not only do I see nothing in this theory, which might be the object of any censure, but indeed I see nothing which is not of the greatest advantage to religion above all, and

[54] From the French at GM 2. 297.

which does not lead to the greater admiration of the sovereign substance. . . .

L'HÔPITAL: Letter to Leibniz, Ouques, 1 December 1695[55]

I have received, sir, the letter which you did me the honour of writing on 30 September last, with your reply to M. Foucher. I shall not fail to take it myself to M. the President Cousin as soon as I return to Paris, which will only be next month, in January. I have no doubt that he is both honoured and pleased that from time to time you are good enough to enrich his journals with some of your discoveries. The law that you give for the direction of bodies at the end of your letter is quite splendid; I would very much like to know where you have demonstrated it. But as for the force of bodies that you insist on distinguishing from their quantity of motion, I must confess that I have a lot of difficulty with it. I cannot understand how a body can act except by its mass and its speed, and I do not see that it has been demonstrated that the same quantity of motion is not conserved in nature. I know perfectly well that motion seems to be lost in experiments that have been done, but could it not be that it was communicated to an invisible matter which was contained in the pores of the colliding bodies? But even if one accepts that the same quantity of motion is not conserved in nature, it does not follow that the quantity of force is any different. It seems to me that in that case we could say that the law that God has established consists in the fact that the same quantity of motion is always conserved not *absolutely* but *relatively*, in a certain direction, which would fit very well with all the experiments done by M. Mariotte and others. In fact, I hope very much that some convincing experiments can be done by which we can be certain whether or not force is different from quantity of motion, because it seems to me that this principle needs to be clearly and visibly demonstrated before any consequences are drawn from it, for it is a necessary presupposition. There is also another principle which we owe to you, and about which I agree with you, which is wonderfully useful in solving a number of questions both physical as well as mathematical, namely that nature does not act *per saltum*, and thus that rest can be considered as an infinitely small motion, and so on. And what is more, your philosophical system avoids many difficulties, and reveals an infinite wisdom in the creator of the world, who has

[55] From the French at GM 2. 303.

combined the laws of the union of minds and bodies so well that what happens in the one in consequence of volitions in the other is always entirely in conformity with the natural laws of each substance taken on its own.

4

Leibniz and Henri Basnage de Beauval

INTRODUCTION

Henri Basnage de Beauval (1656–1710) was the author of *Histoire de la religion des églises réformées* (Rotterdam, 1690), which attacked Bossuet's *Histoire des variations des églises protestantes* (1688), and also editor of the Rotterdam journal *Histoire des ouvrages des savants*, which was begun in 1687. He lived in Holland, and corresponded with Leibniz after they first met, in 1692.

Towards the end of 1695, shortly after the publication of the 'New System', Leibniz outlined in a letter to him some of its main ideas.[1] Basnage, answering Leibniz's expressed hope, must have sent some comments on these, for Leibniz replied to him from Hanover, in an explanatory postscript dated 3 January 1696 (B1). Leibniz left it to Basnage to decide 'whether the explanations I have just given would be appropriate for sounding out the opinions of enlightened persons through the medium of your journal'. In the event, Basnage lost no time, and printed an edited extract, now known as the 'Second Explanation of the New System', in his *Histoire* for February 1696.[2] Leibniz requested that his name not be given, 'just as it was not given in the Paris journal' when the 'New System' was published.

The edited version of what Leibniz had sent to him, which Basnage published in February 1696, was followed in November of the same year by the publication in the *Journal des savants* of some of what Basnage had edited out, together with some further material.[3] This has come to be known as the 'Third Explanation of the New System'; it marks the first public occasion on which Leibniz speaks of 'the way of pre-established harmony'.[4]

---

[1] App. A.

[2] 'Extraits de diverses lettres', *Histoire des ouvrages des savants*, Feb. 1696, art. 14, pp. 274–6 (B 39; R 145). Dutens, who reprints it, entitles it the 'Second Explanation of the System of the Communication between Substances and of the Union of the Soul and the Body'.

[3] See app. B and notes to B1.   [4] See introduction to Ch. 6, esp. n. 20.

B1. LEIBNIZ: Letter to Basnage, Hanover, 3 January 1696[5]

I see quite clearly from your comments, that the idea of mine which a friend had put in the Paris journal needs some explanation. You say, sir, that you do not know how I could prove what I have put forward with regard to the communication or harmony between two substances as different as the soul and the body. Actually I thought I had given the way; here is how I hope to satisfy you.[6]

Imagine two clocks or watches which always tell exactly the same time. This could be done in three ways. The first is by a natural· influence.[7] This is what was discovered experimentally to his great surprise by Monsieur Huygens. He had hung two pendulums (*pendules*, ? gender) from[8] the same piece of wood, and the continual swinging of the pendulums imparted corresponding vibrations to the particles of the wood. But these vibrations could continue as they were and not interfere with one another only if the pendulums kept time together, and so it happened, by a kind of marvel, that even when their swinging was deliberately interfered with, they still came back to swinging together, almost like two strings vibrating in unison.[9] *The second way* of making two clocks (even poor ones) always tell the same time would be to have them constantly looked after by a skilled workman, who adjusts them,[10] and keeps them in time[11] from moment to moment. *The third way* would be to make these two clocks (*pendules*, ? gender), from the beginning,[12] with such skill and accuracy that we could be sure that they would always afterwards keep time together.[13]

---

[5] From the French at G 4. 498–500. As explained in the introduction to this chapter, this letter formed the basis of the published Second and Third Explanations. We have noted important changes; the unnoted changes are mainly in the Second Explanation, which (edited by Basnage) follows B1 less closely than the Third Explanation (written by Leibniz).

[6] For Third Explanation variation, see first para of app. B.

[7] For 'natural', Second and Third Explanations read 'mutual'.

[8] For 'hung two pendulums (*pendules*, ? gender) from', Third Explanation reads 'two large pendulums (*pendules*, f.) attached to'.

[9] Second Explanation omits the previous three sentences.

[10] For '*way* of making two clocks . . . who adjusts to them', Second Explanation reads 'would be to assign a skilled workman to them, who adjusted them'.

[11] Third Explanation omits 'and keeps them in time'.

[12] Second Explanation omits 'from the beginning'.

[13] Third Explanation adds: 'And this is the way of pre-established agreement.' For the historical significance of this addition, see introduction to Ch. 6.

Now put the soul and the body in the place of these two watches.[14] Their agreement or sympathy[15] will also come about in one of these three ways. *The way of influence* is that of the commonly accepted philosophy; but as we cannot conceive either material particles or species[16] or immaterial qualities which can pass from one of these substances into the other, we are obliged to reject this view. *The way of continual[17] assistance[18]* is that of the system of occasional causes; but I maintain that this is to bring in a *deus ex machina* to natural and everyday things, where reason says that God should intervene[19] only in the way in which he concurs with all other natural things. Thus there remains only my theory, *the way of pre-established[20] harmony*, set up by a contrivance of Divine foresight, which formed[21] each of these substances from the outset so[22] that merely by following out its own laws, which were given to it when it was brought into being, each substance is nevertheless in harmony with the other, just as if there were a mutual influence between them, or as if in addition to his general concurrence God were continually operating upon them. Beyond that I do not think I have need of any further proof, unless I need to prove that God is sufficiently skilful to be able[23] to produce a contrivance of such foresight, of which in fact we have instances even among men, where they have the skill. Assuming that God is capable of this, it is quite evident that this is the most admirable way, and the one most worthy of him. You had some suspicion[24] that my explanation was incompatible with the very different ideas we have of the mind and the body. But now, sir, you see that no one has established their independence better, because as long as their communication had to be explained by some kind of miracle, that

[14] For 'watches', Second and Third Explanations read 'clocks' (Second: *pendules*, ? gender; Third: *horloges*).
[15] Second Explanation omits 'or sympathy'.
[16] Second Explanation omits 'or species'.
[17] Third Explanation omits '*continual*'.
[18] Second Explanation adds 'from the Creator'.
[19] For 'intervene', Second Explanation reads 'concur'.
[20] Second Explanation omits '*pre-established*'. For the historical significance of this omission, see introduction to Ch. 6, esp. n. 20.
[21] For ', set up ... which formed', Second Explanation reads '. God made'.
[22] For 'so', Second Explanation reads 'of such a nature', and Third Explanation reads 'in so perfect, so regular and so exact a manner'.
[23] Third Explanation: 'adequate'.
[24] Presumably in Basnage's comments on Leibniz's letter of late 1695 (see introduction to this chapter).

gave many people reason to fear that the distinction could not be as great as we believe,[25] because we had to go to such lengths to sustain it. Now all these scruples are at an end. My *Essays on Dynamics* are relevant to this, where I had to look more deeply into the notion of corporeal substance, which I hold to consist more in the force of action and resistance than in extension, which is only the repetition or diffusion of something prior, namely that force. These thoughts, which appeared paradoxical to some, led me to exchange letters with several famous people, and I could let you have a 'commercium epistolicum'[26] on the subject, which would include the exchange with M. Arnauld of which I spoke in my previous letter.[27] It would contain a curious mixture of philosophical and mathematical thoughts, which might perhaps in parts possess the charm of originality. I leave it to you, sir, to decide whether the explanations I have just given would be appropriate for sounding out the opinions of enlightened persons through the medium of your journal—but without giving my name, just as it was not given in the Paris journal.[28] [29]

Appendix A. LEIBNIZ: Letter to Basnage, late 1695?[30]

... Some friends in Paris extracted some philosophical ideas from me, and they have been printed in the *Journal des savants*. Among other things there is a new theory about the communication of substances, and particularly about the union of the soul with the body. Actually I found it appropriate to disguise my name; few people are able to think rationally about these matters. I claim, then, to have shown that everything happens to the soul, and to the body, in virtue of its own laws, and as a consequence of its original state. But this happens with a harmony between these different substances which is so exact, and so well established from the

[25] For 'could not be as great as we believe', Second Explanation reads 'between the body and the soul was not as real as we think'.
[26] Exchange of letters, collected correspondence.
[27] See app. A.
[28] The last two paragraphs of app. B give the 'Third Explanation' variation of the last five sentences here.
[29] For the last five sentences, Second Explanation reads 'I would not at all mind if some enlightened persons were sounded out on the ideas that I have just explained to you.'
[30] From the French at G 3. 121-2.

outset by the infinite wisdom of the creator of things, that the changes which arise in this way in each one out of its own depths match up to one another just as if there were a transmission of species and qualities, or some real influence, as the majority of philosophers imagine there to be, but which could never happen. It seems to me both more worthy of God and more acceptable to philosophy to make everything happen in accordance with the natural laws that God gave things at the outset, rather than that we should be obliged always to employ him *ex machina* in order to explain what happens in the ordinary course of events, as do the creators of the system of occasional causes. So instead of saying with them that God has made for himself a law always to produce changes in one substance in conformity with those in another, which interferes with their natural laws at every moment, I say that God gave each one of them from the outset a nature whose own laws produce these changes, so that according to me the actions of souls neither add to nor subtract from the quantity of moving force which is in matter, and do not even change its direction, as M. Descartes thought it did. Nevertheless, I do not deny the action of one substance on another; but I believe that the effort that it makes is only within itself, and that the change which happens in the other is only a consequence of pre-established harmony. It is impossible to explain the action of one thing on another in the natural order of events in any other way. We shall see what philosophers make of it. I had already exchanged several letters with the late M. Arnauld, who had been surprised at first by the novelty of the idea, and of various others which are connected with it, but began to get used to it as our correspondence on the subject developed. I am particularly keen to have your opinion on it, and also that of M. Bayle who has studied these matters in some depth. . . .

Appendix B. LEIBNIZ: 'Extract from a Letter by M. Leibniz about his Philosophical Hypothesis . . .', November 1696 ('Third Explanation of the New System')[31]

Some learned and acute friends[32] of mine, who have considered my new theory on the great question of *the union of soul and body*

---

[31] 'Extrait d'une lettre de M. de Leibniz sur son *Hypothèse* de philosofie, et sur le *problème curieux* qu'un de ses amis propose aux Mathematiciens; avec une remarque sur quelques points contestez dans les journaux précédents,

[*See p. 66 for n. 31 cont. and n. 32.*]

have found it to be of value, have asked me to provide explanations of some of the difficulties which have been found with it, and which arise from its not having been properly understood. I think the matter might be made intelligible to all types of mind[33] by the following illustration. . . .

In fact I do have other proofs, but they are deeper, and it is unnecessary to present them here. . . .[34]

Let me say a word about the dispute between two very clever people, the author of the recently published *Principles of Physics* and the author of the *Objections* (which appeared in the journal of August 13 and others),[35] because my theory helps to settle it. I do not understand how matter can be conceived as extended and yet without either actual or ideal (*mentales*) parts; if it can, I do not know what it is for something to be extended. In fact, I hold that *matter* is essentially *an aggregate*, and consequently that it always has actual parts. Thus it is by reason, and not only by the senses, that we see that it is divided, or rather that it is ultimately nothing but a multiplicity. I hold it true that matter (and indeed every part of matter) is divided into a greater number of parts than it is possible to imagine. This is why I often say that each body, however small, is a world of infinitely many creatures. Thus I do not believe there are atoms, that is to say parts of matter which are perfectly hard or of unbreakable solidity; nor, on the other hand, do I believe that there is perfectly fluid matter: my opinion is that each body is

---

entre l'auteur des *principes de Physique*, et celui des *objections* contre ces principes¹, *Journal des savants*, 19 Nov. 1696 (Paris edn., no. 38, pp. 451–5; Amsterdam edn., vol. 24, pp. 687–93) (B 44; R 148). Dutens and Desmaizeaux, who reprint it, entitle it the 'Third Explanation of the System of the Communication between Substances'.

[32] The reference is quite possibly to Basnage, to whom of course Leibniz had originally sent B1, and perhaps also to Foucher.

[33] 'types of mind' possibly echoes Pascal, *Pensées*, art. 7. 1–2. Cf. Ch. 2, n. 23, and esp. Ch. 5, n. 68.

[34] Omitted here is the section of the letter dealing with the problem referred to in the title—the problem of the 'brachistrochrone', or curve of quickest descent, which was set by Johann Bernoulli (1667–1748), Professor of Mathematics at Groningen. His aim in proposing the problem, and Leibniz's in advertising it, was to show that it could only be solved with the help of the new calculus; see Aiton, p. 206.

[35] i.e. Hartsoeker (see Ch. 2, n. 36), whose *Principles of Physics* was published in Paris in 1696, and 'M. La Montre, Professor of Mathematics and Philosophy', who raised criticisms of it in the *Journal des savants* the same year (see nos. 16, 28, 31, 32, 33, 35, 36).

fluid as compared with more solid bodies, and *solid (ferme)* as compared with more fluid ones. I am amazed that people still say that there is conservation of the same *quantity of motion*, in the Cartesian sense; for I have proved the opposite, and some excellent mathematicians have already admitted as much.[36] Nevertheless, I do not regard the solidity or cohesion of bodies as a primary quality, but as a consequence of motion. I hope my Dynamics will explain what it consists in, just as the understanding of my theory will serve to remove several difficulties which still engage the attention of philosophers. In fact, I think I can intelligibly answer all the 'doubts' to which *the late M. Bernier* devoted a whole book;[37] and those who are willing to think about what I have previously published will perhaps be able to see how.

[36] Huygens, e.g. (see Ch. 2, n. 93).
[37] *M. Bernier's Doubts Concerning some of the most Important Chapters of his Summary of the Philosophy of Gassendi* (1684). (The title refers to the *Summary of the Philosophy of Gassendi* (1678) by François Bernier (1620–88).)

5

Leibniz and Pierre Bayle

INTRODUCTION

Pierre Bayle (1647–1706), Professor of History and Philosophy at Rotterdam, had great influence on eighteenth-century thought through his masterpiece, his extensive *Dictionnaire historique et critique*.

Leibniz first corresponded with him in the 1680s, when Bayle published some articles of his in the *Nouvelles de la République des lettres* (a journal which Bayle founded in 1684). They were later in touch through an intermediary, Henri Basnage de Beauval. It was through Basnage that Leibniz not very successfully sought Bayle's views on a manuscript he had circulated on Descartes's *Principles of Philosophy*,[1] and to him that Leibniz expressed the wish to have Bayle's opinion of the 'New System'.[2] This wish was eventually and soundly fulfilled by Bayle's comments on it in an extensive footnote (note H) to the article on 'Rorarius' in the first edition (1697) of his *Historical and Critical Dictionary* (PB1 below).

The subject of this article, Jerome Rorarius (1485–1566), had written a booklet, 'That Animals Use Reason Better than Man' (published posthumously in 1654 as a contribution to the debate over Descartes's view of animals as unthinking machines). In the article Bayle holds that the common view, that animals are capable of reason, has the disadvantage that it obscures the distinction between humans and animals, and so makes it very hard to show that the human soul is immortal. He says that both Descartes (successfully) and the Aristotelians (unsuccessfully) tried to maintain the distinction, but that neither account can make sense of cases of animal cleverness such as those which Rorarius presents. He then continues: 'A great mind in Germany, who has understood these problems, has provided some insights which are worth developing'—at which point he directs the reader to note H.

---

[1] See Barber, p. 60, for details.   [2] See Ch. 4, app. A.

Having read, with evident interest and care, what Bayle had to say about the 'New System', Leibniz sent to their intermediary, Basnage, 'A letter containing ... an explanation of the difficulties which M. Bayle found with the New System ...'. Basnage, as he explained in reply to Leibniz,[3] showed this to Bayle, and so was able to enclose a letter from him about it.

Basnage (as editor of the journal *Histoire des ouvrages des savants*) also told Leibniz that he would publish his 'Explanation'; and in reply, both to Basnage[4] and to Bayle,[5] Leibniz expressed the hope that Basnage would also, and at the same time, publish some reply by Bayle. In the event, Leibniz's piece was published by itself in the issue dated July 1698 (PB3 below).

The reason for there being no accompanying reply by Bayle was not that he had nothing to say, for just a few months later the *Histoire des ouvrages des savants* published a letter from him announcing that he had read Leibniz's 'Explanation' and would say something about it in a second edition of the *Dictionary*.[6]

Bayle evidently also wrote personally to Leibniz about this intention, for in an undated letter Leibniz says that if he had known that the *Dictionary*'s second edition was to appear so soon, he would have preferred to have waited for it and to have had his reply to Bayle's original difficulties published simultaneously with Bayle's further thoughts. Given that this was now out of the question, he asked Bayle to send him a copy of those further thoughts, so that the second edition might include Leibniz's reactions to those instead.[7]

Unfortunately, Leibniz's wish for simultaneous public discussion with Bayle was again thwarted, for, in October 1701, Bayle replied that he had no copy to send, everything having already gone to the printer.[8] He consoled him, however, by saying that Leibniz's reply would surely be published anyway, by Basnage in the *Histoire*. Two months later Leibniz apologized for troubling him, and said that for his reply he would, 'with M. de Beauval's permission ...

---

[3] Basnage to Leibniz, 12 Sept. 1698 (G 3. 139).
[4] Leibniz to Basnage, Hanover, 27 Dec. 1698 (G 3. 140–1).
[5] Leibniz to Bayle, Hanover, 27 Dec. 1698 (G 3. 55–6).
[6] 'Extraits de diverses lettres', *Histoire des ouvrages des savants*, art. 13 (pp. 126–42), Mar. 1699, pp. 135–6 (B 54).
[7] Leibniz to Bayle, n.d. (though Erdmann gives '1702') (G 3. 58). According to Gerhardt (G 3. 58 n.), the letter to which Leibniz is replying is lost.
[8] Bayle to Leibniz, Rotterdam, 5 Oct. 1701 (G 3. 61–2).

use the same expedient as I used before' of publishing in the *Histoire*.[9]

Advance notice of Bayle's comments on Leibniz's 'Explanation of M. Bayle's Difficulties' was given in a pre-publication account of the second edition of the *Dictionary* in the *Histoire* for November 1701.[10] They duly appeared, in the new note L to the 'Rorarius' article (PB4 below), when the *Dictionary*'s second edition was published in 1702.

Not surprisingly, Leibniz was quick to read Bayle's second edition,[11] 'in which', he wrote to him that same year, 'there is so much erudition, intellect and charm that it needed a great effort on my part to tear myself away from it when I had to'.[12] His letter (sent via Bernoulli and de Volder),[13] enclosed the reply which he and Bayle had earlier envisaged.

Concerning this reply, Leibniz explained to Bayle that 'for the moment it is for you, sir, and for certain selected friends, rather than for the public'. Acknowledging (in October 1702) Leibniz's manuscript, 'in which you were good enough to consider my small objections', Bayle said he 'had read it with extreme pleasure, and with renewed admiration for the beauty and depth of your mind'. He expressed the fervent hope that it would be published.[14] About

---

[9] Leibniz to Bayle, Berlin, 27 Dec. 1701 (G 3. 62–3).

[10] Art. 3, pp. 465–92.

[11] In a letter to Bernoulli on 29 May 1702, Leibniz, in Hanover, says that he's 'very recently received' (GM 3/2. 696) the new edn.

[12] Leibniz to Bayle, Berlin, 19 Aug. 1702 (G 3. 63–4).

[13] Leibniz to Bernoulli, 19 Aug. 1702 (GM 3/2. 712); Leibniz to de Volder, 19 Aug. 1702 (G 2. 244). The previous month Leibniz had mentioned this reply to Fontenelle, had said he would send it him, and had asked for his opinion (Leibniz to Fontenelle, Lützenburg, near Berlin, 12 July 1702 (FC1 215–16). Fontenelle said he never received it (Fontenelle to Leibniz, Paris, 18 Nov. 1702 (FC1 216)).

[14] Bayle to Leibniz, Rotterdam, 3 Oct. 1702 (G. 3. 64–5). De Volder (via whom Bayle's letter reached Leibniz) expressed surprise that in his letter Bayle 'seems to decline to reply [to Leibniz's article], either because he thinks that his points still retain their old force, or because of something else that has intervened. This is a great blow to my hopes, because I had hoped that from what he wrote to you I would have derived much illumination by which I could more easily find my way through all the complexities of your theory' (de Volder to Leibniz, Leiden, 7 Oct. 1702 (G 2. 244)). Bayle restricts the substance of his reply to this: 'I understand your theory more clearly, sir, since having read your manuscript, and I count myself lucky to have provided the occasion for you to embellish it with further reflections which develop more and more fully a very sophisticated theoretical point. I am not sending you any further doubts, since so far as I can see everything that I could say in response would only be an appendix to my first objections, and to tell the truth would not say any more than they did, but only come back to the same thing in roundabout ways. It seems to me that we cannot really deny the

nine years later, when Leibniz sent a copy of it to Desmaizeaux in 1711, the reply was still unpublished.[15] However, as Desmaizeaux reports,[16] Leibniz made it known in the *Nouvelles Littéraires* for 1715 that he would be happy to see it published.[17] It soon was, not as Bayle and he had earlier imagined, in Basnage's *Histoire des ouvrages des savants*, but in *Histoire critique de la République des lettres* for 1716 (PB6 below).

Bayle's letter of October 1702 received a reply from Leibniz later that year. As Gerhardt explains,[18] the letter exists in various versions. He himself prints both a 'without place and date' version (PB7a below) and a shorter, later version which Leibniz had endorsed 'not sent' (PB7b below). There is also an even shorter version (which Gerhardt does not print) dated 'Berlin, 5 December 1702'.

At some point after the publication of the *Dictionary*'s second edition Leibniz wrote down for his own use some comments on the whole of the 'Rorarius' article.[19] Those relevant to note H are in PB2 below, those on note L are in PB5.

feasibility of your theory as long as we do not clearly understand the substantial basis of the soul and the way in which it can modify itself from one thought to another. Perhaps if we understood that really clearly we would see that nothing is more probable than what you maintain.'

[15] See D2. § 2.

[16] Desmaizeaux, vol. 1, p. xcvii.

[17] 'Remarques de M. D. L.', *Nouvelle Littéraires*, 2 (9 Nov. 1715), pp. 289 ff., in which, stimulated by an earlier publisher's announcement (*Nouvelles*, 1 (5 Jan. 1715), p. 10) of the *Dictionary*, Leibniz remarks that 'M. Bayle replied in the second edition of his dictionary to my response to his objections on the system of pre-established harmony, and I sent him a second response. I expect he would have given a second reply in some kind of supplement to his dictionary if he had lived. I have since sent that second response of mine to M. Desmaizeaux for the benefit of people who would have been interested in these pieces' (p. 290). Desmaizeaux played a part in its eventual publication in Samuel Masson's *Histoire critique de la République des lettres* (Amsterdam) (see introduction to Ch. 9).

[18] G 3. 69 n.

[19] G 4. 528–54. These must post-date Leibniz's reading of Jaquelot's *Conformity of Faith with Reason* (1705)—see n. 48.

PB1. BAYLE: Note H to *Dictionary* Article
'Rorarius'[20] (concerning 'A great mind in
Germany,[21] who has understood these problems,
[and who] has provided some insights which are
worth developing') (1697)

[1] He agrees[a] with the opinion of some of the moderns, that animals are already organized in the seed, and he also thinks[b] that matter alone cannot constitute a true unity, and therefore that animals are unified by a form,[A] which is a simple, indivisible being, truly unique.[B] In addition, he holds' that this form never leaves its subject,[C] which means th.at properly speaking there is neither death nor generation[D] in nature. He makes the soul of man[E] an exception to all this;[d] he sets it apart, etc.[F] [2] This theory[c] frees us from one part of the problem; we no longer need to reply to the crippling objections that are made against the scholastics. The soul of an animal, it is said against them, is a substance distinct from the body; it must therefore be produced by creation, and destroyed by *annihilation*; it would therefore be necessary for heat[f] to have the power to create souls, and to destroy them,[g] and what could be more absurd than that? The Peripatetics' replies to this objection are not worth reporting, or worth bringing out of the darkness of the classroom where they are expounded to young students; they serve only to convince us that as far as they are concerned, the objection is unanswerable. They are no better at avoiding the precipice towards which they are driven when they are required to find some sense and some shadow of reason in this continual production of an almost infinite number of substances, which are totally destroyed a few days later, even though they are much more noble and much more excellent than matter, which always remains in existence. [3] M. Leibniz's theory parries all these blows, for it

[20] Pierre Bayle, *Dictionaire historique et critique* (Amsterdam, 1696–7), i. 966–7. We have noted important differences between note H as in the *Dictionary's* 1st edn. and as in the 2nd (= B 1696; B 1702). The notes cued a, b, c, . . . are Bayle's own. Those cued A, B, C, . . . are unpublished remarks by Leibniz, additional to and later than his published reply to Bayle (PB3); we give them below in PB2. Unlike PB3 they are written on the basis of B 1702. We have noted important differences between the original text of Leibniz's 'New System' (= L) and Bayle's purported quotations from it. These, as he says in PB1, note a, are from the Amsterdam edn. of the *Journal des savants*.

[21] B 1702 has 'M. Leibniz, one of the greatest minds in Europe'.

would have us believe (i) that at the beginning of the world God created the forms of all bodies, and hence all the souls of the lower animals; (ii) that these souls continue in existence for ever from that time on, inseparably united with the first organized body in which God lodged them.[G] That rescues us from metempsychosis,[H] which would otherwise have been an asylum to which we would have had to run. [4] So that it can be seen whether I have understood his thought correctly, I give here a part of his treatise:[h]

[5] There are some problematic things in M. Leibniz's theory, even though they show the breadth and power of his genius.[I] For example, he holds that the soul of a dog operates independently of its body: 'that everything in it arises from its own nature, with a perfect *spontaneity* as regards itself, and yet with a perfect conformity to things outside it. And . . . thus its internal perceptions[22] must arise from its own original constitution, that is from its representational nature[23] (its ability to express external things which are in relation with its organs), which it has had since its creation, and which constitutes its individual character.'[i] From this it follows that the dog's soul would feel hunger and thirst at certain times, even if there were no bodies in the universe; even if 'there existed nothing but God and that soul.'[J][24] He has explained[j] his thinking by the example of two clocks (*pendules*, ? gender) which are perfectly synchronized: that is, he suggests that because of the particular laws which control its operation, the soul will feel hunger at a certain time, and because of the particular laws which govern the movement of matter, the body which is united to that soul will be modified at the same time, in the way it is modified when the soul feels hunger.[K] [6] I shall wait until the clever author of this system has improved it before preferring it to that of occasional causes: I cannot understand the series of spontaneous internal actions which could make a dog's soul feel pain immediately after having felt pleasure, even if it were all alone in the universe. I can understand why a dog passes immediately from pleasure to pain when, whilst it is very hungry and eating some bread, it is suddenly hit with a stick; but that its soul should be constructed in such a

---

[22] B 1696/1702 omits L's 'in the soul itself'.

[23] For L's 'par la nature representative', B 1696/1702 has merely 'representative' —thus actually saying 'from its own original, that is to say representational, constitution'. We have restored Leibniz's original version, however.

[24] Quoted from NS1, § 14.

way that it would have felt pain at the moment that it was hit, even if it had not been hit, and even if it had continued to eat the bread without being disturbed or prevented, that is what I cannot understand.[L] [7] I also find the *spontaneity* of this soul wholly incompatible with its feelings of pain, and in general with all feelings it finds unpleasant.[M] Moreover, the reason why this clever man finds the Cartesian system not to his taste seems to me to be based on a false supposition; it cannot be said that the system of occasional causes, with its reciprocal dependence of body and soul, makes the actions of God into the miraculous interventions of a *deus ex machina*.[k] For since God intervenes between them only according to general laws, in doing so he never acts extraordinarily.[N] Does the internal active power which M. Leibniz thinks is communicated to the forms of bodies know what succession of actions it has to produce? Surely not; for we know from experience that we do not know what perceptions we will have in an hour's time. It would therefore be necessary for the forms to be directed by some external principle in the production of their actions. Would that not be a *deus ex machina*, just the same as in the system of occasional causes?[l] [8] Finally, as he supposes, with very good reason, that all souls are simple and indivisible, it is impossible to see how they can be compared to clocks (*pendule*, f.); how, that is, their original constitution can enable them to do different things, as a result of the spontaneous activity they received from their creator. It is obvious that a simple being will always do the same thing, if no outside cause interferes with it; but if it were made up of several parts, like a machine, it could do different things, because at any moment the particular activity of one part could interfere with that of the others. But in a unitary substance, where would you find the cause of any change of activity?

[BAYLE'S NOTES]

a. See M. Leibniz's article published in the *Journal des savants* for 27 June 1695, p. 449 in the Dutch edn. [i.e. NS1, § 6].

b. *Journal des savants*, etc. p. 446 [i.e. NS1, § 3].

c. p. 447 [i.e. NS1, § 4].

d. *Journal des savants*, pp. 448, 450 [i.e. NS1, §§ 5, 8].

e. M. Bernier, in his *Account of the Gentiles of Hindustan*, p.m. 200, reports a somewhat similar view held by the philosophers of that country. [The 1671 Paris edn. of Bernier's travelogue has the relevant passage on pp. 200–1. Bayle's 'p.m. 200' seems to mean 'pp. 200 f.'.]

f. Chickens are hatched by putting eggs in a slightly warmed oven. This is the practice in Egypt.

g. Various kinds of animal can be killed by putting them in an over-heated oven.

h. *Journal des savants*, 27 June 1695, p. 449. [Bayle's quote is from halfway through NS1, § 6 ('And here the transformations . . .') to the end of NS1, § 7.]

i. *Journal des savants*, 4 July 1695, p. 457 [i.e. NS1, § 14].

j. In *Histoire des ouvrages des savants* for Feb. 1696, pp. 274, 275 [i.e. 'Second Explanation of the New System'; see Ch. 4, n. 2]

k. Ibid.

l. Refer to the objections which were put to M. Leibniz by M. S. F. [i.e. Simon Foucher] in the *Journal des savants* of 12 Dec. [*sic*] 1695, p. 639 and following [i.e. F1].

PB2. LEIBNIZ: Unpublished comments on Bayle's Note H (*Dictionary*, 1702 edn.), 1705?[25]

A. or soul.

B. truly one.

C. entirely and all at once.

D. of a living thing.

E. and all other minds.

F. Because these rational substances have a double status or position: one physical, like all animals, as a consequence of their bodily mechanism, and the other moral, as a result of which they are in society with God, as citizens of the city of God. This means that they conserve not only their substance, but also their personality and the knowledge of who they are.

G. It is not that a certain mass always remains inseparable from the animal or the soul, but rather that certain organs always remain, at least by the substitution of an equivalent, as happens when a river remains the same, although matter of the same kind is always entering and leaving it.

H. according to which the soul passes all at once into another body, quite differently organized.

I. The objection that M. Bayle puts to me here concerns only half of my theory. He seems to approve of what I have said about the

---

[25] From the French at G 4. 528–33. These notes are signalled at A, B, C, . . . in PB1 above.

immateriality and durability of the souls of non-human animals, and even about the durability and transformation of all animals. But he is still not entirely content with the way I have proposed to explain the communication and commerce between soul and body.

J. I meant this only as a fiction, which is not compatible with the order of things but which might help make my thought more intelligible. For God so made the soul that it must correspond to everything external to it, and indeed represent it, in accordance with the impressions that things make on its organic body, which constitute its point of view. If there were other motions in the body than those which usually accompany the feeling of hunger or thirst, the soul would not have that feeling. It is true that if God were to decide to destroy everything external to the soul, but to keep the soul in isolation, with its affections and modifications, they would bring it, through its own dispositions, to have the same sensations as before, just as if bodies were still there, although this would then be nothing but a kind of dream. But since this is contrary to the designs of God, who wanted there to be agreement between the soul and things external to it, it is clear that this pre-established harmony removes such a fiction: it is metaphysically possible, but it doesn't accord with the facts and their explanations.

K. I have explained the agreement between the soul and the body by a comparison between the agreement of these two beings and that of two differently structured clocks (*pendules*, ? gender) which always exactly coincide in showing the same time at the same moment. This could be brought about in three ways. 1: By connecting them together in such a way that their pendulums would have to swing at the same rate; 2: By employing a man specifically to keep them together; 3: By making them from the outset so accurately and so well that they were able to keep together by their own structure. This is undoubtedly the best way. In the same way, the soul and the body could agree 1: by an influence of the one on the other, as in the common view of the schools. This, however, is inexplicable; 2: By God's continually taking care to make them agree, as in the system of occasional causes, so that the state of one is an occasion for God to make corresponding impressions on the other. This would be a perpetual miracle, which is not[26] in conformity with divine wisdom and with the order of things. 3: By an

---

[26] We have supplied the words 'which is not'.

exact ordering of each of these two beings in isolation, such that they agree in virtue of their own natures. This is the most beautiful and the most worthy of God, and it is my system of pre-established harmony.

L. That is also what I do not say, if it is understood correctly. The pre-established harmony means that pain comes into a dog's soul when its body is hit. And if the dog were not going to be hit at this moment, God would not at the outset have given its soul a constitution which would produce that pain in it at this moment, and that representation or perception which corresponds to the blow of the stick. But if (though this is impossible) God had changed his mind and had changed the history of the material world in such a way that the blow never fell, without changing the nature of the soul and the natural course of its modifications, the soul would feel what corresponds to the blow, even though its body never received it. But, says M. Bayle, I understand the reasons through which the dog's body is hit by the stick, but I don't understand how the dog's soul, which experiences pleasure while the dog is eating hungrily, suddenly passes to pain without the stick's being the cause (in the manner of the schools), and without God's particular action (as with the 'occasionalists'). But neither does M. Bayle understand how the stick can have an influx into the soul, nor how the miraculous operation takes place by means of which God gets the body and the soul continually to agree. I, however, have explained how this agreement happens naturally, by supposing that each soul is a living mirror representing the universe from its point of view, and above all with respect to its body. Thus the causes which move the stick (that is, the man stationed behind the dog, getting ready to hit it while it eats, and everything in the history of the material world which contributes to his being in that position), are also represented in the dog's soul from the outset, exactly and truly, but feebly, by small confused perceptions and without apperception, that is, without the dog's knowing it—because the dog's body also is affected by them only imperceptibly. And just as in the history of the material world these dispositions eventually produce the blow firmly on the dog's body, so similarly the representations of these dispositions in the dog's soul eventually produce the representation of the blow of the stick; and since that representation is prominent and strong (which the representations of the predispositions were not, since the predispositions affected the dog's body only feebly), the dog apperceives it very distinctly, and this is what constitutes its pain. So we don't have to imagine that in this encounter the dog's soul passes from pleasure to pain arbitrarily, and without any internal reason.

M. The crux of M. Bayle's objection here is that we have no spontaneous inclination towards what we find unpleasant. I make a distinction: I admit this when we know that something will displease us, but in this case the dog does not know. We must also distinguish between the spontaneous and the voluntary. The principle of change is in the dog, the disposition of its soul moves imperceptibly towards giving it pain: but this is without its knowing, and without its wanting it. The representation of the present state of the universe in the dog's soul produces in it the representation of the subsequent state of the same universe, just as in the things represented the preceding state actually produces the subsequent state of the world. *In a soul, the representations of causes are the causes of the representations of effects.* And since this subsequent state of the world includes the blow on the dog's body, the representation of that subsequent state in its soul includes the pain which corresponds to that blow.

N. I have more than one reason for not liking the system of occasional causes; but I agree that this is one of them. It isn't sufficient for an action not to be miraculous that it be in conformity with a general law. For if that law had no foundation in the nature of things, perpetual miracles would be needed to implement it. For example, if God made a law according to which a planet had to go round the sun in circles, without arranging something which would make it do so, I say that the planet would not be able to obey that law, unless God himself were continually making it do so. Thus it is not enough for God to ordain that the body should obey the soul, and that the soul should have perceptions of what happens in the body; he must also give them some means of doing so; and I have explained what those means are.

PB3. LEIBNIZ: 'A Letter from M. Leibniz to the
Editor, Containing an Explanation of the
Difficulties which M. Bayle Found with the New
System of the Union of the Soul and Body'
(July 1698)[27]

[1] I am taking the liberty, sir, of sending you this explanation with regard to the difficulties which M. Bayle found with the theory I proposed to explain the union of the soul and body. Nothing could be kinder than the tone he adopted towards me; and I consider myself honoured by the objections he raises in his excellent *Dictionary*, in the article on Rorarius. After all, when a mind as great and as profound as his raises objections it cannot fail to be instructive; and I shall try to profit from the light he has thrown on these matters here, as well as in several other places in his work. He doesn't deny what I have said about the conservation of souls and even of animals, but he doesn't yet seem satisfied with the way I tried to explain the union and commerce between the soul and the body, in the *Journal des savants* of 27 June and 4 July 1695, and in the *Histoire des ouvrages des savants*, February 1696, pp. 274, 275.[28]

[2] Here are his words, which seem to indicate what he found difficulty with: 'I cannot understand', he says, 'the series of spontaneous internal actions which could make a dog's soul feel pain immediately after having felt pleasure, even if it were all alone in the universe.'[29] My reply to this is that when I said that the soul would still feel all that it feels now even if there were only it and God in the world, I was only employing a fiction. In order to show that the feelings of the soul are only a consequence of what is already within it, I was imagining something which could never happen naturally. I do not know whether M. Bayle's argument for the incomprehensibility which he finds in this series of actions is to be found in what he says lower down, or whether it is meant already to be there in the example of the spontaneous transition

---

[27] 'Lettre de M. Leibniz à l'auteur, contenant un éclaircissement des difficultés que Monsieur Bayle a trouvées dans le système nouveau de l'union de l'âme et du corps', *Histoire des ouvrages des savants*, July 1698, pp. 329–42 (B 51; R 153). Where Leibniz significantly misquotes Bayle, this has been noted.

[28] i.e. 'New System' (NS1) and 'Second Explanation of the New System' (see Ch. 4, n. 2).

[29] All of Leibniz's Bayle quotations are from PB1, §§ 6, 7, 8.

from pleasure to pain. Perhaps he is suggesting that such a transition contradicts the axiom that a thing will always remain in the same state if nothing occurs to make it change, and therefore that an animal which once experiences pleasure will have it for ever if it is all alone, or if nothing external makes it move on to pain. In any case, I agree with the axiom, and indeed I claim that it supports me, for it is in fact one of my basic principles. [3] Do we not take this axiom to mean not only that a body which is at rest will always remain at rest, but also that a moving body will always retain its movement or progression, that is to say the same speed and the same direction, if nothing occurs to prevent it? Thus not only will a thing left to itself remain in the state it is in, but also, when that state is one of change, it will continue to change, still in accordance with that same law. Now, according to me it is the nature of a created substance to change continually in accordance with a certain order, which conducts it *spontaneously* (if one may use the word) through all its states, in such a way that someone who saw everything would see in its present state all its past and future states. And this law of order, which constitutes the individuality of each particular substance, exactly corresponds to what happens in every other substance, and in the universe as a whole. I hope it is not too much to claim that I can demonstrate all of this; but for the moment all that matters is to show the possibility of the theory, and its ability to explain the phenomena. So in this way the law of the changes in the substance of an animal takes it from pleasure to pain just when there is a break in the continuity of its body, because the law of this animal's indivisible substance is to represent what happens in its body, just as we know from our own cases, and indeed to represent in some fashion, through its relation to the body, everything that happens in the world. Substantial unities are nothing other than different concentrations of the universe, which is represented in them in accordance with the different points of view which distinguish them.

[4] M. Bayle goes on: 'I can understand why a dog passes immediately from pleasure to pain when, whilst it is very hungry and eating some bread, it is hit[30] with a stick.' I am not sure that we do understand this so well. No one knows better than M. Bayle himself that this is what the great difficulty consists in: how to explain why what happens in the body makes a change in the soul.

---

[30] For 'hit', B 1696 reads: 'suddenly hit'.

This is what forced the defenders of occasional causes to have recourse to God's continually taking care to represent in the soul changes which take place in the body. Whereas I believe that it is its own God-given nature to represent to itself, in accordance with its own laws, what happens in its organs. He goes on:

[5] 'But that its soul should be constructed in such a way that it would have felt pain at the moment that it was hit, even if it had not been hit, and even if it had continued to eat the bread without being disturbed or prevented, that is what I cannot understand.' And I don't remember having said it either. One can speak in this way only by a metaphysical fiction, as when one imagines God as annihilating a certain body to produce a vacuum: the one is as much against the order of things as the other. For since the soul's nature was made from the outset in such a way that it would represent in succession the changes in matter, the case imagined here could never occur in the natural order. God could have given each substance its own phenomena, independent of all others; but in so doing he would have made as many unconnected worlds, so to speak, as there are substances—rather as we say that when dreaming one is in a world of one's own, and one enters the common world on awakening. (Though dreams themselves are related to the organs, and to the rest of the body, but in a less distinct manner.) Let us continue with M. Bayle:

[6] 'I also find', he says, 'the spontaneity[31] of this soul wholly incompatible with its feelings of pain, and in general with all feelings it finds unpleasant.' There certainly would be an incompatibility if spontaneity and voluntariness were the same thing. Everything voluntary is spontaneous, but there are spontaneous actions which are not chosen, and which consequently are not voluntary. The soul is not able always to give itself pleasant feelings, since the feelings it has are dependent on those it has had. M. Bayle continues: 'Moreover, the reason why this clever man finds the Cartesian system not to his taste seems to me to be based on a false supposition; it cannot be said that the system of occasional causes, with its reciprocal dependence of body and soul, makes the actions of God into the miraculous interventions of a *deus ex machina*. For since God intervenes[32] only according to general laws, in doing so he never acts extraordinarily.'

[31] For 'spontaneity', B 1696 reads '*spontaneity*'.
[32] For 'intervenes', B 1696 reads 'intervenes between them'.

[7] This is not the only reason why the Cartesian system is not to my taste; and a little consideration of my own system will clearly show that the reasons why I adopt it are contained within itself. After all, even if the hypothesis of occasional causes did not involve miracles, it seems to me that mine would still have other advantages. I have said that we can think of three systems for explaining the intercommunication we find between soul and body: (1) the system of influence understood literally as a flow from one into the other. This is the system of the schools, which I consider impossible, as do the Cartesians. (2) The system of the perpetual caretaker, who represents in the one what happens in the other, rather like a man who is employed constantly to synchronize two inferior clocks which cannot keep the same time by themselves. This is the system of occasional causes. And (3) that in which two substances naturally agree, as would two perfectly accurate clocks. I find this as possible as that of the caretaker, and more worthy of the creator of these substances, clocks or machines. Let us see, however, whether the system of occasional causes really doesn't involve a perpetual miracle. Here it is said that it does not, because the system holds that God acts only according to general laws. I agree that he does, but in my view that isn't enough to remove miracles. Even if God produced them all the time, they would still be miracles, if the word is understood not in the popular sense, as a rare and marvellous thing, but philosophically, as something which exceeds the power of created things. It isn't sufficient to say that God has made a general law, for in addition to the decree there has also to be a natural way of carrying it out. It is necessary, that is, that what happens should be explicable in terms of the God-given nature of things. Natural laws are not as arbitrary and groundless as many think. If, for example, God decreed that all bodies had a tendency to move in circles with radii proportional to their size, we would have to say that there was some way of bringing this about by simpler laws; otherwise we would have to admit that God brings it about miraculously, or at least by angels expressly charged with it, rather like those that used to be assigned to the celestial spheres. It would be the same if someone said that God has given natural and primitive gravities to bodies, by which they each tend to the centre of their globe without being pushed by other bodies. For in my view this system too would need a perpetual miracle, or angelic help at least.

[8] 'Does the internal active power which is[33] communicated to the forms of bodies know what sucession of actions it has to produce? Surely not; for we know from experience that we do not know what perceptions we will have in an hour's time.' I reply, that this power or, better, this soul or form doesn't know them distinctly, but senses them confusedly. In each substance there are traces of everything that has happened to it, and of everything that is going to happen. But this infinite multitude of perceptions prevents us from distinguishing them, just as I cannot distinguish one voice from another when I hear the loud and confused noise of a crowd.

[9] 'It would therefore be necessary for the forms to be directed by some external principle in the production of their actions. Would that not be a *deus ex machina*, just the same as in the system of occasional causes?' The preceding reply blocks this inference. On the contrary, the present state of each substance is a natural consequence of its preceding state, but it is only an infinite intelligence which can see that consequence, because it embraces the whole universe, souls as well as every portion of matter.

[10] M. Bayle concludes with these words: 'Finally, as he supposes, with very good reason, that all souls are[34] simple and indivisible, it is impossible to see how they can be compared to clocks (*pendule*, f.); how, that is, their original constitution can enable them to do different things, as a result of the spontaneous activity they received from their creator. It is obvious that a simple being will always do the same thing, if no outside cause interferes with it; but if it were made up of several parts, like a machine, it could do different things, because at any moment the particular activity of one part could interfere with that of the others. But in a unitary substance, where would you find the cause of any change of activity?' I find that this objection is worthy of M. Bayle, and it is one of those most deserving of clarification. But I also think that if I had not allowed for it from the outset, my system would not be worth examining. I compared the soul with a clock (*pendule*, f.) only in respect of the ordered precision of its changes, which is imperfect even in the best clocks, but which is perfect in the works of God. In fact, one can say that the soul is a very exact immaterial

---

[33] For 'which is' B 1696 reads 'which M. Leibniz thinks is'.
[34] The word 'are', mistakenly omitted by Leibniz, is provided by B 1696.

automaton.[35] [11] When it is said that a simple being will always do
the same thing, a certain distinction must be made: if 'doing the
same thing' means perpetually following the same law of order or
of continuation, as in the case of a certain series or sequence of
numbers, I admit that all simple beings, and even all composite
beings, do the same thing; but if 'same' means acting in the same
way, I don't agree at all. Here is an example which explains the
difference between these two senses: a parabolic movement is
uniform in the first sense, but not in the second, for the segments of
a parabola are not the same as each other, as are those of a straight
line. (It is true, by the way, that a simple body left to itself will
describe only straight lines, provided that we take the movement of
the centre as standing for that of the body as a whole. But since a
simple rigid body, once it has been given a rotation or circulation
around its centre, will retain it in the same sense and with the same
speed, it follows that a body left to itself can at points away from its
centre describe circles when the centre is at rest, and even (when the
centre is in motion) *certain quadratrices*. These will have an
ordinate made up of the straight line travelled by the centre and the
right sine (*sinus droit*), the versed sine being the abscissa. The arc
(*l'aire* [sic] = ? *l'arc*) will be to the circumference as that straight line
is to a given radius.) [12] We must also bear in mind that the soul,
even though simple, always has feelings composed of several simultaneous perceptions; which for our purposes has the same effect as
if it were composed of parts, like a machine. For, in conformity
with a law of order which exists in perceptions as much as in
movements, each preceding perception influences succeeding ones.
Moreover, for several centuries most philosophers have attributed
thoughts to souls and to angels which they believe are completely
incorporeal (not to mention the intelligences of Aristotle), and have
also admitted spontaneous change in simple beings. I will add that
the perceptions which are simultaneously together in the same soul
involve a truly infinite multitude of small indistinguishable feelings
that will be developed in what follows, so one should not be
astonished at the infinite variety of what emerges over time. All of
this is only a consequence of the representational nature of the soul
which must express what happens, and indeed what will happen, in
its body, and, because of the connection or correspondence of all

[35] Spinoza (*Tractatus de intellectus emendatione*, 85) claims to be the first to
regard the soul as a 'spiritual automaton'.

the parts of the world, it must also express in some way what happens in all the others. It might perhaps have been enough to say simply that God, having made corporeal machines, could also easily have made immaterial ones which represent them; but I thought it would be good to explain things a little more fully.

[13] As for the rest, I read with pleasure what M. Bayle says in the article on Zeno. He will perhaps appreciate that what comes out of it fits in with my system better than with any other; for what is real in extension and in motion consists only in the foundation of the order and regular sequence of phenomena and perceptions. Also, the Academics and the Sceptics, as well as those who have sought to reply to them, seem to have got into serious difficulties only because they looked for more reality in external sensible things than that of regular phenomena. In conceiving of *extension* we are conceiving of an order among coexistences; but we should not think of it, any more than space, as though it were a substance. It is like *time*, which presents to the mind only an order of changes. And as for *motion*, what is real in it is *force* or power; that is to say, what there is in the present state which carries with it a change in the future. The rest is only phenomena and relations. Consideration of this system shows us also that when we get to the bottom of things, we find in most philosophical sects more good sense than we had realized. The Sceptics' lack of substantial reality in sensible things; the Pythagoreans' and Platonists' reduction of everything to harmonies and numbers, ideas and perceptions; the one and the whole of Parmenides and Plotinus (though not of Spinoza); the Stoic connectedness, compatible with the spontaneity maintained by others; the vitalistic philosophy of the Cabbalists and the Hermetics, who attributed feeling to everything; the forms and entelechies of Aristotle and the scholastics; and meanwhile also the mechanical explanations, by Democritus and the moderns, of all particular phenomena, and so on—all these are reunited as in a common centre of perspective from which the object (confused when looked at from anywhere else) reveals its regularity and the congruence of its parts. Our biggest fault has been sectarianism, limiting ourselves by the rejection of others. The formalists criticize the materialists or the corpuscularians, and vice versa. We wrongly set limits to the division and subtlety of nature, as well as to its richness and beauty, when we posit atoms and the void, and suppose certain first elements (as even the Cartesians do) in place of

true unities; and also when we do not recognize the infinite in everything, and the exact expression of the greatest in the smallest, or the tendency of each thing to develop in a perfect order which is the most admirable and most beautiful effect of a sovereign principle, the wisdom and goodness of which leave nothing more to be desired by those who understand its economy.

PB4. BAYLE: Note L to *Dictionary* Article 'Rorarius', 2nd. edn. (1702)[36]

[1] I begin by saying that I am very pleased with the small difficulties I raised against this great philosopher's system, for they have given rise to replies which have further explained the matter to me, and have made me see more distinctly how marvellous it is. I now consider this new system to be an important breakthrough, which advances the frontiers of philosophy. We used to have only two theories: the schools' and that of the Cartesians; the one was a *way of influence* of the body on the soul and the soul on the body, the other was a *way of assistance*, or of occasional causality. But here we have a new acquisition; one which we can call with Father Lamy[a] the *way of pre-established harmony*.[A] [2] We are indebted to M. Leibniz for it, for nothing can be imagined which gives so exalted an idea of the power and intelligence of the author of all things. Together with the advantage that it avoids any implication of miraculous conduct, that fact would incline me to prefer this new system to that of the Cartesians, if only I could see the way of *pre-established harmony* as being at all possible. It must be stressed that when I say that this way avoids any implication of miraculous conduct, I am not retracting what I said before[b] to the effect that the system of occasional causes does not involve God's intervening miraculously. I am still as convinced as ever that for an action to be

[36] Bayle, *Dictionaire historique et critique*, 2nd edn. (Rotterdam, 1702), iii. 2610–13. (The system of references in Bayle's notes, cued a, b, c, . . . , has sometimes been changed for greater clarity.) Bayle introduces the note by saying that he is aware that some readers regard such addenda as mere excrescences, but he thinks that they will not be able to say that 'of the comments that I want to make on M. Leibniz's reflections, which can be seen in M. Basnage's journal [PB3]; for these comments are a natural and necessary extension of one of the parts of the first edition of this article'. The notes signalled A, B, C, . . . are unpublished comments by Leibniz, and they are given below in PB5.

miraculous it must be produced by God as an exception to general laws, and that anything he does immediately according to such laws is not, properly speaking, a miracle. But as I want to cut out of this discussion as many points as I can, I will accept the suggestion that the best way to get rid of any idea of miracles is to suppose that created substances are active, immediate causes of natural effects. So I will not say what I could in response to this part of M. Leibniz's replies. I am also leaving out all those objections which can be made against the views of other philosophers just as much as against his, so I will not raise all the difficulties which confront the idea that God can give created things the power of self-movement. Those difficulties are severe,[c] and almost insurmountable;[B] but M. Leibniz's system is no more open to them than is that of the Peripatetics, and I do not know that even the Cartesians would dare to say that God couldn't give our soul the ability to act. If they do say that he couldn't, how can they claim that Adam sinned? And if they daren't say so, they weaken the reasons they give for saying that matter is incapable of any kind of action. I do not see either that it would be any more difficult for M. Leibniz than for the Cartesians, or other philosophers, to defend himself against the objection of a mechanical fate, that is, the destruction of human freedom. So let us leave all that, and consider only what is particular to the system of *pre-established harmony*.

[3] 1. My first point is that it raises the power and intelligence of divine art far beyond anything that we can understand.[c] Imagine a ship which, without having any senses or any knowledge, and without being steered by any being, either created or uncreated, has the ability to manœuvre itself so perfectly that it always has a favourable wind, avoids currents and rocks, anchors where need be, and goes into harbour exactly when necessary. Suppose that such a ship sails like that for several years, always altering course and manœuvering as required by (*eu égard aux* [*sic*] = ? *en égard aux*) changes of wind and differing circumstances of land and sea. You will agree that even the infinity of God is not too much for giving such a power to a ship (*l'infinité de Dieu n'est pas trop grande pour communiquer à un vaisseau une telle faculté*); and you will also say that a ship is not the sort of thing which could be given such a faculty by God. M. Leibniz, however, supposes that the mechanism of the human body is more admirable and more

astonishing than all this.[D] Let us apply his system of the union of soul and body to Caesar.

[4] 2. According to this system we have to say that Julius Caesar's body exercised its power of movement in such a way that from birth to death it followed out a continual sequence of changes which corresponded in the smallest detail to the incessant changes in a certain soul, of which it had no knowledge, and which had no effect on it.[E] We have to say that even if it had pleased God to annihilate Caesar's soul the day after it was created, the principle, according to which this faculty of Caesar's body had to produce its acts, was such that the body would have gone to the Senate on a certain day at a certain time, and would have uttered such and such words, etc.[F] We have to say that this power of movement produced its changes and modifications punctually to correspond to the volubility of the thoughts of this ambitious mind, and that it moved into some particular state rather than any other, because Caesar's soul moved on from one thought to another.[G] Can a blind force modify itself so appropriately as a consequence of an impression communicated to it thirty or forty years before, when it has not been renewed since, when it is left all by itself, and without ever having had any knowledge of its instructions? Isn't that much more incomprehensible than the voyage I spoke of in the preceding paragraph?[H]

[5] 3. What adds to the difficulty is that the human mechanism has an almost infinite number of organic parts (*organes*), and[d] is continually exposed to the impact of surrounding bodies, which by an innumerable variety of disturbances will stimulate in it a thousand kinds of modification. How can we make sense of the fact that this *pre-established harmony* is never upset, and always stays on course through even the longest life of a man, despite the infinite variety of actions of all these parts one on another, surrounded on all sides by an infinity of corpuscles, sometimes cold, sometimes hot, sometimes dry, sometimes wet, always active, always pricking at the nerves, in this way or that? I think that this multiplicity of parts and of external agents is essential for the almost infinite variety of changes in the human body. But could this variety be as perfectly ordered as this system requires? Will it never disturb the correspondence between these changes and those of the soul? This is what seems to be quite impossible.[I]

[6] 4. It is useless to hide behind God's power, and to maintain

that animals are only automata; it is useless to claim that God was able to make machines which are so cleverly put together that a man's voice, the light reflected from an object, etc., strikes them exactly as is necessary to make them move in such or such a manner. Everyone except some of the Cartesians rejects that idea;[J] and no Cartesian at all would be prepared to accept it, if we were to extend it to man, i.e. if we said that God has been able to make bodies which do mechanically everything that we see other men do.[K] In denying this possibility we are not claiming to set limits to God's power and knowledge; the intention is only to convey that the nature of things means that the faculties which can be given to a created thing must have certain limitations. It is absolutely necessary that the activity of created things be appropriate to what they essentially are (*leur état essentiel*), and that it be carried out in accordance with the character of all machines, for according to the philosophers' axiom,[e] whatever is received is commensurate with the capacity of the receiver.[L] So we can reject M. Leibniz's theory as impossible, since it involves more serious difficulties even than that of automata:[M] it suggests a continuous harmony between two substances which do not act on each other.[N] But even if servants were machines and punctually did this or that every time their master ordered, the master would still be having a real effect on them: he would utter words, he would make gestures, and these would set up a real disturbance in these servants' organs.[O]

[7] 5. Let us now consider Caesar's soul: we will find even more impossibilities. This soul was in the world without being exposed to the influence of any body or any mind. The power God had given it was the sole source of the particular actions it produced at each moment, and if these actions were of different kinds, that was not because some were produced by the operation of agencies which did not contribute to the production of the others, for man's soul is simple, indivisible, and immaterial. M. Leibniz admits this. And indeed, if he did not admit it, and instead were to suppose with the common run of philosophers and with several[f] of the best metaphysicians of this century that something consisting of several suitably arranged material parts is capable of thought, I would regard his theory as absolutely impossible,[P] and there would be many other ways to refute it, which are of no relevance here, since he recognizes the immateriality of our soul and takes it as a starting-point.[Q] [8] Returning to Julius Caesar's soul, let us call it an

immaterial automaton,[g] and let us compare it with an Epicurean atom—I mean an atom surrounded by a void on all sides, and which never comes into contact with any other atom. The comparison is very close; for on the one side this atom has a natural power of self-movement which it exercises without being helped in any way, and without being hindered or crossed by any thing; and on the other side Caesar's soul is a mind which has been given the ability to produce its thoughts, and exercises it without the influence of any other mind, or of any body. Nothing assists it, nothing crosses it. According to common notions and ideas of order this atom will never stop, and having been moving a moment ago, it will be moving now and in all following moments, and the manner of its movement will always be the same. This follows from an axiom accepted by M. Leibniz,[h] 'that a thing will always remain in the same state if nothing occurs to make it change'.[i,37] 'We conclude', he says, 'not only that a body which is at rest will always remain at rest, but also that a moving body will always retain its movement or progression, that is to say the same speed and the same direction, if nothing occurs to prevent it.' It is clear to everyone that this atom (whether it moves itself by an innate power, as Democritus and Epicurus hold, or by a power given by the Creator) will keep on moving forward uniformly and regularly along the same straight line, without ever turning to the right or to the left, or reversing direction. Epicurus was derided for inventing the motion[j] of declination;[38] he introduces it gratuitously only in order to try to escape the labyrinth of everything's being necessitated by fate, and he could give no explanation for this addition to his theory. It conflicts with our most obvious ideas, for we can see clearly that if an atom which has moved in a straight line for two days is to turn aside at the beginning of the third day, it has either to meet some obstacle, or to form some desire to depart from its course, or to incorporate in it some device which comes into play at that moment. The first of these is ruled out in an empty space. The second is impossible, because an atom has no power of thought. The third is similarly impossible in an absolutely unitary corpuscle.[R] Let us now apply all of this.

[9] 6. Caesar's soul is a being which possesses unity in the strictest sense. The ability to give itself[k] thoughts belongs to its nature: it

---

[37] The quotes in this section are from PB3, §§ 2, 3.

[38] See Cicero, *De fato*, x.

received from God both the possession and the use of it. If the first thought it gives itself is a feeling of pleasure,^S it is hard to see why the second should not also be a feeling of pleasure; for when the total cause of an effect remains the same, the effect cannot change.^T Now, in the second moment of its existence, this soul does not acquire a new ability to think, but only keeps the ability it had in the first moment; and it is as independent of the effects of any other cause in the second moment as it was in the first. So it ought to reproduce in the second moment the same thought it had produced before.^U If you object against me that the soul must be in a state of change, and that in the situation I describe it would not, I reply that its change will be like the atom's change: for an atom which keeps on moving along the same line is in a new situation at each moment, but one which is the same as the previous situation. Therefore, for a soul to persist in its state of change, it is enough for it to give itself another thought which is the same as the previous one.^V But let us not take it so narrowly: let us allow that its thoughts might be different; but it would at least still be necessary that the change from one thought to another involved some affinity which connects (*raison d'affinité*) them. Suppose that at one moment Caesar's soul sees a tree with flowers and leaves; I can¹ understand that it might suddenly want to see one which has only leaves, and then one which has only flowers, and in this way how it might make for itself several successive images which arise one out of another. But we could never make sense of the possibility of bizarre changes from black to white or from yes to no, or those wild leaps from earth to heaven which are quite common in human thought. We could never understand how God might have been able to put into Julius Caesar's soul the principle of a change such as the following: no doubt more than once whilst he was suckling he was pricked by a pin; according to the theory we are examining here, the soul would have had to modify itself with a feeling of pain immediately after the pleasant sensations of the sweetness of milk which it had been having for two or three minutes together. By what means was it determined to interrupt its pleasures and suddenly give itself a feeling of pain, without anything's having alerted it to prepare it for the change, and without anything new happening in its substance? If you review the life of this first Roman emperor, you will at each stage find material for an objection even stronger than this one.^W

[10] 7. We could make some sense of this if we supposed that a

man's soul is not a mind but rather a host of minds, each of which has its functions which come into play exactly as required by the changes which take place in the human body. We would then have to say that something analogous to a great apparatus of wheels and springs, or of fermenting material, arranged in accordance with the vicissitudes of our bodily mechanism, arouses or deadens for such and such a time the action of each of these minds. But then man's soul would no longer be a substance; it would, just like a material being, be an *ens per aggregationem*,[39] a mass or collection of substances. What we are looking for here is a single being which experiences now joy, now sadness, etc.; we are not looking for several beings, one of which produces hope, another despair, etc.[X]

[11] The observations you have just read only develop those that M. Leibniz has done me the honour of examining. I am now going to comment on his replies.[Y]

[12] 8. He says that[m] 'the law of the changes in the substance of an animal takes it from pleasure to pain just when there is a break in the continuity of its body, because the law of this animal's indivisible substance is to represent what happens in its body, just as we know from our own cases, and indeed to represent in some fashion, through its relation to the body, everything that happens in the world'.[40] These words give a very good account of the fundamentals of this system: they are, so to speak, its denouement and its key. But at the same time they are the point which provides the perspective from which we can most clearly see the objections of those who think that this new theory is impossible. The law that is spoken of here supposes a decree of God, and shows in what respects this system is similar to that of occasional causes.[Z] These two systems agree on the following point: that there are laws according to which a man's soul must *represent what happens in his body, just as we know from our own cases*. They differ about the way in which these laws are implemented. According to the Cartesians, God implements them: M. Leibniz says that the soul implements them itself. This is what seems impossible to me, for the soul does not have the equipment it would need for this kind of implementation. However infinite God's knowledge and power might be, he couldn't do with a machine which was lacking a certain part something for which that part was necessary. He would

[39] 'being by aggregation'—a scholastic phrase.
[40] The quote is from PB3, § 3.

have to make up for that lack, and then it would be he, and not the machine, which produced the effect. Let us try to show that the soul lacks the equipment necessary for implementing the divine law in question by means of a comparison.

[13] Let us imagine, at random, an animal created by God, and designed to sing incessantly. It will sing all the time, that is obvious; but if God intended it to follow a certain score, it is absolutely necessary that he either puts it in front of its eyes, or imprints it in its memory, or arranges the animal's muscles in such a way that by the laws of mechanics one note is made to follow another exactly according to the score. Otherwise it is inconceivable that this animal should ever be able to follow the complete series of notes which God has written.[AA] [14] Let us consider a man's soul in the same way. M. Leibniz holds that it has been given not only the power of continually giving itself thoughts, but also that of always following a certain sequence in its thoughts, corresponding to the continual changes in the bodily machine. This sequence of thoughts is like the score set down for the musical animal described above. Would it not then be necessary, if the soul is to change its perceptions or modifications at each moment according to that score of thoughts, for it to know the sequence of notes, and to think of it at the time? But experience shows us that it knows nothing of it.[BB] In the absence of such knowledge, is it not necessary that at least there should be in the soul a set of specific devices, each of which is a necessary cause of such and such a thought? Is it not necessary that they should be precisely arranged so that just this one operates after that, according to the 'pre-established' correspondence between the changes in the bodily machine and the thoughts in the soul? But it is quite certain that an immaterial, simple, indivisible substance cannot be composed of this innumerable multitude of specific devices arranged one in front of another according to the order of the score in question. It is therefore not possible for the human soul to implement this law.[CC]

[15] M. Leibniz supposes that the soul has no distinct knowledge of its future perceptions, 'but senses them confusedly', and that 'in each substance there are[n] traces of everything that has happened to it, and of everything that is going to happen.[DD] But this infinite multitude of perceptions prevents us from distinguishing them,[o] . . . the present state of each substance *is a natural consequence of its preceding state*, . . . the soul, even though simple, always has

feelings composed of several simultaneous perceptions; which for our purposes has the same effect as if it were composed of parts, like a machine. For, in conformity with a law of order which exists in perceptions as much as in movements, each preceding perception influences succeeding ones.[p] . . . the perceptions which are simultaneously together in the same soul involve a truly infinite multitude of small indistinguishable feelings that will be developed in what follows, so one should not be astonished at the infinite variety of what emerges over time. All of this is only a consequence of the representational nature of the soul which must express what happens, and indeed what will happen, in its body, and, because of the connection or correspondence of all the parts of the world, it must also express in some way what happens in all the others'.[q 41] [16] I don't have much to say about that: I say only that this suggestion, if it were fully developed, would be the real means of resolving all the difficulties. By the penetration of his great genius, M. Leibniz has perfectly appreciated the full extent and force of the objection, and where the solution to the main difficulty is to be found. I am sure that he will iron out what might otherwise have been most worrying about his system, and that he will be able to teach us some wonderful things about the nature of minds. No one can more usefully or more reliably explore the world of the intellect than he can. I hope that his splendid explanations will dissipate all the impossibilities I have so far imagined, and that he will completely resolve my difficulties, and those[r] of Dom François Lamy. It is because of this hope that I was able to say without flattery that his system should be considered[s] an important breakthrough.

[17] It does not matter that, whereas the Cartesians suppose that there is only one general law for the union of all minds with bodies,[42] he holds that God gives a particular law to each mind, which seems[t] to entail that the primitive constitution of one mind is specifically different from that of another. Don't the Thomists say that in the realm of angels there are as many species as there are individuals?[EE, 43]

[41] The quotes (with Bayle's added italics) in this section are from PB3, §§ 8, 9, 12.

[42] See, e.g. (?), Malebranche, *Search*, 1. 13. 5.

[43] See Aquinas, *Summa Theologica*, I. 50. 4.

[BAYLE'S NOTES]

a. Dom François Lamy, Treatise 2 of *The Knowledge of the Self*, p. 226, 1699 edn. [i.e. L2].

b. See M. Leibniz's article in *Histoire des ouvrages des savants*, July 1698, p. 334 [i.e. PB3, § 6].

c. See M. Sturm in the first volume of his *Elective or Theoretical Physics* (of which an extract can be found in the Leipzig journal 1697, p. 474 and following) and in the article which he published in the Leipzig journal 1699, p. 208 and following, as a reply to an article by M. Leibniz in the same journal 1698, p. 427 and following.[44]

d. Note that according to M. Leibniz that which is active in each substance is something which is reducible to a true unity. So since each man's body is composed of several substances, each of these substances must have a source (*principe*) of action really distinct from that of each of the others. He wants the action of each such source to be spontaneous. But their effects will necessarily be disturbed; and will vary in an infinite number of ways, because neighbouring bodies will to some extent constrain the natural spontaneity of each one.[FF]

e. *Quidquid recipitur, ad modum recipientis recipitur* ['Whatever is received is received in accordance with the capacity of the receiver'].

f. M. Locke, for example.

g. M. Leibniz uses this expression in *Histoire des ouvrages des savants*, July 1698, p. 338; 'the soul', he says, 'is a very exact immaterial automaton' [i.e. PB3, § 10].

h. Article in *Histoire des ouvrages des savants*, July 1698, p. 331 [i.e. PB3, § 2].

i. M. Leibniz says in the same place [i.e. PB3, § 2] that he agrees with the axiom, and 'indeed I claim', he adds, 'that it supports me, for it is in fact one of my basic principles'.

j. See above, p. 1142 [i.e. the *Dictionary* article on Epicurus where, in note U, Bayle discusses Epicurus's account of freedom].

k. This is said from the point of view of M. Leibniz's system.

l. In saying this I am making a concession; that is to say, I am not insisting on the reasons which make it impossible for us to understand how a created spirit could give itself ideas.

m. Leibniz, in *Histoire des ouvrages des savants*, July 1698, p. 332 [i.e. PB3, § 3].

n. This is what is incomprehensible in an indivisible, simple, immaterial substance.

o. Leibniz in *Histoire des ouvrages des savants*, p. 337 [i.e. PB3, § 8].

p. Ibid. pp. 339, 340. [i.e. PB3, §§ 9, 12].

q. Ibid., p. 340. [i.e. PB3, § 15].

[44] The references are to J. C. Sturm, *Physica electiva sive hypothetica* (Nuremberg; vol. 1, 1697; vol. 2, 1698); a review of Sturm's *Physica*, *Acta eruditorum*, Oct. 1697, pp. 474–83; 'G. G. L. De ipsa natura, sive de vi insita, actionibusque creaturarum . . .', *Acta eruditorum*, Sept. 1698, pp. 427–40 (R 154); J. C. Sturm, 'Joh. Christophorus Sturmius de Deo in creaturis corporeis . . .', *Acta eruditorum*, May 1699, pp. 208–24.

r. These are in the second book of *The Knowledge of the Self*, from p. 225 to p. 243, Paris, 1699 [i.e. L2].
s. See above, p. 2610, col. 2 [i.e. [§ 1] above].
t. Two men never have the same thoughts, not merely for a whole month, but even for two minutes. So the principle of thought in each one must have its own rule and its own nature.

PB5. LEIBNIZ: Unpublished Comments on Bayle's Note L (1705?)[45]

A. I had already used this name for it in my reply to M. l'Abbé Foucher in the *Journal des savants* of 9 April of the year 1696 [i.e. F3, § 7], and Revd Father Lamy found it appropriate.

B. They are not so insurmountable, as can be seen from my reply (also in the Latin journal of Leipzig) to M. Sturm's latest article.[46]

C. I agree that it raises it beyond anything we can comprehend (*comprendre*), but not beyond what we can understand (*concevoir*).

D. First I shall reply to the question of whether it is possible to conceive of such a ship. Then I will come on to the comparison which is made here with the machine of the human body. To begin with, I find it strange that without giving any reason M. Bayle ventures to decide the question in the negative, and denies that this is possible for God—for he himself often admits that anything which doesn't imply any contradiction or imperfection could be produced by the divinity. I agree that M. Bayle would be right if the idea were that God gave the ship a certain faculty, perfection, or occult quality, so that it always kept itself on course without any internal understanding and without any external attraction or direction, like the Phocians' boat in Homer's Odyssey.[47] For that kind of supposition would be impossible; it would conflict with the principle of sufficient reason, since no reason could be given for

[45] From the French at G 4. 533–54. These notes are signalled at A, B, C, . . . in PB4 above. Leibniz introduces these comments thus: 'M. Bayle, on p. 2610 of the above [*Dictionary*], responds as follows to my reply which was published in the *Histoire des ouvrages des savants*, July 1698.'
[46] Leibniz's 'De ipsa natura, sive de vi insita, actionibusque creaturarum . . .', *Acta eruditorum*, Sept. 1698 (R 154), replies to J. C. Sturm's 'De natura sibi incassum vindicata', in the second volume (1698) of his *Physica electiva*.
[47] 'For the Phaeacians have no pilots, nor steering-oars such as other ships have, but their ships of themselves understand the thoughts and minds of men' (*Odyssey*, bk. 8, 558–60, trans. A. T. Murray (London, 1919)), i. 299.

such a perfection, and it would require the perpetual miracle of God's continual involvement. Unless, of course, some occasionalist found it appropriate to have recourse to so-called general laws, since God could always pass one in favour of this ship. And M. Bayle, who wants to deny that occasional causes are miracles, could not reasonably object to that. But for my own part I reject such natural laws, whose execution (*exemtion* [sic] = ? *execution*) is absolutely inexplicable (*explicable* [sic]) by the nature of things. So, dismissing this occult quality of the ship, we have to admit that there is nothing to prevent there being a ship so fortunately born (so to speak) as always to arrive in port, without being steered, through winds and tides, past storms and rocks, and all by the mere coincidence of happy accidents. Unmanned ships have certainly sometimes reached their destination. Is there any impossibility which means that this could not happen several times to the same ship, and as a result that it could not happen each and every time it put to sea, since that could only be a certain number of times? Since the number of accidents is not infinite, not only God, but also a very superior finite mind could predict all the accidents to which the ship would be exposed, and would be able to determine, as the solution of a geometrico-mechanical problem, the ship's structure, and where, when, and how it should put to sea, in order to adjust it as necessary to this finite number of accidents. Don't we know that men are ingenious enough to make automata capable of turning at just the right moment at certain street corners, and of thus adjusting to a certain number of accidents? And a proportionally greater mind could provide for a greater number. And if this excellent mind did not have to take these accidents as already given, but had the freedom to make them happen or not as he wished, it would be incomparably easier for it to do what was necessary, and, in advance and by a pre-established harmony, to adjust the ship to the accidents, and the accidents to the ship. Thus it is the greatest mistake to doubt whether the infinity of God is great enough to be able to do this.

E. Bodies do not know what happens in the soul, and the soul makes no physical impression on the body. M. Bayle is right about that; but God makes up for this—not by himself giving the body new impressions from time to time, so as to make it obey the soul, but by constructing this automaton from the outset in such a way that, at the right time and place, it will do just what the soul requires.

F. There is nothing strange in that, once we consider that a craftsman as great as God can make an automaton which resembles a servant and which is capable of acting as one, and of carrying out at the right time the orders it has been given, over a very long period.[48] The body is such an automaton with respect to the mind.

G. It seems that M. Bayle has got confused, and thinks that the ship or the human body is to be given some kind of 'faculty or virtue' or other, capable of adjusting itself to accidents or to thoughts without having any knowledge of them, and indeed without any intelligible reason. He has good reason to reject such a faculty as impossible; but no one ever suggested such a thing. The automaton which acted as a servant would need only a structure which made it perform its functions in accordance with mechanical rules. It wouldn't modify or change itself to fit in with the thoughts of the master. It would follow out its course, and by that alone would fit in exactly with the wishes of the person its maker intended it to serve.

H. It emerges more and more that M. Bayle has not fully grasped my thought, which is that the body modifies itself as necessary not by some kind of received impression or power, but by its structure, which is designed for that purpose. We can again use the automaton which acts as a servant to resolve the whole problem. The structure it has been given is sufficient for all its functions, even though it is left to itself, even though its first impressions are not renewed, and even though it has no knowledge of what it is to do, or of the instructions it was given. And the difference between Caesar's body and this automaton is only one of degree.

I. Why is this so impossible? He should have given a reason. Everything said here is an amplification, which does not increase the difficulties, but merely makes us admire the skill of God even more. And M. Bayle would have found it difficult to set out this objection properly. In fact, since the pre-established harmony extends to the whole universe and all its modifications, and since each

[48] It would appear from the *Theodicy* (G 6. 137) that Leibniz got this servant analogy (which in a letter to Hartsoeker he describes as 'elegant' (G 3. 521)) from Jaquelot (cf. J 7, § 16).

being has been individually adjusted once for all to all the others, it is obvious that accidents are as unable to upset the pre-established harmony as to alter providence, since they have all been foreseen, and God has already taken account of them. The Epicureans, who used to argue against providence, and several other philosophers and theologians, who denied that God knows and governs the detail of things, have thought in the same way: they believed without reason that God's infinity was not sufficiently great to provide for it.

J. It is rejected not as impossible, but as not very likely.

K. The Cartesian would not deny that such an automaton is possible for God; but he would not accept that other people are in fact inanimate automata of this sort. He would rightly say that they are like him. According to me, however, they are all automata, human as well as animal bodies; but they are all animated, animal as well as human bodies. So pure materialists, like the Democriteans, and also formalists, like the Platonists and the Peripatetics, are partly right and partly wrong. The Democriteans had the perfectly justified belief that human as well as animal bodies are automata and do everything completely mechanically; but they were wrong to believe that these machines are not associated with an immaterial substance or form, and also that matter could think. The Platonists and the Peripatetics believed that the bodies of animals and men are animated, but they were wrong to think that souls change the rules of bodily movement; in this way they took away the automatic side of animal and human bodies. The Cartesians were right to reject that influence, but went wrong in taking away the automatic side of man and the thinking side of animals. I think we should keep both sides for both things: we should be Democritean and make all actions of bodies mechanical and independent of souls, and we should also be more than Platonic and hold that all the actions of souls are immaterial and independent of mechanism.

L. M. Bayle always comes back to some unknown faculty given to the body to enable it to adjust to the soul. But this is not being argued for; we have not abandoned the limitations of created beings, nor what bodies and machines essentially are. There is nothing in the workmanship of the divine machine which surpasses God's knowledge and power. Since he knows everything that can be known and can do anything that can be done, he knows the fairly limited number of human volitions, and is able to make a machine capable of carrying them out.

M. This would be a good argument if the theory of automata had been shown to be impossible; but since the opposite is clearly the case, and has been sufficiently well established by the Cartesians, it is only a matter of degree, which is no difficulty at all when we are considering infinite power and wisdom. Although humans can reason about abstract things which go beyond the imagination, there are still signs in the imagination which correspond to these things, such as letters and symbols. There is no act of understanding so pure as not to be accompanied by some imagination. So there is always something mechanical in the body which exactly corresponds to the train of thoughts in a person's mind, in so far as they involve imagination. Consequently, the automaton of his body does not need the soul's influence, or the supernatural assistance of God, any more than does the body of an animal.

N. Why not? They are made by the same creator, who both wanted and was able to make them agree without acting on each other.

O. But there are servants so well primed that they need no signs. They anticipate them. Chiming watches (*monstres* [sic] = ? *montres*), for example, and alarm clocks are servants of this kind. Far from waiting for signs, they give them to us. The artificial servant I described above, who imitates or mimics a real one, does not even need to be wound up or set by us as do watches and alarm clocks; its maker has set it for us. Our body is a servant of this kind.

P. So M. Bayle does not yet regard it as such.

Q. Saying that the soul's God-given force is the only source (*principe*) of its particular actions is not sufficient to give the explanation for those actions. It is better to say that God put into each soul 'the world in concentrated form', or gave it the power to represent the universe according to the point of view appropriate to that soul. It is this which is the source (*principe*) of its actions, and which distinguishes them one from another and from the actions of another soul. For it follows that they will continually undergo changes which represent the universe's changes, and that other souls will have other, but corresponding, changes.

R. It is as well to take note, before going further, of a big difference between matter and the soul. Matter is an incomplete being; it lacks the source of action. And when some impression is produced in it, it registers precisely only that, and what is in it in that moment. This is why matter is not even capable of keeping itself in circular motion, for this movement is not simple enough for it to remember, so to speak. Matter remembers only what happened in the previous moment, or rather *in ultimo signo rationis.*[49] It remembers, that is to say, the direction of the tangent, but has no ability to remember the rule it would need to be given for diverging from that tangent and staying on the circumference. That is why, without something making it do so, a body can't keep moving in a circle, even when it has begun in one. That is why an atom can only learn to go in a simple straight line: it is so stupid and imperfect. It is completely different with a soul or a mind. Because this is a true substance, or a complete being, and the source of its own actions, it, so to speak, remembers (confusedly, of course) all its preceding states, and is affected by them. It retains not only its direction, as does the atom, but also the law of changes of direction, or the law of curvature, which the atom cannot do. And whereas in the atom there is only one change, there is an infinity of changes in the modifications of a soul, each of which has its law; for the Epicurean atom, although it has parts, has a uniform interior, whereas the soul, even though it has no parts, has within it, because of the multitude of representations of external things, or rather because of the representation of the universe lodged within it by the creator, a great number, or rather an infinite number, of variations. M. Bayle would not bring against me the comparison between an Epicurean atom and the human soul, as he does here, if he had considered this difference between the *conatuses* of bodies and those of souls. This is a difference of which I already had a dim notion in my early youth, when I published my 'Physical Theory'.[50] (A notion with which the

---

[49] In order to deal with problems concerning continuous change, the scholastics subdivided instants of time into prior and posterior 'signs', or 'instants'. These were usually called *signa naturae* (see Stephen D. Dumont, 'Time, Contradiction and Freedom of the Will in the Late Thirteenth Century', in *Documenti e studi sulla tradizione filosofica medievale*, 3. 2 (1992), pp. 561–97, esp. 567–8). Dumont has suggested to us that in the present context 'ratio' relates to essence, or nature, rather than to reason; indeed, in the *Theodicy* Leibniz twice identifies 'la priorité de nature' with 'in signo anteriore rationis' (G 6. 346).

[50] *Hypothesis physica nova* (Moguntiae, 1671) (R 13).

late M. Lantin of Dijon was rather taken, as he told me in a letter).[51]

S. I do not think of the soul as 'giving itself' its first feelings. It received them with its existence from God at the moment of creation, for it has had feelings from the outset; and in its first ones it received potentially all the others.

T. The total cause does not remain the same here. Present thoughts involve a tendency towards other thoughts. For the soul has not only perception, but also desire. But though tending towards new pleasures, it sometimes encounters pains.

U. Not at all, for it tends towards change according to the laws of desire, just as the body tends towards change according to the laws of motion.

V. I have already explained above the great difference which exists between the laws of change of a body such as an atom and those of the soul; and it is also shown by the difference between the thought of a soul and the movement of an atom. Spontaneous movement consists in the tendency to move in a straight line; there is nothing so uniform. But thought involves an actual external material object, the human body; and this is a composite object which contains a very large number of modifications, through which it is connected with surrounding bodies and, by means of them, step by step with all others. And the soul's tendencies towards new thoughts correspond to the body's tendency towards new shapes and new movements. And as these new movements can make the object pass from order to disorder, their representation in the soul can also make the soul pass from pleasure to displeasure.

W. Let us review what is said here. It is certainly necessary that the change from one thought to another 'involves some affinity which connects (*raison d'affinité*) them'; this has been shown. If Caesar's soul had only distinct thoughts, and produced them all voluntarily, the change from one thought to another could be as M. Bayle suggests, for example from the thought of one tree to that of another. But besides the perceptions which the soul remembers,

---

[51] Watson, p. 34, says that when in Paris between 1672 and 1676 Leibniz 'met Lantin and La Mare, conseillers to Parlement from Dijon, Foucher was Lantin's friend, and it was probably through Lantin that he met Leibniz'.

there is a mass which is made up of an infinite number of confused perceptions which it does not disentangle. It is through these that it represents outside bodies, and comes to have distinct thoughts which are unlike the preceding ones, because the bodies which the soul represents have suddenly changed to something which strongly affects its own. So the soul sometimes passes from white to black or from yes to no, without knowing how, or at least involuntarily, for what its confused thoughts and its feelings produce in it we attribute to the body. So we should not be surprised if a man who is stung by some insect when eating jam should, despite himself, pass immediately from pleasure to pain. For, in approaching the man's body before stinging it, this insect was already affecting it, and the representation of this was, albeit unconsciously, already affecting his soul. However, in the soul as in the body, little by little the insensible becomes the sensible. That is how the soul changes itself even against its will, for it is enslaved by the feelings and confused thoughts which occur according to the states of its body, and of other bodies through their relation to it. These, then, are the means through which pleasures are sometimes interrupted and followed by pains, without the soul's always being alerted or prepared for it; as for example when the insect which stings approaches without making a noise, or, if it is a wasp for example, when some distraction prevents our noticing the approaching wasp's buzz. Thus we must not say that nothing new happens in the substance of the soul which makes it feel the sting; for what happens is confused presentiments or, better, insensible dispositions of the soul, which represent the dispositions of the body with regard to the sting.

X. M. Bayle is right to deny any such composition to the soul, which would make it destructible and dissipatable, for it would then be a mass. But we have no need for the soul's substance to be composite; it is enough that its thoughts are composite, and involve a large number of objects and modifications distinctly or confusedly understood, as experience in fact shows us. For even though the soul is a simple and single substance, it never has simple and single perceptions. It always has, all at the same time, several distinct perceptions which it can remember, and, associated with them, an infinite number of confused ones which it cannot distinguish. Since this composition of thoughts has only to produce other composite thoughts, it has no need of such a host of minds. Each partial modification of the preceding state of the soul contributes to the next total modification of the same soul, and gives it a new variation.

Y. So all M. Bayle has said so far only reinforces his first objections, and he has been talking as though I had not yet replied to them. He now begins to reply to my answers which were published in the *Histoire des ouvrages des savants*, July 1698,[52] and which should be thought of as though they had been inserted here.

Z. I think of the law of succession of a soul's modifications not as a simple decree of God, but as an effect of an enduring decree within the soul's nature, like a law inscribed in its substance. When God puts a certain law or programme of future action into an automaton, he is not content merely to impose an order on it as a decree; at the same time he provides the means for its implementation—that is, he inscribes a law in its nature or constitution. He gives it a structure in virtue of which the actions which he wants or allows the animal to do are produced naturally and in order. My notion of the soul is the same: I think of it as an immaterial automaton whose internal constitution contains in concentrated form, or represents, a material automaton, and produces in the soul representations of its actions.

AA. All we need do is picture a chorister or opera singer hired to sing at certain times, who finds, at the church or the opera, a book of music in which are written the pieces of music or scores to be sung, and on what days and at what times. This singer sings by sight-reading: his eyes are guided by the book, and his tongue and throat are guided by his eyes; but his soul sings, so to speak, from memory, or something equivalent to memory. For since the music book, the eyes, and the ears can have no influx into the soul, it has to find for itself, though with no trouble or effort, and without searching for it, what its brain and its organs find with the help of the book. This is because the whole score in the book or series of books that are followed in singing is imprinted potentially in his soul from the beginning of its existence; just as the score was in some way imprinted in its material causes before the pieces were put together and made into a book. But the soul is not conscious of all this, for it is encapsulated in its confused perceptions, which

[52] i.e. PB3.

express all the detail of the universe; it perceives it distinctly only when its organs are noticeably struck by the notes in the score.

BB. I have already shown more than once that the soul does many things without knowing how it does them—when it does them by means of confused perceptions and unconscious inclinations or appetitions, of which there are always an extremely large number, so that it is impossible for the soul to be conscious of them, or to distinguish them clearly. Our perceptions are never perfectly uniform, as a straight line is; they are always clothed in something sensible (*desensible* [sic] = ? *de sensible*), which involves something confused, even though it is itself clear. It is in this way that notions of colours are clear, and are easily noticed. But they are confused, for their composition is not manifest in the sensation we have of them. They involve in themselves something of the light source which generates them, of the object from which they come, and of the medium through which they pass. And they are bound to be affected by all that, and as a consequence by an infinity of things which have an effect on the medium they pass through, just as water is always affected a little by its channel. I have shown elsewhere[53] that the confused perception of pleasantness or unpleasantness (*des agremens* [sic] = ? *désagréments*) which we find in consonances or dissonances consists in an occult arithmetic. The soul counts the beats of the vibrating object which makes the sound, and when these beats regularly coincide at short intervals, it finds them pleasant. Thus it counts without knowing it. And it is also in this way that it performs an infinity of other small operations which are very precise, although they are not at all voluntary, and are known only by the noticeable effect in which they eventually culminate. They give us a feeling which is clear but confused, because its sources are not perceived. Reasoning has to come to our aid—as in music, where the proportions which produce an agreeable sound have been discovered.

CC. This is as far as M. Bayle's final objection goes. He gives my reply to it himself, and seems to concede that it is a plausible one, and could well resolve the difficulty. For I had in fact already replied to the objection: the soul has all the devices for which M. Bayle asks, and arranged as necessary. But they are not at all

[53] Perhaps Leibniz has in mind the paper Loemker entitles 'On Wisdom' (G 7. 86–90; L 425–8).

material. They are the preceding perceptions themselves, from which the subsequent ones arise by the law of desires. Here is what M. Bayle says about it [see PB 4, §15].

DD. What is meant here by traces are marks (which can be immaterial) such as relations, expressions, representations; that is, the effects by means of which some past cause can be known, or the causes by which some future effect can be known. And since there is the greatest amount of diversity within the present state of the soul, which knows many things at once and still senses infinitely more, and since this present diversity is an effect of that of a preceding state and a cause of that of a future state, I thought they could be called 'traces', in which a sufficiently penetrating mind would be able to recognize the past and the future; but our own penetration could never reach so far.

EE. Having replied carefully and precisely, point by point, to M. Bayle's difficulties, always consistently and based on the same principles, I hope I have ironed out everything he found worrying; and it does in fact look as though he himself seems more or less prepared to give up his objections. I have also replied elsewhere to Dom François Lamy's difficulties,[54] which were mere misunderstandings. In the end my system comes down to this: each monad is the universe in concentrated form, and each mind is an imitation of the divinity. In God the universe is not only concentrated, but perfectly expressed; but in each created monad there is distinctly expressed only one part, which is larger or smaller according as the soul is more or less excellent, and all the infinite remainder is expressed only confusedly. But in God there is not only this concentration of the universe, but also its source. He is the originating centre from which all else emanates, and if something emanates out from us, it does not do so without mediation, but only because from the outset God wanted to accommodate things to our desires. In fact when we say that each monad, soul, or mind has received a specific law, we must add that this is only a variation of the general law which orders the universe; it is like the way in which the same town appears different from the different points of view from which it is seen. So human souls do not have to be of different species from each other. The contrary is nearer the truth; for it is certain that two leaves, two eggs, two bodies, although of the same

[54] L4.

species, are never perfectly alike, and all these infinite variations, which we could never comprehend under one notion, make up different individuals, but not different species. The marvel is that the sovereign wisdom has found in representing substances a way to vary the same world at the same time to an infinite degree, for since the world already contains in itself an infinite variety, and has that variety diversely expressed by an infinity of different representations, it possesses an infinity of infinities, and could not be more appropriate to the nature and intentions of its inexpressible author, who exceeds in perfection everything that can be thought.

FF. I agree that this will vary in an infinite number of ways the effects of the sources or true unities, but not that it will 'disturb' these unities or souls themselves, or conflict with their spontaneity. The impact of bodies causes changes in mere masses, but not in souls or monads, which spontaneously follow out their courses, adjusted to and representing everything that happens in masses.

PB6. LEIBNIZ: 'Reply to the Comments in the Second Edition of M. Bayle's *Critical Dictionary*, in the Article "Rorarius", Concerning the System of Pre-established Harmony' (1702; pub. 1716)[55]

[1] I published in the Paris *Journal des savants* (June and July 1695) some essays on a new system, which seemed to me to give a good explanation of the union between body and soul.[56] In them, instead of the way of *influence* of the schools, or the way of *assistance* of the Cartesians, I adopted the way of *pre-established harmony*. M. Bayle, who can give to the most abstract thoughts the charm they need if they are to capture the attention of the reader, and yet who goes deeply into them at the same time as bringing them into public view, was kind enough to take the trouble to develop this system in his comments in the article on 'Rorarius' in his *Dictionary*. But as at the same time he also raised some problems

[55] 'Réponse de M. Leibniz aux reflexions contenues dans la seconde édition du Dictionnaire Critique de M. Bayle, article Rorarius, sur le système de l'harmonie préétablie', *Histoire critique de la République des lettres*, art. 4, vol 11 (1716), pp. 78–114 (B 161; R 193). We have noted significant differences between this original and Desmaizeaux's and Gerhardt's (G 4. 554–71) re-publications.
[56] i.e. NS1.

which he thought needed to be cleared up, I attempted to do so in the *Histoire des ouvrages des savants* for July 1698.[57] M. Bayle has now replied to this in the second edition of his *Dictionary* in the same article on 'Rorarius' (p. 2610 let. L).[58] [2] He is good enough to say that my replies have developed the subject further, and that if it were certain that the theory of harmony[59] is a possibility, he would have no hesitation in preferring it to the Cartesian theory, since it gives an exalted idea of the author of things, and avoids any implication of miraculous guidance of the ordinary course of nature. But at present he finds it hard to understand how such a pre-established harmony is possible, and to show why he begins with something which in his view is easier, and yet which we would agree is hardly feasible. He compares my theory with the supposition of a ship, which, without being steered by anyone, manages to get itself to its intended port. He says that it will be agreed that even the infinity of God is not too much for giving this kind of ability to a ship: he does not definitely say that it is impossible, but he thinks that others will say it is; for 'you will also say', he adds, 'that a ship is not the sort of thing which could be given such a faculty by God'.[60] [3] Perhaps he thought that according to the theory in question we would have to think of God as giving the ship a scholastic-style faculty for achieving this effect, like that which the schools attribute to heavy bodies for steering them towards the centre. If this is what he means, I would be the first to reject such a supposition. But if he means a faculty of the ship which is explicable by mechanical rules, through a combination of internal agencies (*ressorts*) and external circumstances, and yet he still rejects the supposition as impossible, then I would ask him to give some reason for doing so. For although, as I shall show below, I have no need of the possibility of anything quite like the ship as M. Bayle appears to understand it, nevertheless I think that if we consider the thing thoroughly, far from there being any difficulty here with regard to God, it would appear that even a finite mind might be clever enough to bring it about. There is no doubt that a man could make a machine which was capable of walking around a town for a time, and of turning precisely at the corners of certain streets. And an incomparably more perfect, although still limited, mind could

[57] i.e. PB3.   [58] i.e. PB4.
[59] For 'harmony' Desmaizeaux and G read: 'pre-established harmony'.
[60] See PB4, § 3.

foresee and avoid an incomparably greater number of obstacles. And this being so, if this world were, as some think it is,[61] only a combination of a finite number of atoms which interact in accordance with mechanical laws, it is certain that a finite mind could be sufficiently exalted as to understand and predict with certainty everything that will happen in a given period. This mind could then not only make a ship capable of getting itself to a certain port, by first giving it the route, the direction, and the requisite equipment (*ressorts*), but it could also build a body capable of simulating a man. The difference, after all, is only one of degree, which is no difference at all in the realm of possibilities; and however large the multitude of a machine's operations, the power and the skill of the workman could increase in proportion, so that to be unable to see the possibility of the thing is just a matter of not considering the intervening stages sufficiently well. [4] In fact, the world is not composed of a finite number of atoms; rather, it is a machine,[62] each part of which is composed of a truly infinite number of devices (*ressorts*). But it is also true that the one who made it, and governs it, is of a yet more infinite perfection, since he encompasses an infinity of possible worlds,[63] and from which he selected the one that pleased him. To return to limited minds, however: we can see from the odd isolated cases which we sometimes come across how far others, which we don't know about, could go. For example, there are people who can do large arithmetical calculations very quickly in their heads. M. de Monconis mentions such a person in Italy in his day, and there is one in Sweden today, who hasn't even been taught ordinary arithmetic, and who, I hope, will be carefully tested as to how he does it.[64] And what is a man, however excellent he may be, in comparison with all the many possible and even actual creatures? — creatures such as angels and geniuses, who in all sorts of understanding and reasoning might surpass us incomparably further than these marvellous possessors of natural arithmetical ability surpass us in the matter of numbers. I realize that ordinary people have no time for these things: they are bemused by considerations where it is necessary to think about what is out of

---

[61] See [§ 8] below.

[62] For 'is a machine' G reads 'is like a machine'.

[63] G adds 'which he has in his understanding'.

[64] Balthasar de Monconys' *Journal des voyages . . . ou les scavants trouveront un nombre infini de nouveautez . . .* (Lyon, 1665–6). Leibniz refers again to the Swedish boy at *New Essays*, i. i.

the ordinary, or even completely unheard of. But when we think about the size and the complexity of the universe, we see things quite differently. M. Bayle above all cannot fail to see the validity of these conclusions. In point of fact, my theory doesn't depend on them, as I shall show presently; but even if it did, and even if it were right to say that it is more surprising than the above-mentioned[65] theory of automata (and I shall show later on that in fact it is only an extension of its good parts, or of what is solid and reliable in it), I should not be at all worried by that, given that there is no other way of explaining things in conformity with the laws of nature. For we must not be ruled by popular notions in these matters, to the prejudice of conclusions which are certain. Moreover, it is not because of its strangeness that a philosopher should object to the theory of automata, but because of its lack of a foundation (*principes*), since there must be *entelechies* everywhere. It is to have a very impoverished idea of the author of nature (who multiplies, as far as he can, his *little worlds*, or *indivisible active mirrors*) to accord them only to human bodies: it is in fact impossible that they are not everywhere.

[5] So far we have only talked of what a limited substance can do; but in the case of God, it is quite another matter, and far from its being the case that what at first seemed impossible actually is impossible, we must in fact say that it is impossible that God should act otherwise, since he is infinitely powerful and wise, and maintains order and harmony in everything as far as is possible. But what is more, that which seems so strange when considered in the abstract is a necessary consequence of the constitution of things; and so the universal marvel dispels and, so to say, absorbs the particular marvel, by explaining it. For everything is regulated and bound together in such a way that these natural mechanisms which never go wrong, that we can compare to ships which steer themselves to port despite all the course changes and all the storms, should not be thought any stranger than a rocket (*fusée*) which runs (*coule*) along a rope, or a liquid which flows (*court*) along a channel. Moreover, since bodies are not *atoms*, but divisibles—and indeed actually divided—to infinity, and since everything is filled with them, it follows that the smallest little body is individually affected by the smallest of changes in any of the others, however distant and however small it may be, and so must be an exact

[65] See [§ 8] below.

mirror of the universe. This means that a sufficiently penetrating mind would, in proportion to its penetration, be able to see and foresee in each corpuscle what is happening and what will happen both in that corpuscle and outside it.[66] So nothing happens to it, not even as a result of the impact of surrounding bodies, which does not follow from what is already internal to it, or which disturbs its internal order. This is even more obvious in the case of simple substances, or the active principles (*principes*) themselves, which, following Aristotle, I call primitive *entelechies*, and which according to me nothing can disturb. [6] This answers one of M. Bayle's marginal notes (p. 2612, let. b) where he objects to me that since an organic body is composed of several substances, each of these substances must have a source (*principe*) of action really distinct from that of each of the others, and since the action of each such source is spontaneous, their effects will vary in an infinite number of ways, because neighbouring bodies will to some extent constrain the natural spontaneity of each one.[67] But we must bear in mind that for all time each one has been accommodated to every other, and adapts itself to suit what the others will demand of it. There is therefore no constraint in substances except in external appearances. And this being so, any point you take in the world develops along a predetermined line, which that point has adopted once and for all, and which nothing can make it abandon. I think this point can be shown very clearly and precisely to the geometrical mind,[68] even though there are infinitely more lines of this kind than a finite mind can comprehend. In fact the line would be straight if the point were all alone in the world; as things are, it owes its shape, in virtue of mechanical laws, to the collaboration of all other bodies, and it is by just that collaboration that it is *pre-established*. So I claim that there is no real spontaneity in a mass (unless we consider the universe as a whole, which encounters no resistance); for if this point could be isolated from everything else, it would continue not

[66] For 'both in that corpuscle and outside it', G reads 'in that corpuscle, and also what is happening and what will happen everywhere, both in the corpuscle and outside it'.

[67] See PB4, note d.

[68] Pascal wrote of the 'geometrical mind' in his *Pensées* (1670), art. 7. 1–2, and also in a manuscript, 'De l'esprit géométrique', written *c.*1658, unpublished during his lifetime but mentioned by Antoine Arnauld and Pierre Nicole in the so-called *Port-Royal Logic*, their *La Logique ou L'Art de penser* (1662), Discours 1, and read by Leibniz by 1684 (R 91); see also Ch. 2, n. 23; Ch. 4, n. 33.

in the pre-established line, but in the straight tangent. So, strictly speaking, what is spontaneous is the *entelechy* (of which this point is the point of view); and whereas the point, because it has no memory, so to speak, nor prescience, can have of itself only the tendency along the touching straight line,[69] the entelechy expresses the pre-established curve itself,[70] so that in this sense, no change is violent with regard to it.[71] [7] This shows us that in fact there is no longer any difficulty in all those marvels such as the ship which gets itself to port,[72] or the machine without intelligence which performs all the actions of a man, and I don't know how many other fictions that might still be raised against me, and which make our suppositions appear unbelievable when considered in the abstract. And it also shows how everything that had seemed strange disappears completely, when we understand that things are determined[73] to do what they have to do. Everything that ambition or whatever other passion produces in Caesar's soul is also represented in his body; and all the movements involved in these passions come from impressions of objects connected to internal movements. And the body is so constructed that the soul never makes decisions to which bodily movements don't correspond, even the most abstract reasonings having their place there, through the symbols which represent them to the imagination. [8] In a word, everything happens in the body with regard to the details of phenomena as if the wicked doctrine of those who, following Epicurus and Hobbes, believe that the soul is material were true; or as if man himself were only body, or an automaton. Thus they[74] have extended to man what the Cartesians maintain with regard to all other animals, since they have in effect shown that man, with all his reason, does nothing which is not a set of images, passions, and movements in the body. We have prostituted ourselves in trying to prove the opposite, and have only prepared the way for the triumph of the mistake by approaching it in that way. The Cartesians came off very badly (rather like Epicurus with his *declination of the atoms*, which Cicero made such fun of[75]), when they tried saying that the soul,

---

[69] For 'touching straight line', G reads 'straight line which touches that line'.

[70] G adds 'since the neighbouring bodies are unable to influence such a soul or entelechy'.

[71] G adds 'Although in so far as this soul has confused and, consequently, involuntary perceptions, change which is usually called violent still takes place.'

[72] G adds 'without a pilot'.   [73] G adds 'or inclined'.

[74] For 'they', G reads 'the materialists'.   [75] See n. 38.

though unable to give motion to the body, could nevertheless change its direction. But it is neither possible nor necessary for it to do either; and since the materialists have no need to resort to any such thing, nothing which happens on the outside of a man is capable of refuting their doctrine—which suffices to establish one part of my theory. Those who point out to the Cartesians that the way they prove that animals are only *automata* could be taken as justifying someone who said that all other[76] men, except himself, are simple automata, have said exactly and precisely what I need for this half of my theory, which concerns the body. But as well as the metaphysical[77] principles which establish the *monads*, of which composites are only resultants, internal experience—the consciousness we have of the 'I' which perceives what passes in the body— refutes the Epicurean doctrine. And perception, since it cannot be explained by shapes and movements, establishes the other part of my theory: we are obliged to admit[78] an *indivisible substance* in ourselves, which must itself be the source of its phenomena. So according to this second half of my theory, everything happens in the soul as if there were no body, just as according to the first half, everything happens in the body as if there were no soul.[79] Besides which, I have often shown that, even in bodies, although in detail phenomena are explicable mechanically, the ultimate analysis of mechnical laws and the nature of substances in the end oblige us to appeal to active indivisible principles; and I have also shown that the admirable order which we find in them shows that there is a universal principle whose intelligence as well as whose power is supreme. And just as we can see from what is good and sound in the false and wicked doctrine of Epicurus, namely that there is no need to say that the soul changes the tendencies of the body, so it is also easy to see that it is not necessary either for the material mass to send thoughts to the soul by the influence of I know not what chimerical[80] species, or for God always to act as interpreter of the body to the soul, any more than he needs to interpret the soul's wishes to the body, as the Cartesians would have it:[81] the *pre-established harmony* is a good mediator between both sides. All

[76] For 'said that all other', G reads 'said that, metaphysically speaking, it is possible that all other'. [77] G omits 'metaphysical'.
[78] For 'we are obliged to admit', G reads 'it makes us recognize'.
[79] G adds 'And reason demands that we judge that other men have the same advantage as we have'. [80] G adds 'scholastic'.
[81] Desmaizeaux omits 'as the Cartesians would have it'.

this shows us that what is of value in the theories of Epicurus and of Plato, of the greatest materialists and the greatest idealists, is united here; and there is no longer anything surprising in it, except the sole pre-eminent perfection of the sovereign principle, now displayed in his work far above anything that had been thought before. So why is it any wonder that it all goes well and smoothly, when all things co-operate and lead each other by the hand, once we suppose them all to be perfectly planned? On the contrary, what would be the greatest of wonders, or rather the strangest of absurdities, would be if the ship which was destined to find port, or the machine whose path was mapped out from all time, were to fail despite the measures which God had taken. *As regards corporeal masses, therefore, we should not compare our theory with a ship which steers itself to port*—but rather with those ferries (*bateaux de trajet*), fixed to a rope, that run[82] across a river. Just as with stage-machines and fireworks, whose perfect operation we no longer find strange when we know how it is all done, we transfer our admiration from the invention to the inventor—just as we do nowadays when we see that the planets have no need of intelligences to guide them.

[9] As yet we have spoken of almost nothing except those objections which concern the body or matter, and no difficulty has been raised up till now[83] other than that of the marvellousness (but beautiful, regular, and universal) which there will have to be in bodies if they are to agree with each other, and with souls. And in my view this should be taken as a proof rather than as an objection by people who correctly assess 'the power and intelligence of divine art'[84]—to quote M. Bayle, who has also said that 'nothing can be imagined which gives so exalted an idea of the power and intelligence of the author of all things'.[85] We must now turn to the *soul*, where M. Bayle has found further difficulties after what I said in resolution of his initial ones. He begins[86] by comparing a soul which is completely isolated and taken by itself, receiving nothing from outside, with an Epicurean *atom*, surrounded by a void; and indeed I do consider souls, or rather *monads*, as *atoms of substance*, for in my view there are no *material atoms* in nature, since even the

---

[82] For 'ferries, fixed to a rope, that run', G reads 'ferries which are fixed to a rope that runs'.

[83] Desmaizeaux omits 'up till now'.   [84] Quote from PB4, § 3.

[85] Quote from PB4, § 1.   [86] PB4, § 8.

smallest piece of matter still has parts. [10] Now, since the atom, as imagined by Epicurus, has a moving force, which gives it a certain direction, it will, assuming that it doesn't meet any other atom, execute that motion without hindrance, and uniformly. In the same way the soul, placed in the same circumstances, where nothing from outside affects it, if it has once received a feeling of pleasure, it seems (according to M. Bayle[87]), that it must always retain that feeling—for when the total cause remains the same, the effect must always remain the same. If I object that the soul should be considered to be in a state of change, and that therefore the total cause does not remain the same, M. Bayle replies[88] that this change must be like that of an *atom* which is moving continually along the same (straight) line and at a uniform speed. And even if it were allowed (he says[89]) that its thoughts might be different, it would at least still be necessary that the change that I am alleging from one thought to the other should involve some affinity which connects (*raison d'affinité*) them. I quite accept the principles underlying these objections, and I use them myself to explain my system. The state of a *soul*, like that of the *atom*, is a state of change, a tendency: the atom tends towards a change of place, the soul towards a change of thought; each of them changes of itself in the simplest and most uniform way that its state allows. So how does it come about (I will be asked[90]) that there is such simplicity in the changes of an *atom*, and such variety in those of the *soul*? It is because the atom (as we are imagining it, for there is no such thing in nature), even though it has parts, has nothing to cause any variety in its tendency, because we are supposing that these parts do not change their relations; on the other hand, the soul, though completely indivisible, involves a compound tendency, that is to say a multitude of present thoughts, each of which tends towards a particular change, depending on what is involved in it, and which are all in it at the same time, in virtue of its essential relatedness to all the other things in the world. [11] It is in fact the lack of this relatedness[91] which rules Epicurean atoms out of nature. For there is no individual thing which must not express[92] all the others, in such a way that the soul, because of the variety of its *modifications*, should be compared not with a

---

[87] PB4, § 9.   [88] PB4, § 9.
[89] PB4, § 9.   [90] PB4, §§ 9, 10.
[91] Gerhardt adds '(among other things)'.
[92] For 'there is no individual thing which must not express', G reads 'each thing or part of the universe must take note of'.

material atom, but rather with the *universe* which it represents from its own *point of view*, and in a way even with God, whose *infinity* it represents *finitely* (because of its confused and imperfect perception of the infinite).[93] And the reason for a change in the soul's thoughts is the same as for the change in things in the *universe* which it represents. For mechanical causes, which work themselves out in the body, are brought together, and, so to speak, concentrated in souls or *entelechies*, and indeed originate there. In fact, not all entelechies are, like our soul, *images of God*; for they are not all intended to be members of a society or a state of which he is the head. But they are all still *images of the universe*. They are in their own way scaled-down *worlds*: fertile *simplicities*; *unities* of *substance*, though, because of the multitude of their modifications, *virtually infinite*; centres, which express an *infinite circumference*. [12] And it is necessary that they should be like this, as I have explained previously in correspondence with M. Arnauld.[94] And their enduring should cause no one any difficulty, any more than the enduring of the Gassendists' *atoms*. As for the rest, as Socrates in Plato's *Phaedo* remarked of a man who scratches himself, often it is only a step from pleasure to pain: *extrema gaudii luctus occupat*.[95] So we need not be surprised by this change; it sometimes seems that pleasure is only a complex of small perceptions, each of which, if it were large, would be a pain.[96]

[13] M. Bayle has already recognized that I have done my best to reply to a good part of his objections. He also observes that in the system of occasional causes God has to implement his own laws, whereas in mine the soul does it; but he objects that the soul has no tools for doing so. I reply as I have replied, that it has: it has its

---

[93] Gerhardt adds 'The idea of pleasure seems to be simple, but it is not, and if we analysed it, we would find that it involves everything which surrounds us and, consequently, everything which surrounds those surroundings.'

[94] Perhaps Leibniz has in mind his letter of 9 Oct. 1687 to Arnauld (G 2. 111–15, 126). He misleadingly speaks here as though his correspondence with Arnauld is in the public domain. Though it appears not to have been widely circulated, its publication was twice announced (*Journal des savants*, 31 Mar. 1708 (vol. 39, p. 595) and in *Mémoires de Trévoux*, July 1708 (vol. 22, p. 2283)). R. C. Sleigh, Jr., to whom this information is due, suggests that in this piece 'perhaps Leibniz was engaging in a little pre-publication advertising' (personal communication).

[95] The reference is to *Phaedo*, 60b, but the quotation is directly from *Proverbs* 14: 13 ('the end of that mirth is heaviness', in the Authorized Version).

[96] According to G (G 4. 563 n.) '; it sometimes seems that pleasure . . . would be a pain' replaces the original MS's 'in the bodies of animals. We get pleasure from resisting a certain pressure, but when it gets too violent, it turns to pain.'

present thoughts, from which the subsequent ones are born; and one can say that in the soul, as everywhere else, *the present is big with the future.*

[14] I think M. Bayle will accept, and all other philosophers with him, that our thoughts are never simple, and that in the case of some thoughts the soul can of itself pass from one to the other, as it goes from premises to a conclusion, or from the end to the means. Even the Reverend Father Malebranche agrees that the soul has internal voluntary actions. Why shouldn't this be the case with all thoughts? Perhaps because it has been thought that confused thoughts are *toto genere* different from distinct thoughts, whereas they are only less well distinguished and less developed because of their multiplicity. This has meant that certain movements, which are rightly called involuntary, have been attributed to the body to such an extent that they have been believed to have nothing corresponding to them in the soul: and conversely it has been thought that certain abstract thoughts were not represented in the body. But both of these are mistaken, as often happens with this sort of distinction, for we have taken note only of what is most obvious. [15] The most abstract thoughts need some imagination: and when we consider what confused thoughts (which invariably accompany the most distinct that we can have) are,[97] we realize that they always involve the infinite, and not only what happens in our body but also, by means of it, what happens elsewhere. Confused thoughts thus serve our purpose as the tool which seemed necessary for the functions I attribute to the soul much better than the legion of substances of which M. Bayle speaks. It is true that the soul does have these legions in its service, but not in its interior.[98] It is, then, present perceptions, with an orderly tendency to change,[99] that make up the musical score which tells the soul what to do. [16] But (says M. Bayle) 'would it then not be necessary that it know (distinctly) the sequence of notes, and be thinking (distinctly) about them?'[100] I reply that this is not so: it is enough that the notes are

---

[97] G adds 'such as those of colours, smells, tastes, of heat, of cold, etc.'.

[98] G adds 'For there is no soul or entelechy which is not dominant over an infinity of others which enter into the parts of its body (*ses organes*), and the soul is never without some organized body appropriate to its present state.'

[99] G adds 'in conformity with what is outside'.

[100] This is a somewhat impressionistic quote from PB3, § 14. The word 'distinctly' is added as Leibniz's own parenthesis.

contained in its confused thoughts;[101] otherwise,[102] every *entelechy* would be God. For God distinctly and[103] perfectly expresses everything at once, the possible and the actual, past, present, and future. He is the universal source of everything, and created *monads* imitate him as far as created things can: he has made them the sources of their phenomena, which contain relations to everything, more or less distinct according to the degree of perfection of each substance. What is impossible about that?[104] I want to see some positive argument which leads me to some contradiction, or the denial of some established truth. It would be no objection just to say that it is surprising. Far from it: everyone who accepts immaterial indivisible substances attributes to them a simultaneous multitude of perceptions, and a *spontaneity* in their reasonings and their voluntary acts. I am therefore only extending that *spontaneity* to their confused and involuntary thoughts, and showing that their nature is to contain relations with everything that is external.
[17] Can it be proved that that cannot be, or that everything which is in us must be distinctly understood? Isn't it true that we can't always remember even things that we know, and which can immediately be brought back by some little reminder? Then how many other kinds of thing might there not be in the soul, which we cannot get at so easily? Otherwise the soul would be a God, when it is enough for it to be a little world, that is as *imperturbable* as the big one, once we realize that there is just as much spontaneity in the confused, as in the distinct. In another sense, however, it is reasonable to call those things which consist in confused thoughts, and in which there is involuntariness and incomprehension, *perturbations* (as the ancients did) or passions. And this is what in ordinary speech we not unreasonably attribute to the conflict of the body with the mind, since our confused thoughts represent the body or the flesh, and constitute our imperfection.
[18] When I gave substantially this response before, that confused perceptions implicitly contain everything that is external, and involve infinite relations, M. Bayle recorded it, but did not refute it; instead, he said 'that this suggestion, if it were fully developed,

[101] G adds 'in the way the soul has a thousand things in its memory without thinking of them distinctly'.
[102] G adds 'if entelechies distinctly understood all the infinity which they contain'.   [103] G omits 'distinctly and'.
[104] G adds 'It seems rather that this is necessary to bring created things close to God, as far as can reasonably be done.'

would be the real means of resolving all the difficulties';[105] and he does me the honour of saying that he expects that I will completely resolve his own. Even if he said this only out of politeness, I would not have failed to try to resolve his difficulties. I believe I have not missed any out; and if I have left something out without trying to resolve it, it must have been because I didn't understand exactly what objection was being put to me—something which sometimes makes it most difficult for me to reply. I would have liked to see why it is thought that there could not be the multitude of perceptions that I suppose there to be in an *indivisible substance*; for I believe that even if experience and common sense did not force us to recognize a large variety in our soul, it would still be possible to suppose it. It is no proof of the impossibility of something merely to say that one cannot conceive this or that, when one doesn't make clear where it conflicts with reason, and when the difficulty is only one of imagination, and not of understanding.

[19] It is pleasant to have to deal with an opponent at once so fair and so profound as M. Bayle, who is so even-handed that he often foresees the answers—as when he remarks that my view that the primitive constitution of each mind is different from that of every other should seem no more extraordinary than what the Thomists say, following their master, about the diversity of species of all separated intelligences. I am very glad to find that I agree with him about that too, for somewhere I have cited this same authority.[106] In fact, in accordance with my definition of *species*, I do not call this a *specific* difference; for since, according to me, no two individuals are ever perfectly alike, we would have to say that no two individuals are ever of the same species, which would not be correct. I am sorry that I have not yet been able to see the objections of Dom François Lamy in (so M. Bayle tells me[107]) the second treatise of his *The Knowledge of the Self* (1699 edition), otherwise I would have already sent my replies. [20] M. Bayle was kind enough to make a point of sparing me those objections which apply equally to other systems, and I am obliged to him for that, too. With regard to the force given to created things, I shall say only that I believe I have replied in the journal of Leipzig for September 1698 to all the

---

[105] PB4, § 16.
[106] See n. 43. Leibniz is perhaps referring to *Discourse on Metaphysics*, § 9 (G 4. 433).
[107] Perhaps Leibniz is referring to PB4, note a. These objections are in L2.

objections in a learned man's article in the same journal for 1697, which M. Bayle cites in the side margin,[108] and indeed I have demonstrated that without an *active* force in bodies there would be no variety in phenomena, which would be the same as if there were nothing at all. It is true that this learned opponent has replied (May 1699),[109] but he really only expounds his view, without paying sufficient attention to my arguments against it: as a result, he omits to reply to this demonstration, as if he regarded what I said as useless for persuading or clarifying things further, or even as harmful to a good understanding. I admit that this is the usual fate of disputes, but there are exceptions; and what has gone on between M. Bayle and myself seems to be of a different kind. For my part I always try to make sure that moderation is preserved, and to strive to clarify things, in order that the disagreement should not only not be harmful, but might even become useful. I do not know that I have managed this here; but although I cannot flatter myself that I have given complete satisfaction to a mind as penetrating as M. Bayle's in a matter as difficult as that with which we are concerned, still I shall be content if he finds I have made some progress in so important an inquiry.

[21] I have been unable to resist renewing the earlier pleasure I had found in reading with close attention several articles in his excellent and rich Dictionary, among others those which concern philosophy, such as the articles on the Paulines, Origen, Pereira, Rorarius, Spinoza, and Zeno. I was surprised all over again at the fecundity, the force, and the brilliance of his thought. No Academic, not even Carneades, could have brought out the problems better.[110] Although very clever in such meditations, M. Foucher was nowhere near it, and for myself I find that nothing in the world is of more use in resolving these problems. This is what particularly pleases me about the objections of clever and reasonable people, for I feel that it gives me new strength, like Anteus in the fable when he is thrown

---

[108] i.e. PB4, note c.

[109] For details of these references see n. 44.

[110] Carneades (*c.*214–*c.*129 BC) was an Academic sceptic who taught, e.g., that nothing can be proved—since any proof rests on unproved assumptions, and since there is always something to be said on both sides of a question. According to Cicero, 'Carneades distinguished himself by a quickness of wit, that was in a manner divine, and a peculiar force of eloquence' (*De oratore*, 3. 18; in *Cicero on Oratory and Orators*, trans. J. S. Watson (London, 1871), p. 351; see also *Academiea*, 1. 2. 46).

to the ground.¹¹¹ And what lets me speak with some confidence is that since I made up my mind only after having looked at the question from all sides and in a balanced way, I can perhaps say without vanity, 'omnia praecepi atque animo mecum [ante] peregi'.¹¹² But objections are useful, and save me a lot of trouble; for it is a great deal of trouble to try to go back over every detail in an attempt to guess or anticipate what other people will find to criticize, since people's presuppositions and inclinations are so different. There have been some very penetrating people who have immediately fallen in with my theory, and have even gone so far as to recommend it to others. There have also been other very clever people who have said that they already in effect agreed with it; others have also said that they understood the theory of *occasional causes* in just that way, and did not distinguish it from my own, with which I was very pleased. But I am no less pleased when I see people set about investigating it properly.

[22] Turning now to the articles of M. Bayle which I have just mentioned, and whose subject is very relevant here,¹¹³ it seems that the reason why evil is permitted has to do with the eternal *possibilities* according to which a universe such as this, which allows evil and yet which has been allowed into actual existence, turns out to be overall the most perfect of all the possibilities. But it is a mistake to try to show in detail, as the Stoics did, what St Augustine perfectly understood in general: how useful evil is for drawing attention to the good, and, so to speak, for getting us to step back in

¹¹¹ According to Greek myth, the giant Anteus, born of Poseidon and Earth, forced people to wrestle with him, and killed them when he overcame them. Every time *he* was thrown to the ground, he gained new strength from this contact with his mother, Earth.

¹¹² 'All this ere now have I forecast and inly traversed in thought' (Virgil, *Aeneid*, 6. 105; trans. H. Rushton Fairclough, *Virgil*, 2 vols. (London, 1932), i. 515).

¹¹³ The following discussion of evil relates to Bayle's *Dictionary* articles on Origen and on the Paulines (seventh-century Manichaeans led by a man named Paul). Like the 'Rorarius' article, that on Pereira (which Leibniz also mentions in [§ 21]), a sixteenth-century Spanish physician, is relevant to the question of animal souls. Leibniz's discussion (in [§ 23]) of time, extension, and motion might allude to Bayle's article on Zeno of Elea (who denied the reality of motion and extension), though the reference in [§ 24] to 'the article on Zeno' is to that on Zeno the Epicurean (see n. 125 below).
Leibniz's rejection in this paragraph of the idea that created things cannot produce their modifications obviously leads on to a discussion of Spinoza (Bayle's article on whom is the other which Leibniz mentioned in [§ 21], and which contains a lengthy discussion of 'modifications'). But the idea is perhaps Malebranche's (see, e.g., *Search*, 3. 2. 3).

order to jump forward the further.[114] For how can we grasp all the infinite particularities of the *universal harmony*? However, if I had to make a rational choice between the two, I would be in favour of the Origenist, and never of the Manichaean.[115] Neither does it seem to me that we have to deny action or power to created things on the grounds that if they produced modifications (*modalités*) they would be creators. For it is God who conserves and continually creates their power, that is to say, the *source* of modifications (*modifications*) within a created thing, or a state of that thing from which it can be seen that there will be a change of modifications. Otherwise, it seems to me (as I have said above that I have shown elsewhere) that God would have produced nothing, and there would be no substances other than God—which would bring back all the absurdities of the God of Spinoza. And indeed it seems that the error of that author comes only from his having worked out the consequences of the doctrine which takes away the power and action of created things.

[23] I hold that time, extension, motion, and in general all forms of continuity as dealt with in mathematics, are only ideal things; that is to say that, just like numbers, they express possibilities. In the same way, Hobbes defined space as *phantasma existentis*.[116] But, to speak more accurately, extension is the order of *possible coexistences*, just as time is the order of *inconsistent* but nevertheless connected *possibilities*, such that[117] these orders[118] relate not only to what is actual, but also to what could be put in its place, just as numbers are indifferent to whatever may be *res numerata*.[119]

[114] 'reculer pour mieux sauter': an old French proverb (see James Woodrow Hassell, Jr., *Middle French Proverbs, Sentences, and Proverbial Phrases* (Toronto, 1982), p. 214).

[115] The followers of Mani (third century AD) taught the real existence of the two principles of good and evil. The followers of Origen of Alexandria (AD *c.*185–253) held that even fallen angels will ultimately be saved.

[116] Actually *phantasma rei existentis*. 'I . . . define *space* . . . [as] *the phantasm of a thing existing (phantasma rei existentis) without the mind simply*' (*De corpore*, 2. 7. 2, as in Hobbes, *English Works*, ed. W. Molesworth (1839), i. 94).

[117] For '*possibilities*, such that', G has '*possibilities*. Thus the one concerns things which are simultaneous or which exist together, and the other concerns those things which are incompatible, but which are nevertheless conceived as existent, which is what makes them successive. But taken together space and time make up the order of possibilities of a whole universe.'

[118] G adds '(space and time, that is)'.

[119] 'The thing which is counted'. G adds 'And this encapsulating of both the possible and the existent produces a uniform continuum, which is indifferent to all division.'

Yet in nature there are no perfectly uniform changes such as are required by the idea of movement which mathematics gives us, any more than there are actual shapes which exactly correspond to those which geometry tells us about.[120] Nevertheless, the actual phenomena of nature are ordered, and must be so, in such a way that nothing ever happens in which the law of continuity (which I introduced, and which I first mentioned in M. Bayle's *Nouvelles de la République des lettres*[121]), or any of the other most exact mathematical rules, is ever broken. Far from it: for things could only ever be made intelligible by these rules, which alone are capable — along with those of *harmony* or of perfection, which the true metaphysics provides — of giving us insight into the reasons and intentions of the author of things. In fact the unmanageable multitude of infinite combinations means that when we try to apply metaphysical rules, in the end we get lost and have to stop, just as when we apply mathematical rules to physics. And yet these applications never mislead us, and if there is any mistake after a careful calculation, it is because we can never examine the facts sufficiently closely, so that there is some imperfection in the assumptions. And we are the more capable of carrying this application further, the better we are able to deal with the infinite, as our latest methods have shown. [24] So the utility of mathematical meditations is not in any way diminished by their being ideal, because actual things could never go against their rules; and in fact we can say that this is what the reality of phenomena consists in, and what distinguishes them from dreams. However, mathematicians have no need at all of metaphysical discussions, or to puzzle over the real existence of *points*, *indivisibles*, the *infinitely small*, or *strict infinities*. I noted this in my reply to *Mémoires de Trévoux* for May and June 1700,[122] which M. Bayle cites in the article on Zeno; there I suggested in

---

[120] G adds 'because the actual world did not remain in an indeterminate state of possibility, but arrived at actual divisions and quantities, whose results are the phenomena which occur, and which vary in even their smallest parts'.

[121] In 'Extrait d'une lettre de M. L. sur un principe général . . . ; pour servir de réplique à la réponse du R. P. M.', *Nouvelles de la République des lettres*, July 1687 (B 15; R 99), Leibniz maintains that 'When instances (or what is given) approach each other continuously and eventually disappear into one another, the consequences or outcomes (or what is sought for) must do so also'. He says that this principle depends on a more general one: 'datis ordinatis etiam quaesita sunt ordinata' ('that the order of what is sought for is the same as that of what is given').

[122] For '1700', G correctly (see next note) reads '1701'.

the same year (*Mémoires de Trévoux*, November/December, 2nd part)[123] that it is sufficient for the rigour of their proofs that mathematicians should consider, instead of *infinitely small quantities*, quantities small enough to show that the error is smaller than any value assigned to it by an opponent, and therefore that no value can ever be assigned to it. So that although *genuine* infinitesimals, which are the termination towards which the reduction in assigned values tends, are only like imaginary roots, this will not adversely affect the *infinitesimal* calculus, or the calculus of sums and differences, which I proposed (and which some excellent mathematicians have developed) and in which, since it carries with it its own proof, you can never go wrong except by a failure to understand, or by a lack of application. It has since been acknowledged in the journal of Trévoux (ibid.), in the same place, that what had previously been said in it did not conflict with my explanation. It is true that it is still claimed that it goes against that of M. le Marquis de l'Hôpital; but I do not think that he would want, any more than I do, to burden geometry with metaphysical questions.[124]

[25] I almost laughed at the airs which M. le Chevalier de Méré gave himself in his letter to M. Pascal that M. Bayle reports in the same article.[125] But I see that the Chevalier knew that this great

---

[123] Bayle's somewhat incomplete citation ('*Journal de Trévoux*, May/June 1701, art. 33, p. 423, Dutch ed.', and 'p. 430') is to an anonymous article, 'Nouvelle méthode pour déterminer aisément les rayons de la developpée dans toute sorte de courbe algebraïque. Par Monsieur Jacques B[ernoulli], Acta Eruditorum, mensis Novembris anni 1700. Lipsiae', *Journal de Trévoux* (May/June 1701), art. 33, pp. 422–30. (This appeared only in the Amsterdam edn., not also in the Trévoux edn.) The article objected to the infinitesimal calculus on the grounds that, because it deals with infinities, it can never be as clear and certain as geometry. As he says, Leibniz replied to this in 'Mémoire de M. Leibniz touchant son sentiment sur le calcul différentiel', *Mémoires de Trévoux* (Trévoux edn., Nov./Dec. 1701, pp. 270–2; Amsterdam edn., Jan./Feb. 1702, art. 13, pp. 48–9 (B 64; R 161). (For more details see Aiton, p. 241).

[124] The acknowledgement to which Leibniz refers is in an italicized (editorial?) addition to his article (as in n. 123) in defence of the calculus. In that article he cites the Marquis de l'Hôpital's *Analyse des Infiniment Petits* (Paris, 1696), a book generally regarded as the first textbook on the calculus, as having shown how reliable it is. Writing to Pierre Varignon (GM 4. 91, 1702?), Leibniz says that the point of his article was to show that there is no need to make mathematical analyses depend on metaphysical controversies (see Aiton, p. 241).

[125] In his *Dictionary* article on Zeno the Epicurean, who wrote a work against mathematics, Bayle (as an 'assez bon préjugé' against mathematics), cites the fact that even before Pascal became devout, he had lost his passion for, and become contemptuous of, mathematics. Bayle reports that it was thinking about some things written by the Chevalier de Méré that led Pascal to give up mathematics. De

genius had his weak points, which sometimes made him too susceptible to the influence of extravagant spiritualists, and at times turned him against genuine learning. We have seen the same thing happen, but without recovery, to MM. Stenonis and Swammerdam,[126] for want of joining true metaphysics to their physics and mathematics. M. de Méré takes advantage of it to talk down to M. Pascal. He seems to be rather mocking, like men of the world, who have a ready wit and a mediocre understanding. They try to persuade us that what they don't properly understand is unimportant. . . .[127] It may still be, however, that this Chevalier had some real inspiration, which transported him into 'this invisible and indefinitely extended world' he speaks of,[128] which I believe is that of forms or ideas, to which several scholastics also referred in putting in question *utrum detur vacuum formarum.*[129] For he says that in it 'we can discover the reasons and the principles of things, the deepest truths, the agreements, the exactness, the proportions, the true originals and the perfect ideas of everything we seek'. This intellectual world of which the ancients spoke so much, is in God, and in us also, in a way. But what the letter says against infinite divisibility shows clearly that its writer was still very much a stranger to this higher world, and that the *pleasures* of the visible world, of which he wrote, did not leave him time to acquire citizen's

Méré's airs and his talking down are clear in passages from the letter to Pascal which Bayle quotes. De Méré boasts of his own accomplishments in mathematics, and then goes on to say that there are things more important than it. 'I must tell you that beyond this natural world, which falls within the scope of our senses, there is another, invisible one, and it is in that world that one can attain the highest knowledge. Those who investigate only the corporeal world usually draw the wrong conclusions, and always crude ones ... [I]t is in this invisible and infinitely extended world that we can discover the reasons and the principles of things, the deepest truths, the agreements, the exactness, the proportions, the true originals and the perfect ideas of everything we seek.'

[126] Nicholas Steno (1638–87), Danish anatomist and geologist, abandoned science for religion, taking Catholic holy orders in 1667. Towards the end of his life Swammerdam (see Ch. 2, n. 35) came under the influence of the mystic and religious enthusiast Antoinette Bourignon.

[127] We have omitted a passage concerning de Méré's contribution to the beginnings of probability theory.

[128] See n. 125. We have changed Leibniz's version of de Méré ('dans ce monde invisible, et dans cette étendu infinie') to Bayle's version ('dans ce monde invisible, et d'une étendue infinie').

[129] 'whether there exists a vacuum of forms'. Leibniz refers to the question of a vacuum of forms ('Are there possible kinds of thing which do not actually exist?') at various places: e.g. in a letter to Arnauld, 9 Oct. 1687 (G 2. 125) and in 'Reflections on Vital Principles' (G 6. 548). (See also RB, p. lxxix.)

rights in the other. M. Bayle is right to say, with the ancients, that God is a geometer, and that mathematics is a part of the intellectual world, and more suitable than anything else for gaining entry to it. But for myself I believe that within it there is something more. I have suggested elsewhere that there is a calculus more important than those of arithmetic and geometry, and which depends on the *analysis of ideas*. This would be a universal characteristic, whose construction seems to me to be one of the most important things that could be attempted.

PB7a. LEIBNIZ: Letter to Bayle, 1702?[130]

[1] *I have had the honour of receiving your letter, but the piece that I wrote*[131] *has remained with M. Bernoulli, Professor* of Mathematics *at Groningen, so as to be more available if anyone should wish to see it again.*

[2] *I am delighted that you were not displeased by it, but it would be wrong to take out the parts which do you justice, and which recognize the obligation I feel towards you for having contributed to the development of this subject by your excellent and profound comments.*

[3] *If your difficulty, sir, now concerns principally only the spontaneous progression of thoughts, I shall not give up hope that it might one day disappear,* since everything that is active is in a state of transition, or succession, and I know of nothing in nature which is not so. Otherwise where would change come from? If someone were to say, with some recent philosophers, that only God is active, they must say that God at least is in a spontaneous progression from action to action on the things he created. So such a spontaneous progression is a possibility, and it would then be necessary to prove that it is possible only in God. But why couldn't

---

[130] From the French at G 3. 65 ff. As explained in the introduction, this letter exists in various drafts. The passages italicized are taken over into what, on the basis of much internal evidence, is the later PB7b. For example, according to PB7a ([§ 5]), Leibniz has not yet seen Lamy's book, so it must be dated earlier than 30 Nov. 1702, when he received it (see n. 141); similarly, PB7b ([§ 4]) must on the other hand be later than that date. (See also the references to Toland's movements at PB7a, § 7, and PB7b, § 5.)

[131] i.e. a MS of PB6 which Leibniz had sent to Bayle on 19 Aug. 1702 (see nn. 12, 13).

souls be imitations of God in this? And to tell the truth, if we take away their activity, and therefore the consequences of their activity, or the transition to other actions, I do not see what they have left. But if it *were* said that only God is active, it would be enough for our purposes that the soul or other substance has in it a progression which is spontaneous in all other respects, that is to say that in that instance this spontaneous progression would then come only from God and from itself. And leaving aside that general concurrence of God's, and speaking only of relations between created things, there must be some tendency, or a spontaneous progression, in all substances. It is that force or tendency which I can call by no better name than an 'entelechy', which has been so little regarded. Yet amongst fundamentals there is almost nothing which is more significant or of greater importance, although Aristotle seems not to have sufficiently well understood, or at least explained, what he called by that name. And so since it seems to me that the soul is allowed to have such spontaneity on some occasions, the theory that it also has it on others is all the more plausible. But in the end it is something more than a theory, as is the maxim which I put in what I wrote, that 'the present is always big with the future', or that 'every substance must express in the present all its future states'.

[4] Moving on, I should not be in too much of a hurry to publish what I have written, the point of which was only to provide some clarification for you, sir, and for some other people, so as to receive the same in return. For I write not so much to make an impression as to investigate the truth, which it is often useless, and even harmful, to publish — on account of the uninitiated, who are incapable of appreciating it, and quite capable of taking it the wrong way. . . .

[5] I have not yet been able to see the book by the Benedictine Father Lamy on *The Knowledge of the Self*, and I do not even know if he has treated me well or badly in it — or rather, if he has treated the truth well or badly, that is to say, whether he has merely quibbled, or has shown a genuine desire for the truth. But I always assume the best. It would seem, sir, that you attribute to him the term 'pre-established harmony'. I have no objection, and it is only because of the following circumstance that I tell you that I myself gave it to my theory in a paper[132] that I sent to M. Cousin, the President, for his journal, in which I made use of the account which

that journal had given of the first edition of the Father's book, and of the claim it made that the union of the soul and the body, as he, along with the new Cartesians, understands it, is something supernatural. I imagine that that paper, which as far as I know has not been published, was communicated to Father Lamy, and provided the occasion for what he said about my system in the second edition.

[6] I do not know, sir, whether you know of anyone else who has made any comments on my theory. M. de Volder made some which were different from yours.[133] He asks whether the mere impulsions (*impetuosités*) which there are in matter wouldn't be enough, without primitive entelechies. But in that way we would lose the substantial unities, without which—that is, without simple things— compounds and resultants would be nothing. There would also be modifications, with no substantial subject to be modified; for what is purely passive could never have active modifications, since a modification, far from adding some perfection, can only be a variable restriction or limitation, and as a result cannot exceed the perfection of the subject. Not to mention for the moment a number of other reasons which have led me to fill everything with souls and entelechies, I think that the unfounded fear that people have had of allowing the indestructibility of non-rational souls, and the lack of understanding they have had of the full indestructibility of the animal, and indeed of the machine, and of the fact that death is only part of a progression, has put off those who could already have arrived at this position.

[7] *The learned Englishman who brought me your kind regards* is going back to *Holland*.[134] *He has shown me what he wrote to you about a piece in your Dictionary in the part about Dicaearchus*, who according to Cicero denied that the soul was something substantial, and reduced it to a temperature or modification of matter or of extended mass, rather as did one of the interlocutors in Plato's *Phaedo*, who said that the soul was a harmony.[135] It seems to me that Epicurus, Hobbes, and Spinoza are of the same opinion. Epicurus allows only the interplay of small bodies. Hobbes, reduces everything to body, and explains feeling by reaction, like that of an

[133] See, for examples, de Volder to Leibniz, 12 Nov. 1699 (G 2. 198–9), 25 July 1702 (G 2. 243).
[134] John Toland; see Leibniz to Bayle, 19 Aug. 1702 (G 2. 63).
[135] Simmias, at *Phaedo*, 85b–86d.

inflated balloon.[136] And Spinoza claims that the soul is the idea of the body, so that it becomes like what the shape or the mathematical body is to the physical body.[137] It is in some such way that the Cartesians think of the souls of animals. But they rightly do not allow them any perception: they see them purely as machines. Our learned Englishman seems also to claim that matter can become able to think, as it can become round, and thus that a certain organization, or a certain shape, can produce thought, and that when that organization is destroyed, thought will cease. But I took the liberty of telling him that thought seems to be of a completely different kind. Even if we had eyes as penetrating as you like, so as to see the smallest parts of the structure of bodies, I do not see that we would thereby be any further forward. We would find the origin of perception there as little as we find it now in a watch, where the constituent parts of the machine are all visible, or in a mill, where one can even walk around among the wheels. For the difference between a mill and a more refined machine is only a matter of greater and less. We can understand that a machine could produce the most wonderful things in the world, but never that it might perceive them. Among visible things there is nothing which gets nearer to thought than does an image in a mirror (and brain traces could be no more accurate than that is), but the accuracy of that image doesn't produce any perception in the thing it is in. We do not even come close to it, whatever mechanical theory we make up; we remain infinitely far away from it, as must happen with things which are absolutely heterogeneous, just as a surface, when folded up on itself as often as you like, can never become a body. We can also see that since thought is an action of one thing on itself, it has no place among shapes and motions, which could never provide the basis of a truly internal action. Moreover, there must be simple beings, otherwise there would be no compound beings, or beings by aggregation, which are phenomena rather than substances, and exist (to use the language of Democritus) by *nomos* [convention] rather than *physis* [nature], that is, notionally, or conceptually, rather than physically. And if there was no change in simple things, there would be none in compound things either, for all their reality

---

[136] See Hobbes, *Elements of Philosophy*, 4. 25. 2; *Leviathan*, 1. 1; *Human Nature*, 2. The image of the balloon seems to be Leibniz's own.

[137] *Ethics*, pt. 2, prop. 13. The explanation of this claim is Leibniz's rather than Spinoza's.

consists only in that of their simple things. Now, internal changes in simple things are of the same kind as that which we understand to be in thought, and we can say in general that perception is *the expression of a multitude in a unity.* You have no need, sir, of this clarification of the immateriality of thought, of which you have talked admirably in many places. However, putting these considerations together with my specific theory, it seems to me that the one helps to throw some light on the other. . . .

PB7b. LEIBNIZ: Letter to Bayle, 1702?[138]

[1] *I have had the honour of receiving your letter, but the piece that I wrote has remained with M. Bernoulli, Professor at Groningen, so as to be more available if anyone should wish to see it again.* [2] *I am delighted that you were not displeased by it, but it would be wrong to take out from it the parts which do you justice, and which recognize the obligation I feel towards you for having contributed to the development of this subject by your excellent and profound comments.* [3] *If your difficulty now concerns principally only the spontaneous progression of thoughts, I shall not give up hope that it might one day disappear*; and indeed I had written a letter to help bring that about,[139] but I have changed my mind, and have left out all those arguments, because you may have no need of them, sir, and there is perhaps something else, other than what you have mentioned, which prevents you from entering fully into my opinion. It seems you also have a fear of falling into repetition,[140] though if we proceed in an orderly way through argument, exception, reply, and counter-reply, we can avoid it.

[4] I have finally received the extract from *The Knowledge of the Self*[141] by the Benedictine Father Lamy covering what concerns my system, but I have found it hard to understand what it might be that can have caused him difficulty. And whereas you, sir, were careful not to raise as objections points which could be brought against all

[138] From the French at G 3. 69–72. The passages italicized are taken over from the earlier PB7a (see n. 130).

[139] i.e. PB7a.

[140] Cf. Bayle to Leibniz, 3 Oct. 1702 (n. 14).

[141] Leibniz's first written remarks on this (L3) record that he received it 30 Nov. 1702. (See Ch. 6, n.37.)

systems, nearly everything he says against me counts no less against all the others. It is as if he fancies that my system ought to make things better than they could, or should, be. For he accuses me of taking away freedom from the soul, and of blaming God for things that go wrong. But the soul's voluntary actions spring from its nature, in conformity with the freedom which is natural to it, and its involuntary actions, feelings, or passions, while they do not come from the body, come from the fact that its nature is expressive of the body. And since God is the author not only of the nature of the soul, but also of that of the body, it doesn't matter whether disorders and wildness, whether voluntary or involuntary, come from the nature of the soul alone, or from the nature of the soul together with the impressions or influences from the body, or from the nature of the soul together with impressions from God—and indeed we might add that this last alternative, which is that of occasional causes, is the most problematic. And since according to this author God can produce pains and other more advantageous feelings in the soul, why should it not be permitted for God, as I claim, to give to the soul a nature which produces these things successively in the course of time?

[5] *The learned Englishman who brought me your kind regards* will be *back* in *Holland. He has shown me what he wrote to you about a piece in your Dictionary in the part about Dicaearchus,* who removes all souls from nature. He wanted to reply to the objection you make to Dicaearchus. But I made no pretence of not being of your opinion, that matter cannot become able to think, as it can become round. I have shown, sir, as you know, that when it is appropriately organized, matter can become suitable for allowing clear thoughts, but not for giving rise to thoughts where there were none—just as an assayer cannot create gold, but can bring it out (*il le développe*) it. It is true that if the disarranging of matter were capable of ending thought, its arrangement would also be capable of creating it. But that must be understood as applying only to clear thoughts which catch our attention well enough for us to remember them. . . .

[6] Before finishing, I will say something with regard to your letter, where you say, sir, that the plausibility of my theory cannot be assessed unless we understand clearly the substantial basis of the soul, and how it can modify itself. I do not know if it is possible to explain the constitution of the soul any better than by saying

(1) that it is a simple substance, or what I call a true unity; (2) that this unity nevertheless expresses a multitude, that is, bodies, and that it does so as well as is possible according to its point of view, or its relations; (3) and that therefore it expresses phenomena according to the metaphysico-mathematical laws of nature, that is, according to the order most befitting to intelligence or reason. From which it follows finally (4) that the soul is an imitation of God as far as is possible for a created thing, for like him it is simple and yet also infinite, in that it contains everything implicitly through confused perceptions — though with respect to clear perceptions it is limited, whereas everything is clear to the sovereign substance, from which everything emanates, which is the cause of existence and of order, and is in a word the ultimate reason for things. God contains the universe eminently, and the soul or unity contains it actually, being a central mirror, though active and vital, so to speak. Indeed, we can say that each soul is a world apart, but that all these worlds agree, and represent a different relation to the same phenomena. And this is the most perfect way of multiplying beings as far as possible, and in the best way possible.

6

Leibniz and François Lamy

INTRODUCTION

François Lamy (1636–1711) was a French Benedictine physicist, philosopher, and theologian. Among his works is *Le Nouvel Athéisme renversé, ou Réfutation du système de Spinoza* ... (Paris, 1696). Most important here, however, is his rare and little known *De la Connoissance de soi-même* in which he discusses Leibniz's 'New System'. The different editions of this very rare work are usually confused, to the detriment of an adequate understanding of the relation between his texts and Leibniz's.[1]

The first edition of Lamy's book was published in Paris between 1694 and 1698 in five volumes (*tômes*) (Paris: André Pralard, 1694, two in 1697, two in 1698).[2] The final two volumes were noted by the *Journal des savants* on 25 August of the year of their publication, 1698. Commenting that they have a 'close connection' with its earlier parts, the anonymous reviewer says he will give an analysis of the whole work. He proceeds to do this, through successive issues of the journal.[3] Lamy's book consists basically of three treatises (*traités*), and on 8 September the reviewer had reached part 2 of the second, 'Where the question of the union of the mind with the body is examined'.[4] He explains (in this and the following issue) that Lamy denies that the mind and the body have any power to act on each other, and that he argues for occasionalism. Lamy, the reviewer says, holds that these two substances can only be united

---

[1] For further details see our 'Leibniz, Lamy, and "the way of pre-established harmony"', *Studia Leibnitiana*, 36/1 (1994), pp. 76–90.

[2] Their title-pages give no indication of authorship; but the first volume contains a letter of dedication signed by 'F. F. L.' (= Frère François Lamy) and a concluding 'Approbation des Docteurs de Sorbonne' which attributes the work to 'le Révérend Père Dom F. L.'.

[3] 25 Aug. 1698 (no. 33, pp. 393–6); 1 Sept. (no. 34, pp. 397–406); 8 Sept. (no. 35, pp. 416–20); 15 Sept. (no. 36, pp. 421–7); 17 Nov. (no. 37, pp. 434–44); 24 Nov. (no. 38, pp. 445–53); 1 Dec. 1698 (no. 39, pp. 457–66).

[4] Vol. 1 (1694), pp. 423–532.

by a 'supernatural relation between their diverse manners of being, which can only come from the purely arbitrary institution of the author of nature'.[5]

Leibniz read at least the 8 and 15 September parts of this review, for they form the basis of, and are quoted in, a manuscript which Gerhardt entitles 'Supplement to the Explanation of the New System Regarding the Soul and the Body, Sent to Paris on the Occasion of a Book Entitled *The Knowledge of the Self*' (L1 below). Though the Lamy passages in question had been in print since 1694, Leibniz says that Lamy would have avoided all problems had he considered 'a new system published not long ago' (i.e. Leibniz's own 'New System' of 1695 (NS1)).

A second, now six-volume edition ('Seconde Édition, retouchée et augmentée considérablement') of Lamy's book was published in 1699 (Paris: André Pralard).[6] In this second edition Lamy is able to, and *does*, consider Leibniz's 'New System' of 1695, making reference also to his 'Third Explanation'[7] and his 'Explanation of Bayle's Difficulties' (PB3). The discussion occurs in the 'Fifth Reflections' ('on the way in which God brings about the union between mind and body'), which fall in the second part of the second treatise.[8] He introduces the discussion by noting, at the end of his 'Fourth Reflections', the suggestion of 'a famous philosopher ... M. Leibniz', that an occasionalist theory of the sort which he has been favouring up till then demeans, rather than honours, God. This, says Lamy, 'is what I must consider in some reflections'. A later 'Analysis or abridgement' of the second treatise, summarizes the Fifth Reflections.[9] All of these extracts from the *The Knowledge of the Self* are given below at L2.

Leibniz came to know of Lamy's discussion of his 'New System' through Pierre Bayle. Bayle's *Dictionary* note L of 1702 directs its readers to 'treatise 2 of *The Knowledge of the Self*, p. 226, 1699 edition'.[10] But, having thus learnt of Lamy's remarks, it was some

---

[5] No. 35, pp. 417–18.

[6] The dedicatory letter and 'Approbation' are carried over from the 1st edn., with the approbation now appearing at the end of the second volume. The changed title-page now attributes the work to 'un Religeux Bénédictin de la Congrégation de Saint Maur'. This 2nd edn. was reprinted in 1701 (Paris: Nicolas le Clerc), with a title-page explicitly attributing it to 'le R. P. Dom François Lamy, Bénédictin de la Congrégation de S. Maur'.

[7] See Ch. 4, app. B.   [8] Vol. 2, pp. 225–74.

[9] Vol. 2, pp. 387–92. This summary is written in the third person, and refers to 'the author' and 'our philosopher'.   [10] PB4, note a.

time before Leibniz read them. His reply to note L, which on
29 May 1702 he sent on its way to Bayle, reports: 'I am sorry that I
have not yet been able to see the objections of Dom François Lamy
in (so M. Bayle tells me) the second treatise of his *The Knowledge
of the Self* (1699 edition), otherwise I would have already sent my
replies'.[11] By the end of the year, however, he had seen what Lamy
had to say, for a manuscript dated 30 November 1702 discusses it
(L3 below). He also wrote a formal reply (L4 below) which he sent
to the *Journal des savants* in 1704, but which was not published till
1709.[12]

  Though Leibniz intended that what he wrote about Lamy on the
basis of the review of the first edition of *The Knowledge of the Self*
(L1 below) should be published in *Journal des savants*, it never was.
An undispatched, undated letter to Bayle refers to 'a paper that I
sent to M. Cousin, the President, for his journal, in which I made
use of the account which that journal had given of the first edition
of the Father's book, and of the claim it made that the union of the
soul and the body, as he, along with the new Cartesians,
understands it, is something supernatural. . . . [A]s far as I know
[that paper] has not been published.'[13] Leibniz goes on to conjecture

[11] PB6, § 19.
[12] He remarked to Coste in 1706 that Lamy's objections to the system of pre-
established harmony are easily dealt with: 'I tell you in passing, sir, that in this
same book [*The Knowledge of the Self*] the Reverend Father Lamy has also
written against my system. He says that its simplicity is dazzling, but that after
examining it he found it a false brilliance. Nevertheless it seemed to me very easy
to answer his objections. . . . The good Father seemed upset about the fact that
what in the system of occasional causes is attributed to nothing but the immediate
operation of God alone in my system is made to arise from within our own being
(though with the concourse of God). But he does not take account of the fact that
it is appropriate to the sovereign wisdom to give to his works which are part of the
natural order a nature in which everything is connected by reason, in such a way
that someone sufficiently clear-sighted could read the future and the past in the
present, and indeed the state of the whole universe in that of each of its parts. This,
however, could not be the case unless there were everywhere actual subdivisions to
infinity, so that everything can feel the effects of everything else. And by this
means each soul or substantial unity, in primarily representing its body, is
representative of the whole universe according to its capacities. So it is very far
from being the case that the perceptions of the soul and the motions of the body
have only an arbitrary relation, as these men suppose' (Leibniz to Coste, Hanover,
4 July 1706 (G 3. 383)).
[13] PB7a, § 5. In this draft letter Leibniz says: 'I have not yet been able to see the
book by the Benedictine Father Lamy on *The Knowledge of the Self*, and I do not
even know if he has treated me well or badly in it—or rather, if he has treated the
truth well or badly, that is to say, whether he has merely quibbled, or has shown a
genuine desire for the truth. But I always assume the best' (PB7a, § 5). In a later

that the paper may nevertheless have been communicated to Lamy, and thus may have 'provided the occasion for what he said about my system in the second edition'.

On the other hand, Leibniz's 'Reply to the Objections [of Lamy]' (L4), a piece written on the basis of Lamy's second edition, was published—though not until 1709, rather later than he intended. In September 1704 Fontenelle, the Secretary of the Paris Academy of Sciences, wrote to him that Bignon had not thought it appropriate for the *Journal des savants*, which printed 'nothing polemical';[14] and in December of the same year Varignon wrote that the editors of the journal did not want to publish 'disputes'.[15]

Leibniz was rather cross with Fontenelle, for in an undated reply he said that had he been told of this decision earlier, he might already have found some other way of publicly defending himself against Lamy's criticisms. He went on to ask that Fontenelle pass the piece on to Pinsson.[16] At the end of 1704, however, Varignon told him that Fontenelle was 'trying to find out to whom he has given it'.[17] And two years later Leibniz reports that the article 'was sent to the people who are currently in charge of the *Journal des savants*, but they have lost it'.[18] It appears that, having already rejected it for the *Journal des savants*, it was the Abbé Bignon who brought about its eventual publication, in 1709, in one of the *Journal*'s supplements.[19] Lamy, who died two years

version of the same letter he reports: 'I have finally received the extract from *The Knowledge of the Self* by the Benedictine Father Lamy covering what concerns my system, but I have found it hard to understand what it might be that can have caused him difficulty. And whereas you, sir, were careful not to raise as objections points which could be brought against all systems, nearly everything he says against me counts no less against all the others. It is as if he fancies that my system ought to make things better than they could, or should, be' (PB7b, § 4).

On 5 Aug. 1703 Leibniz wrote to Queen Sophie Charlotte: 'Meanwhile I have had some new philosophical discussions. A French Benedictine, who is author of a book *The Knowledge of the Self*, and who follows the principles of Father Malebranche, has raised some objections against me in his book, of which I have been sent an extract from Paris. I have done a reply to defend my system of unities and of the union of the soul and the body, the simplicity of which he says he was struck by. He wanted to drag me by the hair into the argument about freedom, which is a good way to blacken people's names. But I know too much about this matter to fall into his trap' (Klopp, 10. 212).

14 Fontenelle to Leibniz, Paris, 9 Sept. 1704 (FC1 232).
15 Varignon to Leibniz, Paris, 6 Dec. 1704 (GM 4. 114).
16 Leibniz to Fontenelle (FC1 233); for Pinsson see LB, p. 221.
17 Varignon to Leibniz, Paris, 6 Dec. 1704 (GM 4. 114).
18 Leibniz to Coste, Hanover, 4 July 1706 (G 3. 383).
19 Leibniz to Bignon, 4 May 1710; Bignon to Leibniz, Paris, 29 May 1710 (Feder, pp. 246, 249).

later, made no reply—a fact about which Leibniz was uncertain as late as 1714.[20]

[20] Leibniz to Remond, Vienna, 26 Aug. 1714 (G 3. 625). What prompted Leibniz in his undispatched letter of Dec. 1702 (PB7a, § 5) to Bayle to refer to his, Leibniz's, unpublished comments on the 1st edn. of Lamy's book was Bayle's suggestion in his then recent note L that the phrase 'pre-established harmony (*harmonie préétablie*)' was due to Lamy (PB4, § 1). Leibniz said that it was in those comments of his that the phrase had first been used. He imagined, he goes on to say, that these comments had been communicated to Lamy, who, picking up the phrase from them, then used it in the 2nd edn. of his book (PB7a, § 5).
Except for the fact that the phrase *is* in fact his and not Lamy's, Leibniz is quite wrong about this, however. The paper Leibniz is referring to is his 'Supplement to the Explanation of the New System' (L1), and, whether Lamy did or did not get to read it, he could not have got the phrase 'pre-established harmony' from it—for it does not occur there. Moreover, even if Leibniz had used the phrase there, and even if Lamy had read it there, that would not have been either Leibniz's first use of it or Lamy's first encounter with it.
Leibniz tells a different, but probably still only half-correct, story in some undated manuscript comments which he made (PB5, comment A) on Bayle's *Dictionary* note L. Here he remarks on Bayle's attribution of the phrase to Lamy that 'I had already used this name for it [my system] in my reply to M. l'Abbé Foucher in the *Journal des savants* of 9 April of the year 1696 [i.e. F3], and Revd Father Lamy found it appropriate'.
Leibniz does indeed use the phrase then (i.e. at F3, § 6), and he uses it as though consciously for the first time: 'what follows ... in other substances is only in virtue of a "pre-established harmony" (if I may use the expression)'. But this, his first published use, was not his first use. One earlier use is in a letter of 30 Sept. 1695 to l'Hôpital (GM 2. 298). Presumably the *composition* of the 'First Explanation' dates from around this time. Two others are in letters to Henri Basnage de Beauval. One of these two letters dates, according to Gerhardt, from late 1695 (G 3. 122), and the other is dated 3 Jan. 1696 (B1). This latter says more about the 'new system', and Leibniz left it to Basnage to decide whether to publish it in his *Histoire des ouvrages des savants*. In the event Basnage published an edited version (see Ch. 4, n. 2), but, while Leibniz's original (B1) speaks of 'the way of pre-established harmony, set up by a contrivance of Divine foresight', the published version, edited by Basnage with no eye for a catch-phrase, speaks only of 'the way of harmony' (see Ch. 4, n. 20).
Leibniz suggests (in his manuscript comments on Bayle's *Dictionary* note L; PB5, comment A) that Lamy came across the phrase in what is its first published use, in the 'First Explanation' of Apr. 1696. That this is what happened is certainly a possibility; on the other hand, Lamy does not refer to this article in his discussion of Leibniz in the 2nd edn., so he may not have read it. Out of the three pieces he does refer to, two (the original 'New System' of 1695 (NS1) and the 1698 *Histoire des ouvrages des savants* 'Letter to the Editor Containing an Explanation' (PB3) do not speak of 'pre-established harmony'. The third (the Nov. 1696) piece (see Ch. 4, n. 31), however, the so-called 'Third Explanation', does use the phrase. More particularly, it refers, as does Lamy, to 'the *way of pre-established harmony*', and also, as does Lamy, to the two contrasting ways as 'the way of assistance' and 'the way of influence'. It seems likely that it was on this occurrence of the phrase, in the 'Third Explanation' of Nov. 1696, that Lamy 'found it appropriate'.

L1. LEIBNIZ: 'Supplement to the Explanation of the New System Regarding the Soul and the Body, sent to Paris on the Occasion of a Book Entitled *The Knowledge of the Self*' (1698?)[21]

[1] In the *Journal des savants* for 8 and 15 September (numbers 35 and 36) 1698, there is an abstract of a book entitled *The Knowledge of the Self*, published in Pans by Pralard, where the union of soul and body is much discussed. Several very good things are said on the subject: the matter is examined with care, and in more than usual detail. In explanation of the basis of this union it is said that the two substances can only be united 'by a relation, between their diverse manners of being, which is supernatural (so to speak), and can only come from a purely arbitrary institution on the part of the creator of nature'.[22] But if the clever author of this book had considered *a new system published not long ago*, he would have been saved from the difficulties he encounters here. The relation is anything but *supernatural*, for it is a natural consequence of what God has created; and it is not at all *arbitrary*, except in so far as it can be said that the creation of this universe depends on the free choice of the creator. The School opinion, that the soul and matter have something incomplete about them, is not so absurd as people think. For matter without souls and forms or entelechies is purely passive, and souls without matter would be purely active. A complete corporeal substance, which is really one—what the School calls *unum per se* (as opposed to a being by aggregation)—must result from an active principle of unity, and also from a mass of the kind which makes up a multitude, and which would be solely passive if it contained only primary matter. By contrast, secondary matter, or the mass which makes up our body, contains parts throughout, all of which are themselves complete substances because they are other animals, or organic substances, which are individually animated or active. But the collection of these corporeal organized substances which makes up our body is united with our soul only by the relation which arises between the sequences of phenomena which develop from the nature of each separate

---

[21] 'Addition à l'explication du système nouveau touchant l'union de l'âme et du corps, envoyée à Paris à l'occasion d'un livre intitulé Connoissance de soy même' (G 4. 572–77)

[22] Leibniz is quoting in this paragraph from *Journal des savants*, pp. 417–18.

substance. [2] And all of that shows how one can say on the one hand that the soul and the body are independent of each other, and on the other hand that the one is incomplete without the other, since the one is never naturally without the other. Thus it does not seem that it can be generally said, with the author of the treatise on *The Knowledge of the Self*, 'that the (organic) body could perform most of its functions before the soul was united to it, and that the soul will never perform its functions better than when separated from the body'. On the contrary, so far as plants, animals, and all kinds of living thing in general are concerned there is reason to believe that just as soon as the body is truly organic in itself the soul is united to it, and that death can naturally strip away from the soul only some of the grosser parts of its organic body. I am speaking here only about the souls and substantial entelechies that God leaves to the course of nature, such as those of beasts. I am not here saying anything about the origin and separation of our souls, or about how it is with minds, or about the *kingdom of grace* as opposed to that of *nature*.

[3] Convinced of the *supernatural* relation between the soul and the body, the author says that 'if the soul were to reflect that the pleasant feelings which it receives and which are occasioned by its body can only come to it immediately from God, and that he has no need of the body to give it them, it would have no inclination but to unite itself with God'.[23] It is agreed that originally these sensations can come only from God, but not immediately, except in the general way in which all realities continuously emanate from God. For present feelings are a consequence of preceding feelings, and all together follow from *the nature of the soul itself*, which essentially is only the *regular tendency* from which there must spontaneously arise a *series* of phenomena such as to represent the functions of its body, exactly as if this body could give them to it by the influx of species, as the School used to imagine. But it is not clear that to incline us to love God we need to believe that at every moment he gives us agreeable feelings in some *immediate supernatural* or miraculous way. On the contrary, this view would lower the opinion which we should have of the grandeur and wisdom of God, and of the perfection of his works. It is true that strictly speaking 'God has no need of the body to give the soul the feelings that it has', but he does have need of it in order to operate through the

[23] Ibid. p. 419, for the quotes in this para.

order of nature that he has established, for he has given to the soul, once for all from the beginning, this force or tendency which makes it express its body.

[4] Our author maintains 'that the mind is united to the body passively but not actively',[24] because, according to him, there is no part of the body which does not act on the mind, whereas there are parts of the body on which the mind does not act. But it seems rather that such action must always be reciprocal, and that there is never action between created things without reaction. He also maintains 'that the body is united to the mind as a whole actively but not passively', because, the mind being indivisible, the body can only affect it throughout; whereas, according to him, the mind has pure intellectual thoughts which do not affect the body. And yet it seems that the body reacts to our abstract thoughts also, and experience shows that meditation is capable of harming it; for in addition to the fact that attention tenses the fibres of the brain, even the most abstract thoughts always employ *signs* which affect the imagination. It also seems that it is *more correct* to say that minds are where they immediately operate, than to say, as here, 'that they are nowhere'. I have explained elsewhere what I mean when I say that minds act on bodies.

[5] *Confused thoughts* are usually understood as being of an entirely different kind from *distinct* thoughts, and our author thinks that the mind is more united to the body by confused thoughts than by distinct ones. That is not unreasonable, for confused thoughts are a mark of our imperfection, passions, and dependence on the assemblage of exterior things or on matter, whereas the perfection, force, control, liberty, and action of the soul consist principally in our distinct thoughts. However, that does not mean it is not true that confused thoughts are in the end nothing else but a multitude of thoughts which are in themselves like distinct ones, but which are so small that each by itself does not capture our attention and is not distinguished from the rest. In fact we can say that there is a truly infinite number of them, all at the same time, contained in our feelings. This is what the big difference between confused and distinct thoughts really consists in—a difference exactly the same as that between natural machines and artificial ones, as was explained when the new system was published in the *Journal des savants*. [6] So it can be said that confused thoughts are 'essentially different

---

[24] *Journal des savants*, pp. 419, 420, for the quotes in this para.

from each other'[25] only in the same way as it can be said that bodies or motions are different from each other. In fact, our author seems to be of another opinion, believing that 'the feeling of pain differs essentially from that of heat, although the difference between the motions of fire which cause pain and those which cause heat is only one of degree'. However, we can say that the pleasant feeling of moderate heat and the painful feeling of excessive heat are equally representative of the motions of matter, and differ only as they do, leaving aside the reflections of the soul. So we should certainly not understand confused sensations as something basic and inexplicable, or otherwise we would be putting them on virtually the same footing as the old 'qualities' of some scholastic philosophers. If we insist on maintaining that there is an essential difference, we will only be substituting these sensations for those qualities, and so merely shifting the difficulty. And although it is true that it is beyond our powers to explain them completely, because the number of variations involved is much too great, that doesn't prevent us from understanding them more and more by means of experiments which reveal their basis in distinct thoughts. [7] Light and colours provide examples of this. These confused feelings are not at all 'arbitrary', either, and I don't agree with the opinion accepted by many today, and followed by our author, that there is no resemblance or relation between our sensations and corporeal traces. It seems rather that our feelings represent and express them perfectly. Perhaps someone will say that the feeling of heat has no resemblance to motion: yes, without doubt it does not resemble a sensible motion, like that of a carriage wheel; but it does resemble the assemblage of small motions in the fire and in the organs, which are its cause; or, rather, it is only their representation. It is like the way in which whiteness bears no resemblance to a convex curved mirror, even though it is nothing but an assemblage of a number of small convex mirrors, such as on close inspection froth is seen to be. If we could always discover the cause of our sensations with the same facility, we would find that it is always something similar. So all the jibes and ranting against the schools and against the ordinary philosophy, according to which our sensations bear a resemblance to the traces of objects, are useless, and arise only from a too superficial consideration. We can also see from this that God 'does not present ideas of any kind he pleases to the soul on the occasion of traces in the brain',

---

[25] Ibid. pp. 422, 424, 426, for the quotes in this para.

as the author says, but only the ones which resemblance requires. [8] And there is room to be astonished that excellent philosophers today can suppose that God acts in a way which is so arbitrary and so undetermined (that is to say, so destitute of reason) in establishing the laws of nature, whether for thoughts or for motions. This would be an insufficient use of his wisdom, which is always directed towards choosing the most suitable. So 'if God had attached the sensation of taste to the trace which results in the brain on the occasion of the vibrations in the ear' (as our author thinks that he was free to do), it would be as though a painter were to represent the cupola of St Peter by the shape of a pyramid. And then it could really be said that our senses deceived us. But in the objection that our author builds on another foundation, to the effect that someone could say that God leads us astray through our senses by making us attribute to bodies sensible qualities which are only modes (*manières*) of our minds, he supposes what is not so. For these sensible qualities are modes (*manières*) or modifications of bodies and not of our mind, while our sensations are in truth ways of being of the soul, but ones which represent those of bodies. It is true that our feelings bear no resemblance to mere modifications of extension or of space, and our author has made this very clear; but I have also sufficiently well shown that there is something more in bodies than extension. As regards 'the combats' that are supposed to take place 'between the body and the soul', they are nothing other than the different inclinations which arise from distinct thoughts and from confused thoughts, that is to say, from reason and from instincts and passions (*instinct* being, so to say, a long-lasting innate passion, and *passion* being a transitory and chance instinct; to which one can add *habit*, which falls between these two sorts of inclination, as being more lasting than a passion, but not innate like an instinct).

[9] Before finishing, I shall add with regard to the author's belief that we have only the idea of God and not those of created things, that I have shown elsewhere that it is useless to discuss the matter unless one has a criterion of a true idea. Here is the one I have proposed elsewhere:[26] *Ideas are confused in us, but we see them distinctly* when we can demonstrate a priori the possibility of the object. Anyone who can do that has the right to claim an understanding of ideas; otherwise he boasts vainly of that great advantage. That is how we put an end to controversies on the subject by means of a practical proof.

[26] The reference seems to be to 'Meditationes de cognitione, veritate et ideis per G. G. L.', *Acta eruditorum*, Nov. 1684 (R 91) (see Loemker, p. 293).

L2. LAMY: Extracts from *The Knowledge of the Self* (2nd edn. 1699)[27]

L2.1. LAMY: Extract from 'Fourth Reflections: On the Same Subject [as the Third Reflections "in which we ask what is the Effective Cause, or who is the Author, of the Union of the Mind and the Body"]' (volume 2, treatise 2, part 2 (p. 224))

But, my God, in thus trying to honour the sovereign being, am I not dishonouring him? Isn't it demeaning him to tie him down like this to continually having to notify the mind as to what is happening in its body and activate the springs of the body whenever the mind wants? Isn't this asking continual miracles of God? And wouldn't it be much more worthy of his wisdom (as a famous philosopher claims[a]) to have given to the mind and the body all in one go the power or the force each to adjust itself in accordance with the dispositions of the other? This is what I must now consider in some new reflections.

[LAMY'S NOTE]

a. Monsieur Leibniz.

L2.2. LAMY: 'Fifth Reflections: On the Way in which God Brings about the Union between Mind and Body' (volume 2, treatise 2, part 2 (pp. 225–43)).

[1] I freely admit that I find something very attractive about the thought which struck me at the end of my last reflections; for one can, it seems to me, think of only three ways in which the union between mind and body might be brought about.[a] (1) By means of a reciprocal communication of species and qualities between the two substances —this would be called *the way of influence*. (2) By means of a perpetual supervisor who from moment to moment is responsible for producing in each of these substances impressions corresponding to those taking place in the other—what could be termed [225/6] *the way of assistance*. (3) By means of a divinely pre-established natural agreement; that is to say, one which results precisely from the

---

[27] François Lamy, *De la Connoissance de soi-même*, 2nd edn. (Paris: André Pralard, 1699). The square bracketed pairs of numbers record the pagination of the original.

constitution of the natures that God gave these substances at the outset, rather like that between two very accurate clocks—what could be called *the way of pre-established harmony.*

[2] In my last reflections the first of these three ways, which is that advocated by common philosophy, seemed to me absolutely untenable. I so clearly saw that the soul cannot be the true cause of movements in the body, nor the body really act on the mind and give it thoughts, that it seemed to me impossible to accept any real influence between them.

[3] The second, which is that of occasional causes, really seemed to me very sound and [226/7] acceptable, except that it in a way devalues divinity; it makes it a slave to its creation, and has God producing perfectly natural effects purely by miracles. Isn't the third way infinitely more simple and sensible? And doesn't it testify to an incomparably greater intelligence and acuteness in the sovereign workman?

[4] Indeed, can one imagine anything simpler and more straightforward than initially to have given the two substances (mind and body) a 'nature', or 'internal force', by which they change themselves, and 'produce in an orderly way all their changes in such a way that everything in them arises from their own nature with a perfect spontaneity, so that merely by following out its own laws, given to it when it was brought into being, each substance is nevertheless in harmony with the other—just as if there were [227/8] a mutual influence between them, or as if, in addition to his general concurrence, God were continually operating upon them?'[28]

[5] In this way the human body, for example, following only the laws of a physical machine, is brought to act and move its hand or foot, say, not because the soul wills it, but at precisely the same time as the soul, in virtue of its own laws and the constitution of its nature, is determined to wish it, or to produce that act of will. And the soul would in fact produce that act of will even if there were only it and God in the world. And on the other hand the various thoughts and perceptions of the soul occur in sequence because of the soul's own laws: 'as in a spiritual automaton',[29] a feeling of pain comes to it at just the right time, at the moment when the body, in virtue of the mechanical laws [228/9] of matter, is stabbed with a sword.

---

[28] The 'quotation' is a composite of passages in NS1, §§ 14, 15, and 'Third Explanation of the New System' (Ch. 4, n. 31; cf. B1).

[29] Quoted from NS1, §15.

[6] It's clear from this that this way of uniting these two substances and of correlating their modalities, which involves a detailed prevision of all their various changes, and the establishment of laws which will produce them in an order such as to make each modality of the one coincide with the appropriate modality of the other; it's clear, I say, that this way involves an infinite intelligence and wisdom. What more does it need in order to make it acceptable, and to make it preferable to the two others, than to be more suitable to honour the wisdom and power of the infinitely perfect being?

[7] But am I perhaps being partial? And how dangerous it is to look at a system from only one side! In fact, [229/30] looking at this one from another angle, a moment's thought makes me begin to see difficulties and even impossibilities which certainly deserve examination and a closer look.

[8] First: Either these two substances were destined, pre-established, and made for each other from the beginning: that is, God gave them the nature that was necessary in order to establish a perfect correspondence between them, and in virtue of which the soul, for example, has a sensation of pain just when the body is stabbed by a sword as a consequence of the mechanical laws of matter; or alternatively, without having been destined for each other, they have each received separately, and as if they were alone with God, such a nature that, coming to exist at the same time, [230/1] they find their respective modalities in exact correspondence.

[9] On the first of these alternatives this system is little different in this respect from that of occasional causes. For according to this, God, on the occasion of the sequence of movements that he foresaw would occur in due course as a consequence of the laws of the nature which he had given to the body, gave to the soul another nature, from the laws of which there would originate as many different thoughts as would correspond to the different movements of the body. The only difference between this system and that of occasional causes of the Cartesians, therefore, is that in the latter it is God who, on the occasion of modalities of one of these two substances, immediately produces impressions in the other; whereas in the new system he produces these impressions only [231/2] mediately, in that he has given these substances powers and forces

appropriate for producing them for themselves, each within its own bosom.

[10] On the second of these alternatives, according to which these substances have not been made for each other, the sequence of thoughts and perceptions that God gave to minds is not at all wise, but purely capricious. After all, what wisdom, and indeed what justice, is there for example in making a soul pass suddenly from joy to pain merely by the laws of the constitution of its nature, without its having deserved that punishment through some wrong-doing? Even if Adam, for example, had never sinned, the sufferings of his soul since his wrongdoing, being in this system only a natural consequence of the constitution of his soul, would still have tormented him as much. [232/3] What a lot there would be to say about that with regard to religion!

[11] Second: Whichever of these alternatives we choose, the author of this system still holds that it is the substances which modify themselves by their own forces and which, by I don't know what *spontaneity*, produce all the changes and all the thoughts which occur in them. It is therefore not very clear whether, in an intelligent substance, that production is free or necessary. If it is free, and the soul, for example, freely gives itself thoughts, then why does it give itself such disagreeable and painful ones? What pleasure does it find in tormenting itself? On the other hand, if all these changes come over it necessarily, by virtue of the constitution of its nature, and without its being able [233/4] to prevent them, however disagreeable they may be, then where is God's wisdom in thus allowing the soul, without cause and without reason, to undergo an infinite but bizarre and capricious variety of thoughts, feelings, and perceptions?

[12] Third: Moreover, this soul is therefore not at all free. And in fact it seems as if minds cannot be free in this system, whatever its author says. Admittedly, he claims that 'it has the advantage that instead of saying that we are free only in appearance and in a way which is sufficient for practical purposes, as several clever people have held, we must rather say that we are determined only in appearance, and that, in strict metaphysical language, we are perfectly independent of the influence of all other created things'.[b][30] But in the end, it doesn't seem that he recognizes any genuine

___

[30] The quote is from NS1, § 16, where for 'advantage' Leibniz has 'great advantage'.

liberty in the soul: for (1) [234/5] he says that 'it is not able always to give itself pleasant feelings, since the feelings it has are dependent on those it has had'.[c]

[13] (2) He adds that 'the present state of each substance is a natural consequence of its preceding state'.[d] But a natural consequence of a preceding state is a necessary consequence. (3) Finally, he says that 'in conformity with a law of order which exists in perceptions as much as in movements, each preceding perception influences succeeding ones'.[e] But the law of communication of motion is necessary. Therefore the influence of earlier perceptions on later ones is also necessary.

[14] Fourth: Although it must be admitted that this system is possible, we still cannot fail to observe that it is not the one which God actually followed, and that in fact he established that of [235/ 6] occasional causes. For example, I admit that one could possibly say that when a man is stabbed with a sword, it isn't because of the blow, nor on the occasion of it, that the soul suffers pain, but instead that as a consequence of its own laws, it would have felt it at precisely that moment, even if there were only God and that soul. But can we say in the same way that when a man becomes mad, it isn't because of the derangement that has taken place in his brain that his mind wanders? Can we deny that it is because of a disturbance of the animal spirits caused by an excess of wine that the mind of a drunken man comes to have only deranged, bizarre, and extraordinary, etc. thoughts? And is it credible that such wildness is only a natural consequence of the constitution of that soul, and that it is only [236/7] conforming to the natural laws which God has given it? How complimentary this is to his wisdom! What a spectacle worthy of the infinitely perfect being, that a soul should leave his hands with a nature which puts it under a real necessity of being crazy for sixty or eighty years—and perhaps even for all eternity, for that which stems from the nature and essence of a thing must last as long as that thing itself. Doesn't this clearly make God the originator of these disorders? And would such a system do him much honour?

[15] I say much the same in connection with what happens in the body. When a man takes and eats a piece of bread, I admit that one could possibly say that his will has no part in these movements, and that it isn't because the will desires and commands them that the body carries them out, but [237/8] that the body was itself already

disposed in virtue of mechanical laws to perform them at the same moment as the soul willed it, and that it would indeed have done them even if there had been no soul in the world. But can one say the same of the action of writing? Can one pretend with any conviction that it isn't by the direction of the mind and by the command of the will that the various movements which are necessary to make the various shapes of the letters are carried out? Can one say that at the time, for example, that I set about writing these reflections against the new system, my hand, in virtue of its own laws and natural constitution, was already completely disposed of itself to form the various movements necessary to give sensible expression to my thoughts, and that it would actually have formed them [238/9] even if there were no soul? Isn't it obvious that this prodigious diversity of movements, so ordered in one sense, and so bizarre in another, cannot result from general mechanical laws, so that it is necessary that in this respect the body depends on the direction and authority of the soul?

[16] Fifth: This system supposes that to each of these substances, I mean the mind and the body, God has given laws in virtue of which all that is to happen to them develops in sequence independently of the influence of any other created thing. But who controls the operation of these laws? Are they wise laws? And if they are, do these substances actually follow them? Let us consider: everyone says that one of these laws is that beings tend of themselves to their own preservation, and avoid, if only [239/40] mechanically, everything that tends to their destruction. The wisdom of God demands this. And yet we observe bodies which throw themselves into the flames, which jump to their deaths, which cut themselves to pieces. We observe minds which live perpetually in pain and bitterness. What a charming law it would be by which a soul which is engaged in abstract thought about religion, or in contemplating the deity, finds itself gripped by a sharp pain which makes it break off and abandon its train of thought! What a wise law it would be by which a soul engaged in professing its love of God is surprised by a blasphemous thought, and moved by that to a hatred of that divine object to which it wanted to pay court! There is no wisdom or order in this, nothing worthy of God, and this system, which at first dazzled me by I know not what air [240/1] of simplicity and uniformity, now seems to me so dislocated, so shaky, and out of

true in so many places, that I now believe it untenable, despite the great intelligence of its illustrious author.

[17] Sixth: But there is a final place in which it seems even more out of true, and yet which is the most important and most fundamental of the system. This is its supposition of a certain 'active nature', a 'power', a 'force', an 'energy', distinct from the power of God, in virtue of which beings 'produce in an orderly way all their changes in such a way that everything in them arises from their own nature with a perfect spontaneity'.[31] For this supposition is directly contrary to the weakness and dependence essential to created things, and to the sovereign power essential to the Creator. [241/2] It is a false idea to suppose that it would be unworthy of God to commit himself continually to act on his creatures, and to produce by himself all the changes which happen to them. As there is no better demonstration of the infinite dependence of a created being, and of the sovereignty and extent of the power of the Creator, nothing is more honourable to him. Having him thus produce all the impressions which occur in the mind and the body does not mean his performing perpetual miracles, for he does it only in accordance with certain general and ordinary laws, and miracles are only exceptions to these laws.

[18] So it seems to me that to make it one of God's perfections that he rids himself of his power by communicating it to what he has created is to rob him of an essential and incommunicable perfection [242/3] and give it to a created thing. In a word, it is to support a system on contradictory and chimerical ideas, since it is certain that God produces everything that really happens at every moment in the things he creates; and that only he is able to act on them, and to produce their changes as a true cause. I remember that I have a document to this effect written by one of my friends, where these truths are proved and clearly demonstrated by the method of the geometers.[32] I must reread it at the first opportunity, in order to fortify myself more and more against the false brilliance of this new system.

---

[31] The 'quotation' is a composite of NS1, § 14 and 'Third Explanation of the New System' (Ch. 4, n. 31; cf. B1).

[32] Presumably Lamy is referring to the third treatise of *his own* (but also anonymous) *Le Nouvel Athéisme renversé* (Paris, 1696), in which he overturns Spinoza's system 'suivant la méthode des Géomètres'.

[LAMY'S NOTES]

a. Everything said about the 'New System' in these Fifth Reflections is taken from what M. Leibniz says about it (1) in the *Journal des savants* of Aug. 1695,[33] (2) in the same journal for Nov. 1696,[34] and (3) in *l'Histoire des ouvrages des savants* for July 1698.[35]
b. In the *Journal des savants*, 4 Aug. 1695 [*sic*, actually 4 July 1695].
c. In a letter to the editor of *l'Histoire des [ouvrages des] savants*, July 1698. [i.e. PB3, § 6].
d. Ibid. [i.e. PB3, § 9].
e. Ibid. [i.e. PB3, § 12].

L2.3. LAMY: Extract from the 'Analysis, or Summary of the Second Treatise of the Book on the Knowledge of the Self' (volume 2, pp. 387–92)

[1] In the *Fifth Reflections* our philosopher examines the system of M. Leibniz concerning the union of mind and body. At first he finds himself very agreeably impressed, and so taken that he very nearly adopts it. Indeed, he observes with this illustrious savant that we can think of only three ways in which the union between mind and body might be brought about. First: That of a reciprocal communication of species and qualities between the two substances, such as is maintained by the common philosophy. But, having shown as he does that the mind and body cannot really act the one on the other, this way, which can be called *the way of influence*, seems to him absolutely untenable.

[2] (2) Second: That of a perpetual supervisor responsible for producing from moment to moment in each of these beings impressions corresponding to those taking place in the other. This way, which can be called *the way of assistance* and is that of occasional causes, seems to him to devalue divinity, to make it a slave to its creation, and has God producing perfectly natural effects purely by miracles.

[3] (3) Third: That of a divinely pre-established natural agreement, which consists in God's having given to these two beings (the mind and the body) such a nature and such a force that each modifies itself, and produces out of its being, in virtue of its own laws, all the changes of which it is capable, without connection to

---

[33] Lamy is obviously referring to the 'New System', whose June and July dates he wrongly gives as August.
[34] 'Third Explanation' (see Ch. 4, n. 31).
[35] Leibniz's reply to Bayle's *Dictionary* note H (i.e. PB3).

what happens in the other. They nevertheless agree with each other so well, that the body is ready to move, and actually does move, just when the soul, in virtue of its own laws, is determined to will it. And on the other hand the soul is seized with pleasure or pain, precisely at the moment when the body, in virtue of its own laws, is violently or moderately stimulated. And it is this third way (which we can call the way *of pre-established harmony*) which at first captivated our philosopher, for it seemed to him to involve greater simplicity and greater wisdom.

[4] But second and more mature reflections successfully freed him from this deceitful spell, and showed him not only difficulties but even kinds of impossibilities in this system. For, first: either these two substances (the mind and the body), each with the force to produce within its own bosom all the impressions of which it is capable, were created and destined for each other from the beginning; or alternatively, without having been made for each other, they each received separately, and as if they were alone with God, such a nature that, coming to exist at the same time, they find their respective modalities in exact correspondence. If the former, then this system does not differ from that of occasional causes, except for the alleged forces and powers that God gave these substances by which to modify themselves. If the latter, then the sequence of thoughts that God gave to a mind is not at all wise, but purely capricious. For example, what wisdom, and indeed what justice, is there in making a soul pass suddenly from joy to pain merely by the laws of the constitution of its nature, without its having deserved that punishment through some wrongdoing?

[5] Second: To speak only of the mind and of this supposed force that it has for producing all its thoughts. Either this production is free or it is necessary. If it is free, what pleasure does this mind take in tormenting itself and so often giving itself painful feelings? If, on the contrary, it is necessary, so that these feelings come over it necessarily, by virtue of the constitution of its nature, then, yet again, where is the wisdom and justice of God, in making laws for minds which are not free, and giving them commandments?

[6] Third: This system is based on the supposition of a nature acting by a force or a power distinct from the power of God. This supposition is directly contrary to the weakness essential to created things, and to the sovereign authority essential to the Creator.

[7] Fourth: Our philosopher shows that although it will certainly

be admitted that this system is possible, it is still certain that it is not that which God actually followed and that, on the contrary, in fact he established that of occasional causes. He shows that this latter is the only system which is able to show the wisdom and justice of God in the series of different changes which take place in the mind and the body, and that by contrast the new system makes God act in a bizarre, capricious, random, and unjust manner.

L3. LEIBNIZ: Remarks on Lamy (November 1702).[36]

[1] At last I have received[37] the extract of the book *The Knowledge of the Self* which discusses my system. It consists of five reflections on how God brings about the union of soul and body. The author, who has some merit and thinks deeply, after declaring that he thinks *the way of influence* of soul on body and body on soul, which was taught in the schools, is impossible, states (p. 227) that it seems at first that *the way of occasional causes* in a way devalues the divinity, that it enslaves it to its creation, and 'has God producing perfectly natural effects purely by miracles'.[38] Compared with this, *the way of pre-established harmony*, which I have put on the table, is 'infinitely more simple and sensible and testifies to an infinitely greater intelligence and acuteness in the sovereign workman'.[39] But the same author claims to show a little later (p. 229) that it appears like this only 'so long as one looks at the system from only one side, but when one looks at it from another angle, one sees difficulties and impossibilities which deserve closer inspection'.[40] Let us look at that inspection.

[2] 'First, either these substances', which are in pre-established harmony, 'were made for each other', says he, 'or, without having been destined for each other, they have each received separately, or as if they were alone with God, such a nature that their modalities agree'.[41] If it is *the first*, then the new system differs from that of

[36] From the French at G 4. 577–90.
[37] Gerhardt reports that Leibniz noted on the manuscript here: '30 November 1702, Berlin'.
[38] Quote from L2.2, § 3.
[39] Near-quote from L2.2, § 3. Leibniz's 'infinitely' misquotes Lamy's 'incomparably'.
[40] See L2.2, § 7.   [41] Near-quote from L2.2, § 8.

occasional causes only in that in the new system God produces impressions only indirectly, through the force which he has given to each substance. If *the second*, then the sequence of perceptions that God gave to minds, is not at all wise, but purely arbitrary.

[3] I reply that there is no room for doubt as to which alternative I take, and that I have clearly declared in favour of the first. There is therefore no problem to raise here, since he seems to agree that in that case there would be none, and my system has no problem not shared with that of occasional causes. For I hold that not only the soul and the body, but also all other created substances in the universe are made for each other, and mutually express one another, though they may be related either more or less closely depending on the closeness of the relation. It can thus be said that in the intentions of God and in the order of final causes, one substance depends on another; for God considered one when producing the other, even though so far as physical influence, or efficient causation, goes, they have as little dependence on each other as if each were alone in the world with God. And there was no need to produce this dilemma, for I had already firmly come down on the side of wisdom in the operations of God, against any suspicion of capriciousness; indeed, the greatest conceivable wisdom, greater than had ever been thought before, as our author admitted earlier, along with M. Bayle. Nothing shows the need and the necessity for the existence of an infinitely powerful and wise maker better than my system does, since it is necessary for pre-establishing the harmonies: and this is a new and irrefutable way of proving the existence of God.

[4] Second: He faces me with another dilemma: the spontaneous production of perceptions in the soul is either free or necessary. If it is free, why does the soul give itself unpleasant feelings? And if these perceptions come to it necessarily, despite itself and in virtue of the constitution of its nature, where is the wisdom of God in making it undergo this variety of sensations without cause and without reason? I am amazed that he raises difficulties of this sort, which, if they had any foundation, would apply equally to all other systems. We have to distinguish between voluntary thoughts, which no doubt are free, and involuntary thoughts, like feelings of pain, for example. Now it is always God who produces these feelings: he does it directly in the system of occasional causes; in the other two systems he does it indirectly, through the natures which he has

established. For in the system of influences, which is the usual one, he does it through the nature of bodies, which communicate something to the soul, and have some influence over them; in mine he does it through the constitution of the soul, in that it must express the body. These sensations then are not free, and nor should they be, since they are not voluntary, and I can't see why they are contrary to the wisdom of God in my system any more than in the others. And their occurrence is not without cause and without reason, since they happen because the soul must express the body.

[5] Third: He objects again that the soul is not free in my system, and produces three proofs of this. *The first proof*, which is basically the same as the preceding objection, is that I say that the soul can't always give itself pleasant sensations, since the sensations it has depend on those it has had. But I ask the author of this objection whether it isn't true in the other two systems also, that sensations which are unpleasant to the soul come from something which doesn't depend on its free will?

[6] *The second proof* against freedom is that I say that the present state of each substance is a natural consequence of the preceding state. He infers from this that a natural consequence of a preceding state is a necessary consequence. But that is a conclusion which I do not accept. If it is in the nature of a substance to be free in the actions in question, that natural consequence will be free and voluntary; for voluntary actions are no less natural to the soul than any others; one can even say they are more natural, because in them the soul is exercising a perfection of its nature, which is freedom. In effect, the same objection can be made against the other systems. For in the popular system, which is that of influence, the present state of the soul, in the case of something involuntary, is in part a natural consequence of the influences of the body; and in that of occasional causes, it is a natural consequence (at least partly) of the impressions made by God. But in regard to what is voluntary, the system of influences, just like mine, makes the soul independent of the body in some way, and dependent on its own fancies—and this is a perfection of its nature. By contrast, the system of occasional causes is the one which has most problems with this, especially when the voluntary actions are evil.

[7] *The third* alleged *proof* that there is no liberty in my system is that according to me there is a law of order among perceptions just as there is with movements. And according to the author of the

objection, the communication of motion is necessary. But without laying any stress on the fact that the laws of motion are established in accordance with the divine wisdom, and are not geometrically necessary, it is sufficient to say that the perceptions which express the laws of motion are linked together just like those laws, which they express according to the order of efficient causes. But the order of voluntary perceptions, which is that of final causes, is in conformity with the nature of the will.

[8] Fourth: It is objected that even if my system is possible, it isn't what God followed, and that it must be said that it does not accord with the phenomena. I cannot see how this can be maintained if it is granted that God could create a nature capable of producing those phenomena in succession. But let us move on to the details of the objection. It claims that on my system it must be for no reason, and not because of the destruction of traces in the brain (for example) that the mind becomes confused. But I reply that I can perfectly well say that the soul becomes confused because of the body, just as well as the other systems can. For the soul's nature is to express the body and to be in agreement with it, exactly as if the body had an influence on it. I am amazed that anyone can choose to lay at the door of my system all the inconveniences which are there in the nature of things, as if these were not problems for the other systems too, and as if the difficulties were not even worse for that of occasional causes, where all agreement between body and soul can only come immediately from God.

[9] I am asked whether it is 'credible that such wildness', which we see in the thoughts of a drunken man, 'is only a natural consequence of the constitution of that soul, and that it is only conforming to the natural laws which God has given it'.[42] But our nature is corrupted by free actions produced from the core of human nature itself, and which have combined their effects with that of the original constitution which comes from God; and our nature is originally made in such a way that our modifications depend heavily on the modifications of the body which are expressed in us; so neither our sins nor our involuntary wildnesses, such as those which can happen in a fit of madness, need be imputed to God more in my system than in any of the others. For couldn't we similarly ask how these disorders can all be consequences of the impressions made by God in the system of occasional

[42] Quote from L2.2, § 14.

causes? Or, in the usual system, how God came to create the body in such a way that it suffers these disorders capable of upsetting the soul, or why he should, as it were, condemn the soul to reside in such a body? Really this is asking for the cause of evil.

[10] And when the author of this objection adds: 'What honour this does to the divine wisdom!',[43] does he not see that this is a plea for the Manichaeans who wanted two principles? If he accepted that my system is the only true one, I could undertake to answer this point, and to reply to the Manichaeans; but when it is a matter of comparing my system with the others, why should I entangle myself and my readers with difficulties common to all systems, when it hasn't been shown that mine makes them any worse? In fact, quite the contrary: I can very easily show that mine can cope with these difficulties even better than the others. But this is not the place to enter into such a discussion. M. Bayle saw this perfectly, for he said he didn't want to raise objections against me which applied to all theories.

[11] This is why, when the author continues with his exclamations: 'What a spectacle worthy of the infinitely perfect being, that a soul should leave his hands with a nature which puts it under a real necessity of being crazy for sixty or eighty years or perhaps for all eternity!',[44] he must have barely understood my works, since he thinks I am so unwise as to allow this supposed necessity about the actions of the soul: me, to whom the late M. Arnauld initially imputed something of the sort, but generously withdrew it when he had a better understanding of the basis of my views. Isn't it true that in the other systems too the nature of the soul, just as much as that of the body, comes from the hands of God? And that sins and wildnesses nevertheless originate in it, whether we say that the body influences the soul or not? For, according to me, the soul is made to act as if the body influenced it because it expresses it, and according to our author, because God produces what he wants to happen in it, which comes about as occasioned by the body.

[12] The author of the objection again claims that these wildnesses of the soul should, according to me, last for ever: 'Since', says he, 'that which stems from the nature or essence of a thing must last as long as that thing itself'.[45] But he must excuse me if I say that this is

---

[43] See L2.2, § 14.
[44] Near-quote from L2.2, § 14.
[45] Near-quote from L2.2, § 14.

somewhat ambiguous. We always distinguish between what is essential and what is natural, as in the writings of jurists, who distinguish between what is essential and what is natural in a contract. Properties are essential and eternal, but modifications can be natural even when they are changeable. There are, in fact, degrees of naturalness among modifications. The most natural is that which is entirely in conformity with the perfection of the nature which produces it. But when that nature is corrupted, errors can become natural to it. Second, we must not confuse what we call natural in an ordinary sense with what could be called natural in a more metaphysical sense. For example, in the ordinary sense, it is natural for us to die, but it isn't at all natural to be killed by a cannon shot. This is what we call accidental or violent, and rightly; and I am not trying to change this way of speaking. Thus, when I say that everything that happens to a substance can be seen to be in some sense natural to it, or to be a consequence of its individual nature, I mean the complete nature, which includes all that belongs to that individual. I mean it, therefore, in a kind of transcendental sense, according to which the complete nature of each individual implicitly contains everything that will happen to it, and (because of the relations between them) all other individuals. In truth, this implicit containment is in conformity with strict metaphysical language, even though common usage takes no account of it. But I am not denying the ordinary distinctions for that reason, and I use words in an unusual sense only when I can't find better terms to express myself. If this isn't taken account of, I will have a thousand ludicrous and empty objections raised against me, which are appropriate only to an ill-informed man in the street who knows nothing of the real nature of things, and who treats the opinions of Copernicus or of Descartes, for example, as wildnesses. And I am sure that the author of *The Knowledge of the Self* is too wise to insist on it, when he has properly understood my views.

[13] And when he continues with these words: 'Doesn't this clearly make God the originator of these disorders? And would such a system do him much honour?',[46] this is only a consequence of the misunderstanding that I have just put straight. According to the schools, sins and wildnesses, whether voluntary or involuntary, come from the soul or from the influences of the body: and the natures of the soul and of the body come from the hand of God. In

---

[46] Quote from L2.2, § 14.

the system of occasional causes, wildnesses found in the soul can have their origin only in the soul and, in place of the influences of the body, in God's impressions on the soul on the occasion of the body. And according to me, they come only from the soul, whether through its will, or as a result of the involuntary perceptions which arise in it because its nature is to express the body—which I put in place of the influences of the body. Why, then, should one have more difficulty with my theory than with the others in saving the honour of God and legitimizing these disorders? Since, after all, the soul and the body both come from God, it is the same thing whether we attribute them only to a soul which represents the body, or to a soul which also has impressions from the body, or to a soul which also has impressions from God. And if there is something offensive here with respect to God, it is rather in the theory which puts impressions from God in place of those from the body or of those from ideas of the body, because it seems that this is blaming God more immediately for what happens.

[14] As regards the difficulty which makes up the second part of the fourth objection, that the actions of the human body which show intelligence, such as speaking, writing, etc., could never be the result of mechanical laws, it is the most deserving of clarification; and I have amply done so in the last reply to M. Bayle. Several ancient and modern thinkers, such as Gassendi in his objections, and in his defence of them, who have argued against the Cartesian and other similar proofs of the spirituality of the soul, have believed that everything that happens in nature, even the actions which we see in man, can be explained by the modifications of matter, or mechanically: and even the Cartesian idea which makes animals into automata, implies that men also could be automata. In fact, the body could be an automaton, and really is one; but the internal action of the soul must be kept separate from that. I shall say nothing at present about the principle of mechanical laws itself, which could never be derived from the modifications of extension. Thus the objection stems only from a lack of understanding of the admirable mechanism that God exercises. I was careful from the outset, and I asked when proposing my system if it wasn't possible for God to make an automaton which performed the actions of a man. And given that possibility, I inferred from it that since my system was possible, it was preferable to the others. For by freeing us from a kind of miraculous guidance and raising to its highest the

wisdom of God, it takes away all the difficulty concerning the union of the soul and the body. Also, the author of these objections having said, on p. 235 at the beginning of the fourth objection, that while he would agree that my system is possible, we find that God in fact didn't follow it, cannot in the same objection deny that possibility, in saying that 'all these actions, so ordered in one sense, and so bizarre in another, cannot result from general mechanical laws'.[47] But he doesn't say why they cannot. These general laws, so simple in themselves, produce in their application an infinite variety, and the Cartesians must acknowledge this, since they consider animals to be machines. Even men are capable of making machines whose effects seem to require intelligence. Why can't God, who is infinitely more intelligent and more powerful than we are, both in inventing the means and in putting them into effect, go infinitely further, or rather, why should he not in fact have done so? Thus the difficulty stems only from the limits that we tacitly and unthinkingly put on the divine wisdom and divine power.

[15] *The fifth objection* is: if each substance has received a nature from God, in virtue of which its modifications develop successively and in conformity with certain laws, independently of the influence of any other created thing, the question arises, 'are these wise laws, do these substances actually follow them, and who is it that controls their operation?' I reply that without doubt they are wise, that substances do follow them, and that their own nature ensures their operation. To that it is objected that 'so far as mechanics goes bodies tend to their own preservation, but we observe bodies which throw themselves into the flames, which jump to their deaths, which cut themselves to pieces'. But I find I am having objections put to me of a kind that a savage from deepest America would put to any philosopher, or such as men would have made to the first philosopher, as though I had to answer for everything. And it seems to me that the able author of *The Knowledge of the Self* is by a kind of ingenious fiction stripping himself of all his learning, as if to make me start philosophy again from the beginning. For can't that objection be made to all theories? And these crashing bodies which destroy themselves in collisions, are they not consequences of the natural laws that God has put into bodies, whether one accepts my system or some other? Each thing preserves itself in its present state, if there is no reason which obliges it to change, and the law of

---

[47] Near-quote from L2.2, § 15.

conservation has never been understood otherwise. But it is again necessary to distinguish between a substance and an assemblage of substances which makes up a mass. Each substance conserves itself; but masses in virtue of the laws of their own nature tend to destroy themselves, for they break themselves up by their internal movement, and tend to move out from the centre, if the pressure of things around them is not enough to keep them together.⁴⁸

[16] The same objection is also applied to the mind. 'We see' (he says) 'minds which live perpetually in pain. What a charming law it would be by which a soul engaged in contemplating the deity is surprised by a sharp pain which makes it abandon its train of thought'.⁴⁹ But I say what an amusing *question*, which asks my system to make things better than they should or could be, and asks that the law which, according to my view, God put into nature, should do more than God does himself according to the opinion of the author. For since God himself acts on the soul by continual impressions, according to the doctrine of occasional causes, and doesn't avoid, or rather produces, pains, why should he not be allowed to give to the mind at the outset a nature which produces these same feelings later when the time comes? Has there ever been such partiality, and haven't I reason to be surprised to find such objections being put to me?

[17] In fact, I find it difficult to see how anyone could come up with these difficulties, and from whatever side I look at my system, I can find nothing which gives me reason to consider them. One needs to look at it through a very strangely shaped lens to make it look as distorted as he says. 'There is' (he says) 'no wisdom or order in this, nothing worthy of God'. By the same reasoning we will find no wisdom, no order, and nothing worthy of God in the whole of nature; for why should God be obliged to do better according to me than according to any of the others? And despite the fact that God's infinite wisdom and power are never more clearly shown than on my theory, and almost never less so than on that of occasions, where God is made to look like a man who lives from one day to the next, or like a workman who is always kept busy adjusting his creation; still despite that, an advocate of a doctrine which, to use our author's words, itself seems 'to devalue divinity', can go so far as to say that 'the system of pre-established harmony which dazzled

⁴⁸ The near-quotes in this section are from L2.2, § 16.
⁴⁹ Near-quote from L2.2, § 16.

me by I know not what air of simplicity and uniformity, now seems to me so dislocated, so shaky, and out of true in so many places, that I believe it untenable'. As for me, I have more trouble finding out what the problem is in these objections than I have in replying to them.[50]

[18] *The sixth objection* is, 'the place in which this system seems even more out of true, and yet which is the most important, is its supposition of a certain active nature, a power, a force or energy distinct from the power of God, in virtue of which beings produce in an orderly way all their changes in such a way that everything in them arises from their own nature with a perfect spontaneity. For this supposition', he continues, 'is directly contrary to the weakness and dependence essential to created things, and to the sovereign power essential to the Creator.'[51] But we are not told why and in what way my supposition is contrary to that. Do created things, because they are weak and dependent, have to be completely without power? And must the Creator, because he is the sovereign power, be the only powerful and active being? Can there be no perfections in creatures just because God is infinitely perfect? The same reasoning would show that because he is a sovereign being, he is the only being, or at least the only substance.

[19] He goes on: 'that it is a false idea to suppose that it would be unworthy of God to commit himself continually to act on his creatures, and to produce by himself all the changes which happen to them'.[52] I agree that God acts on his creatures continually in conserving them: but if he alone is active, what perfection has he given to them? I would very much like him to say, for there is none which does not involve some action. And if he had given no perfection to them, his work would be unworthy of him. Moreover, the author of these objections had acknowledged at first, as also did M. Bayle, 'that the way of pre-established harmony testifies to an infinitely greater wisdom'. And isn't that enough to show that all other theories are beneath God?

[20] Again, it is said that 'Having him thus produce all the impressions which occur in the mind and the body does not mean his performing perpetual miracles, for he does it only in accordance with certain general and ordinary laws, and miracles are only

[50] The quotes and near-quotes in this section are from L2.2, §§16, 3, 16.
[51] Quote from L2.2, § 17.
[52] The near- or quasi-quotes in this section are from L2.2, §§ 17, 3.

exceptions to these laws'. I have already replied to this on another occasion, that to think in this way is to have a false idea of what a miracle is. For according to this idea, the laws of nature would be arbitrary, and whatever God had chosen to establish would be the nature of things, and exceptions to them would be miracles: consequently the natural and the miraculous would not differ in themselves, but only in the extrinsic denomination (*denominatione extrinseca*) of their antecedents and consequents. For what was preceded and followed by the same kind of thing would be natural, and what was not would be a miracle. But we need to realize that not every kind of regularity or law is suitable to be a law of nature, and that there is an essential difference between the natural and the miraculous, so that if God acted continually in a certain way, he would be performing perpetual miracles. For example, if God had laid down that a planet should of itself always travel along a curved line, such as for example an ellipse, without providing anything intelligible which caused or maintained this elliptical movement, I say that God would have established a perpetual miracle. It could not be said that the planet moved in this way because of its nature, or following natural laws, because it would not be possible to explain it, or to give a reason for such a phenomenon—as we would need to, however, because this movement is composite, and so the reason for it must derive from simpler movements. And if God had nevertheless wanted there always to be this elliptical movement of the planet, without the contribution of any other physical causes, it would be necessary for him always to intervene, or to put it in the charge of some intelligence. That would be necessary, I say, unless other bodies combine to maintain the movement, and the reason for it can be found in various simpler movements of other bodies which cause the composite movement. But then the nature of the thing will consist of these simpler causes, for example of the straight-line movement of the planet, combined with the impression made by the motion of the surroundings capable of weighing the planet down towards the sun. Thus if God wanted a body to move of itself in a straight line, that would be a law of nature, but if he wanted it of itself to go in a circle or an ellipse, that would be a continual miracle. In the same way it is truly a perpetual miracle if God always has to serve as an interpreter to the body with regard to the soul, by carrying out the soul's wishes in the body, because there is no explanation of how it is done in terms of something simpler, and there is no reason for this agreement of the substances taken from the natures of the things themselves, as I have taken care to provide in my theory.

[21] Lastly, the author of the book *The Knowledge of the Self* concludes the matter by saying 'that God rids himself', according to me, 'of his power by communicating it to what he has created, and is robbed of an essential and incommunicable perfection, so that this system is supported on contradictory and chimerical ideas'.[53] But this is simply begging the question, because he supposes that God alone has the power to act. 'It is certain', says he, 'that God produces everything that really happens at every moment in the things he creates; and that only he is able to act on them, and to produce their changes as a true cause'. In a way I agree with the first point, that God continually produces all that is real in created things. But I also hold that to do so he continually produces or conserves in us that energy or activity which according to me constitutes the nature of a substance, and the source of its modifications. And so I don't at all agree that God alone is active in substances, or is the sole cause of their changes, and I believe that this would make created things completely vain and useless.

[22] The author remembers 'having seen a document to this effect written by one of my friends, where these truths are proved', says he, 'and clearly demonstrated by the method of the geometers. I want to reread it at the first opportunity, in order to fortify myself more and more against the false brilliance of this system.'[54] I have always thought that the only reason or seeming proof which has given rise to and can offer some justification for the Cartesians' occasional causes is the impossibility of influences. It is this that has made these authors turn to what came most easily to their minds; for pre-established harmony is something more profound, and can only be the fruit of the greater maturity of philosophy which comes with time, that is to say, it is due more to God than to men. I nevertheless would be very interested to see this document, and I have given enough evidence of my willingness to learn to show that if these demonstrations are good I will withdraw. Although I have often read what has been written in favour of occasional causes, I have never seen anything (with the exception of the refutation of

[53] The quotes and near-quotes in this section are from L2.2, § 18.
[54] Near-quote from L2.2, § 18. Leibniz's 'having seen' misquotes Lamy's 'having' (see n. 32 above).

influences) approaching a proof of it. In devising it, the hope was to bring out our dependent nature and the power of God; and this would be praiseworthy if it were not at the expense of his wisdom, and if it did not have the effect of destroying our substantiality. For all my reasonings and, I will go so far as to say, my proofs lead me to believe that to rob substance of energy and action is to leave it with nothing at all. The mistaken notion of extension which the Cartesians developed, as if it were a primitive attribute capable of constituting a substance, leads them seriously astray by making them think we can conceive of a substance without action, whereas the notion of extension, rather like that of number and time, is derivative, and incapable of constituting substance. For extension or extendedness is relative, and presupposes some nature which is extended or repeated, just as number presupposes something which is numbered (*res numeratam*). Now we will find that this nature which is continually repeated in extension, and which extension presupposes, must involve dynamics or force, or there will be nothing that can be attributed to it. As for the mind, which is the other substance which Cartesians allow, the Revd Father Malebranche, M. Sturm, and others, if I am not mistaken, accord an internal activity to it; and that is the only activity I accord to any created substance. But according to me, corporeal masses are not substances. I have many other arguments to present, and several of them serve to show that according to the view which completely robs created things of all power and action, God would be the only substance, and created things would be only accidents or modifications of God. So those who are of this opinion will in spite of themselves fall into that of Spinoza, who seems to me to have taken furthest the consequences of the Cartesian doctrine of occasional causes. I have no intention of imputing these Spinozan views (which I think are very evil and absurd) to all those worthy persons who follow the Cartesian opinion. I am, however, entitled to indicate the consequences of that opinion. But I would have less right to do this, if I did not produce a way of avoiding them, and a way which, moreover, has all the advantages that one could want in a theory, and which indeed must be accepted as something more than a theory.

L4. LEIBNIZ: 'Reply to the Objections that the Author of the Book *The Knowledge of the Self* made against the System of Pre-established Harmony' (1704; pub. 1709)[55]

The celebrated author of these objections, who has some talent and who thinks deeply, acknowledges (pp. 225 ff.)[56] that he found something very attractive about the system of *pre-established harmony* which I use to explain the relation between the soul and the body. He says that the way of influence is untenable, and that of occasional causes seems at first unworthy of God, as it has him continually acting by miracles in purely natural effects, whereas the way of pre-established harmony attributes to the sovereign workman an incomparably greater level of skill. But he also adds (p. 230) that a moment's reflection enabled him to see difficulties in it — and indeed impossibilities — which deserve examination. Let us proceed to that examination with him, and see how he carries out his declared plan of fortifying himself against what he calls the false glitter of this new system.

The first difficulty lies in the question of whether the two corresponding substances are made for each other. I reply 'yes', for if they agree, God has made them so as to agree. But it is inferred from this that the system therefore differs little from that of occasional causes. All well and good, say I; but I don't at all see how this follows. In the system of occasional causes the substances agree because God always produces such agreement; their preceding state does not bring them to it naturally, as is the case in the new system. And the difference between the two systems is even more obvious from the fact that the author of the objection wants us to accept that such natural agreement would be impossible. (See the fifth difficulty, below.) But in any case, if someone wants to understand the system of occasional causes in a way which transforms it into mine, I will have no objections.

The second difficulty (p. 233) lies in another question: namely,

---

[55] 'Réponse de M. Leibniz aux objections que l'auteur du livre de la Connoissance de soi-même, a faites contre le système de l'harmonie préétablie', *Supplément du Journal des savants du dernier de juin 1709*, 1709, pp. 276–81 (Amsterdam edn., *Journal des savants, avec les suplémens pour les mois d'avril, juin 1709*, vol. 44, pp. 593–603) (B 110; R 176).
[56] Leibniz's page references are to L2.

whether the soul is free in the production of its feelings. It seems to me that a question is not an objection; nevertheless, I will reply to it, and the reply is easy—or, rather, I have already replied to difficulties of this kind right at the beginning, when the system was first proposed.[57] The soul is free in its voluntary actions, when it has distinct thoughts and shows reason; but since confused perceptions are dependent on the body, they arise from preceding confused perceptions, without the soul's necessarily wanting them, or foreseeing them. So although pains do not come to the soul because it wants them, this does not mean that they therefore come to it without cause or without reason, for the sequence of confused perceptions is representative of the motions of the body, the great number and small size of which do not allow them to be perceived distinctly.

The third difficulty (p. 234) is that it does not seem to the author of these objections that there is any real liberty in this system. But this is an accusation for which I can see no grounds. If I did say (as he alleges) 'that the soul is not able to give itself pleasant feelings',[58] was I not right? Does our 'liberty' extend as far as that in *any* system? Wouldn't that be a 'sovereignty' like that of God? To accuse me of that is not to raise an objection against my system, but to raise an objection against liberty, which is taken here in an exaggerated sense. Another charge against me: I said that 'the present state of each substance is a natural consequence of its preceding state'.[59] Now, it is said, a natural consequence is a necessary consequence. I reply that I do not accept that at all, and I am astonished that he should take up such positions in order to accuse me of errors. What is natural is appropriate to the nature of the thing, but what is necessary is essential, and cannot be changed. Leaves grow on trees naturally, but they still fall off. It is natural for wicked people to commit crimes, but it is not necessary that they should commit them. It is also natural to the habit of virtue to perform good actions. Are such actions any the less free for that? A third charge: I said that 'in conformity with a law of order which exists in perceptions as much as in movements, each preceding perception influences succeeding ones'.[60] The response is easy. Does a law of succession exclude liberty? Doesn't God always act in accordance with such a law? Confused perceptions are ordered just

----

[57] Leibniz perhaps has in mind PB3, § 6.   [58] See PB3, § 6.
[59] PB3, § 9.   [60] PB3, § 12.

like the laws of the motions which they represent. The motions of bodies are explained by efficient causes, but in the distinct perceptions of the soul, where there is liberty, final causes reappear. But there is order in the one of these *series* just as much as in the other; I am a little surprised to find that there is not even the semblance of order in nearly all of these objections.

The fourth difficulty (p. 235) amounts to saying that the new system, even if it were possible, is not the one which God chose, because it is not worthy of him. Consider a disturbance in a man's animal spirits, produced by an excess of wine. Is it credible (asks the author of the objection) that such wildness is only a natural consequence of the constitution of that soul, and that it is only conforming to the laws which God has given to it? How complimentary this is to his wisdom! The exclamation collapses if one thinks about it even for a moment. When there is a disturbance in the body, it is natural that our confused perceptions should represent it. Moreover, the nature of the body and that of the soul are corrupt, and in following out its nature the soul does not always conform to the laws of God: that corruption is a consequence of will and of liberty. To attack the new system for that is to hold it responsible for all the difficulties which we encounter in the nature of things and which are there whichever system is employed. In just the same way we could ask with the ordinary system why God has created the body and the soul in such a way that disturbances happen to them through the influence of the one on the other, which is natural to them according to that system. And it is even worse in the occasionalist system, where they go so far as to say that these disorders are immediate consequences of continual impressions from God. All these are really asking for the cause of evil. Does the author of the objection, in denying that these disorders which crop up in the works of God do credit to his wisdom, want to plead for the Manichaeans?[61] Should we not rather agree with St Augustine, that apparent disorder is corrected by order on a larger scale?[62]

I count as the *fifth difficulty* that when the author comes back a little later to question the possibility of the new system, he denies that God could make an automaton capable of doing without reasoning everything that a man can do with it. M. Bayle denied

[61] Ch. 5, n. 115.
[62] Augustine, *De ordine (Divine Providence and the Problem of Evil).*

this in the same way.[63] But I am astonished that they should presume to set limits to the power and wisdom of God, and do so without bringing forward any proof. But that aside, there are innumerable examples of such works of God which do even more than that. The thing which forms the foetus is an automaton whose cleverness surpasses anything that men can do by reason; the most beautiful poem or other product of intelligence gets nowhere near it. It is true that it works by divine *preformation*; but just the same is true in the pre-established harmony.

The sixth difficulty (which comes down more or less to the fourth) is that it seems that the laws of harmony lack wisdom. Beings tend towards their own preservation, yet there are nevertheless some bodies, such as moths for example, which burn themselves; and there are souls which drown themselves in sorrow. What a charming law, he says, which makes a soul abandon a pleasant thought when it is pricked by a needle. What a fine objection, rather, whose author does not see that it can be made against all the systems, and above all against his own. M. Bayle did much better in sparing me all objections of this kind, as he said from the start he would do.[64] Do we want to criticize God for having made things in such a way that moths get burnt in trying to warm themselves, and for having made our souls, to an extent, subject to the motions of bodies? Whether that happens because of a sudden influence or through a harmony pre-established in advance, it is still in conformity with the nature of things. Why should we demand that the soul's own nature should give it more perfection under the new system than God himself directly gives it according to the system of occasionalism? And is it not a great deal harder to say that God continually and by his immediate action subjects the soul to a disordered body than it is to say that the soul is subjected to it by its own corrupt nature? If in virtue of the laws of nature bodies sometimes destroy themselves when tending towards their own preservation, is the new system more responsible for that than the others are? It can still be said that the wisdom of God is never seen more clearly than in the system of harmony, where everything is connected together by reasons deriving from the natures of things, and never less so than in that of occasionalism, where everything is done forcibly by an arbitrary power.

The seventh difficulty brings out what has most shocked the wise

<hr />

[63] PB4, § 3.   [64] PB4, § 2.

author of these objections. It is that I attribute to created things a certain active nature, power, force, energy, distinct from the power of God. But in doing that, am I not doing what nearly all philosophers, the Church Fathers, and all theologians have always done? And to speak the truth, I don't understand the opposite view at all. If we act, we have the power to act; if we do not act, we do not sin either. If the opposite view were taken to extremes, it could lead us, without our realizing it, to a dangerous doctrine. Anyone who holds that God is the only one who acts could easily go on to say, like a much decried modern author,[65] that God is the only substance, and that created things are only transitory modifications. For up until now nothing has been a better test of substance than the power of action.

I count as the *eighth difficulty* what the author says about miracles. He wants to rescue his system from the imputation of perpetual miracles, but he doesn't explain very well what a 'miracle' is. M. Bayle failed in the same way. According to them, a miracle is only an exception to rules or general laws that God has arbitrarily established. So since God has made it a law or general rule always to attune the body to the soul and vice versa, there is therefore no miracle in it. In this sense a miracle differs from any other action of God only by an 'external denomination', that is to say, by its rarity. But I do not agree that such a rule would be a law of nature, nor that general laws of nature are purely arbitrary. There was no absolute necessity for God to establish them; but he was nevertheless led to do so by some reason, in accordance with his supreme wisdom, and by a certain suitability to the nature of things. Thus a miracle is an exception to those laws only if it is not explicable by the natures of things. And if God had resolved continually to bring into existence an event which was not in accordance with these natures, he would not thereby have made a law of nature, but would have resolved to produce a perpetual miracle, and always to interfere himself in order to produce what was beyond the forces of nature. And that is what would happen under the system of occasional causes, that is, if the soul and the body were always in agreement, but their natures, and what we can understand about them, did not produce that agreement; that is to say, if the automaton of the body did not lead it to do what the soul wanted, and if the natural sequence of the soul's confused perceptions did not lead

[65] Spinoza, *Ethics* I. 14.

it to represent what was happening in the body. But here is an easier example, which will clarify the difference between a law of nature and a general rule whose implementation depends on continual miracles. Suppose that God decreed a law according to which all free bodies, that is, those which were not prevented, had to tend of themselves to move in a circle around some centre, and, consequently, had to do this without its being possible for us to understand how and by what means it was done. I say that this law could not be implemented except by continual miracles, since it is not at all in accord with the nature of the motions of bodies, which is such that a body which is moving in a curved line will continue its movement, if it is free and nothing prevents it, along the straight tangent. Such a law of circular motion would not therefore be natural, assuming that the nature of bodies were such as it presently is. Thus, to avoid miracles, it is not sufficient that God should decree a certain law if he does not also give to created things a nature capable of carrying out his orders. It is as if someone were to say that God had ordained that the moon should move freely through the air or in the ether in a circle around the globe of the earth without there being any angel or intelligence which steered it, or any solid sphere which held it, or vortex or liquid sphere which carried it, or any heaviness (*pesanteur*), magnetism, or other mechanically explicable cause which stopped it from leaving the earth and going off along the tangent of the circle.[66] To deny that this would be a miracle would be to return to absolutely inexplicable occult qualities, which are so rightly decried today.

[66] Leibniz lists here the standard types of explanation of planetary motion. Examples of such theories can be found in: Aquinas, *Summa Theologica* 1a. 70. 3 (angels/intelligences); Aristotle, *De caelo*, 289b–290a, 293a5–10 (solid spheres); Descartes, *Principles of Philosophy*, 3. 25–33, 149 (vortex); Kepler, *Astronomia nova* (1609), introduction; Borelli, *Theoricae mediceorum planetarum* (1666), p. 51 (heaviness); Kepler, ibid. 3. 34, Gilbert, *De Mundo nostro sublunari philosophia* (1631) (magnetism).

7

Leibniz and Isaac Jaquelot

INTRODUCTION

Isaac Jaquelot (1647–1708) was Court Chaplain to the French colony in Berlin, where he met Leibniz in 1702. Over the next four years, when Leibniz was in Berlin or relatively nearby in Hanover or Wolfenbüttel, they discussed various matters, face to face or by letter, beginning with Jaquelot's interest in proofs of the existence of God. In a meeting on 21 March 1703 they must have touched on the notion of substance, for Jaquelot wrote the next day with various thoughts he had had on what Leibniz had said. Taking Leibniz to have defined matter as 'a substance which acts and which is acted on', he tried to show that acting and being acted on are contradictory, that matter is purely passive, and that the only active substance is mind.[1] Leibniz's reply of that same day reaffirmed his belief that everything in the mind develops out of its own nature and that this is true of all substances. Obviously referring to the 'New System', he says that this is 'as I have shown elsewhere in explaining the union of the soul with the organic body'.[2]

Replying with a barrage of questions and objections, Jaquelot said that on the matter of substantial force and activity, and pending further illumination from Leibniz, 'the system of a God who imprints on matter the motion which produces the effects that we see, seems to me much clearer and more consistent'. Also he asked where Leibniz had written about the union of the mind with an organic body. Was it in the Leipzig *Acta eruditorum*? How long ago? 'I have read nothing except something about pre-established harmony in M. Bayle's *Dictionary*.'[3] Leibniz replied[4] impatiently

---

[1] Jaquelot to Leibniz, Berlin, 22 Mar. 1703 (G 3. 454–6).
[2] See app. A.
[3] Jaquelot to Leibniz, 26 Mar. 1703 (G 3. 459–61).
[4] Leibniz to Jaquelot, n.d. (G 3. 461–2).

that it would take 'a book to clear up' all the questions Jaquelot had
thrown together, and 'an infinity of letters before we could agree'.
He suggested also that in saying he preferred the occasionalist
system Jaquelot had 'hardly understood' him: 'For I agree with that
system; but I believe that in developing it one will fall into mine,
provided that one assumes that God never acts miraculously, as the
occasionalists think he does, but only in a manner conformable to
the nature of things.' He did not, however, inform Jaquelot where
he could find the 'New System'.

Jaquelot evidently did some more reading on the matter in the
next months, for in February 1704 he wrote that he had taken the
opportunity afforded by confinement due to ill health to think
about pre-established harmony (J1). Some few days later Leibniz
addressed himself, point by point, to the difficulties which Jaquelot
had raised (J2). The following month Jaquelot compared Leibniz's
system with that of occasional causes, and concluded that the two
differed only in that Leibniz's has 'all the soul's ideas put into it
in advance, whereas in the system of occasional causes ideas
are produced only when they are occasioned by the physical
traces' (J3). Recurring to the point he had first raised a year earlier,[5]
he said that Leibniz's philosophy 'seems to me to destroy free will
entirely'.

Repeating a point he had made previously,[6] Leibniz patiently
replied that though he would be delighted to find that the occasionalists agree with him, they differ in holding that things are
brought about by a continual miracle and not as a consequence of
the natures of things (J4). What reason, furthermore, did Jaquelot
have for saying he denied free will? After all, 'everything that
happens in the soul follows from its nature, so voluntary actions
are done freely'. Moreover, they are no 'necessary consequence' of
the soul.

The question of free will continued to be a cause of disagreement
between them (J5, J6), even though Leibniz found entirely in
conformity with his own views,[7] the sketch of 'the little system that
I have devised for the human soul'[8] which Jaquelot sent him in May.

Later that year Jaquelot sent Leibniz a copy of his book *La
Conformité de la foi avec la raison*, which (with some changes) he

---

[5] Cf. n. 1.   [6] See the second paragraph of this introduction.
[7] Leibniz to Jaquelot, n.d. (G 3. 479).
[8] Jaquelot to Leibniz, Berlin, 6 May 1704 (G 3. 476).

published the next year, in 1705. This further prolonged the dispute over free will, for its appendix, 'Système abrégé de l'âme et de la liberté' (J7), criticizes the system of pre-established harmony on the grounds that it allows only for the illusion of freedom. Because Leibniz was now faced with the prospect of being accused *in print* of holding opinions potentially dangerous to religion, matters became even more heated.

He sent rather angry comments on this pre-publication copy of Jaquelot's 'Brief System' in September 1704 (J8).[9] Jaquelot replied in three letters, of 6 September (J9, on which Leibniz made some comments, as in J10), 7 September,[10] and 12 September (J11). Leibniz's answer, which develops his comments on J9 and also replies to the other two, is undated (J12).

The upshot of all this was withdrawal on Jaquelot's part. He made additions to his 'Brief System' which involved his moving from his first statement that Leibniz makes freedom into a 'pure illusion' to saying that, 'if . . . correctly understood', Leibniz 'can be seen as not destroying freedom'.[11] No doubt it was this volte-face

[9] It needs to be realized that what Leibniz read in 1704 was not the whole of the 'Brief System' as published in 1705. The published version (J7) quite evidently consists partly of what Leibniz must have read and commented on in 1704 (§§ 1–13) and partly of additional material which Jaquelot seems to have written in response to Leibniz's comments. A number of features of the piece and of Leibniz's comments point to this.

In the first place, in his comments on what Jaquelot had sent him, Leibniz refers (J8, § 6) to what Jaquelot claims 'at the end' about his system's being possible. This claim occurs only half-way through his piece as published (J7, § 13). In the second place, Leibniz's comments do not refer to anything later than this paragraph. In further support of the suggestion that paragraphs 14 ff. are a later addition, made in response to Leibniz's comments, is the fact that they are strikingly inconsistent with the previous ones. After 13 paragraphs of complaints about the inadequacies of the 'New System', Jaquelot suddenly switches to a very sound defence of it. As a consequence of this switch, Leibniz's rather angry reply, while wholly appropriate to the first 13 paragraphs of J7, is not really appropriate to J7 taken as a whole.

Finally, there is reason to think that Leibniz's initial angry assessment (in J8) of what Jaquelot said about him in the early draft of the first 13 §§ of J7 changed after the publication of the whole in 1705. For in December of that year, after the publication of Jaquelot's *Conformity of Faith and Reason*, Leibniz used a Latin translation of Jaquelot's 'Brief System' to explain his own system, quoting material partly before and partly after § 13. ('Observatio ad recensionem Libri de Fide et Rationis consensu, a Domino Jaqueleto . . .', *Acta eruditorum*, Dec. 1705 (R 168)). His doing this seems to show a very different reaction to it from that in J8.

[10] G 6. 563. Jaquelot talks in this letter mainly of his own views, and concludes by saying: 'I shall leave for another time discussion of M. Leibniz's own system, which seems to me little different from that of occasional causes.'

[11] J7, §§ 4, 14; see n. 9 for details concerning the additions.

that allowed the correspondence to continue,[12] albeit in ways which are of diminishing interest here.

J1. JAQUELOT: Letter to Leibniz, 2 February 1704[13]

I have, sir, considered your *pre-established harmony* more than once since being confined to my fireside by poor health; and there is no one I could better turn to than yourself in order to extricate me from the difficulties I find in it. Let us suppose that the body and the soul are indeed 'like *two clocks* (*pendules*, ? gender)', and so on. Then,

(1), did the creator give the soul the power of producing its own thoughts? Or does God produce thoughts immediately in the soul? The latter case will be the system of occasional causes, unless we are supposing that the soul has no relation at all with the body; whereas your opinion is that the soul has the power of producing its own thoughts.

(2), if the soul does produce its own thoughts, does it do it with the help, or at least in the presence, of bodily ideas?[14] Or does it produce them independently of such ideas, and without the necessity of any relation to them? If it is in the presence of such ideas, then we are back, or almost, with occasional causes. If it is with their help, we need to know how it is done, for it seems incomprehensible.

If the soul produces its thoughts independently of bodily ideas, and without the necessity of any relation to them, I ask

(1) how it is possible for the soul to form the ideas it has, without being stimulated to it by any object? That seems to me as great a miracle as the creation: to form the thought of an elephant without ever having seen an elephant is more than a miracle.

(2) Why is it that the soul in a 1-year-old child doesn't form thoughts, if to do so it has no need of the child's body? Does God keep the power of thought that he has given it inactive during this time?

---

[12] G 3. 480–2.   [13] From the French at G 3. 462–4.
[14] An 'idea' here—as the adjective 'bodily' (*corporelle*) indicates—is presumably something in the body rather than the soul (cf. Descartes, *Treatise on Man* (AT xi. 177)).

(3) Why is it that the soul forms foolish thoughts when the brain is disturbed by some emotion? If it acts independently of the brain and without any relation to it, why should the soul be unsettled in its thoughts because of some disturbance in the brain?

(4) Why is it that there are peoples as unruly as the Hottentots, etc.? Are their souls of another kind, incapable of producing a sequence of reasonable and well-connected thoughts?

(5) Why is it that there are bodily actions which seem always to have an effect on the soul—such as sounds, objects which catch the eye, and some lesser feelings of pain—but yet which make no impression when the soul is deeply occupied in thought? It seems that in such circumstances these bodily ideas are like shots which miss their targets, stray ideas which have neither consequence nor company in this harmony.

(6) If, in virtue of this harmony, bodily ideas always move in tandem with thoughts in the soul, why can we understand through the power of reasoning so many things of which we cannot form ideas in the imagination?

I do not mean to attack your opinion; I have no other aim than to understand it properly and to be better informed about your system.

J2. LEIBNIZ: Letter to Jaquelot, Wolfenbüttel, 9 February 1704[15]

Since you have been so good as to pass the time by thinking about my system, I will say to your *first question*, that I maintain that God gave the soul the power of producing its own thoughts. The Cartesians themselves, I think, allow this power to souls with regard to some of their thoughts, and I say the same about all of them. Indeed, according to me, the nature of each substance consists in this force, that is to say, in something which leadsit to change in accordance with its laws. It is true, however, that God concurs in everything by his continual preservation of beings. {And it is through him as a common cause that all substances agree. My system is a new proof of the existence of God, which shows at the same time that God's wisdom surpasses anything that we had previously understood.

[15] From the French at G 3. 464–6.

M. Bayle acknowledged in his Dictionary that here on earth we could not easily give a higher idea of it.}

To the second: The soul produces its thoughts in the presence of bodily ideas and not by their help or influence. And I would be delighted if the system of occasional causes could be explained in such a way as to make it compatible with mine.

To the third: The soul is stimulated to its next thoughts by its internal object, that is to say, by its preceding thoughts. For there is a sequence, or connection, as between moments of time. The miracle, or rather the marvel, is that each substance is a representation of the universe from its own point of view. This is the greatest richness and perfection that can be attributed to created things and to the operations of the Creator; it is like a reduplication of worlds in innumerable mirroring substances, by means of which the universe is infinitely varied. These simple substances, once they have begun, are all like separate little divinities, because as for an end, they have none. Now, sir, once we have established the point that the universe is represented in each monad, everything else follows, and your questions seem to answer themselves.

To the fourth: The reason why children do not form the thoughts of grown men is that the parallel between their thoughts and external phenomena is proportional to their bodies. This is a consequence of the harmony. However, souls are never inactive, and never without thoughts, although those thoughts are confused and obscure when the phenomena do not contain anything very striking or distinguished.

To the fifth: This natural harmony between thoughts and what happens in the organs of the body is also the cause of apparent disturbances of those thoughts. But at bottom, and taking the entire sequence of things together, nothing is really disturbed: the greatest disorders are corrected and compensated for with interest in the entire sequence of things.

To the sixth: The unruliness of certain people also comes from this relation between the soul and the body. For there is nothing in the soul which is not also expressed in the organs of the body. There are never two perfectly identical souls; indeed, they are completely different right from the start. For each soul is made so as to represent the universe in its own way. A Hottentot is not M. Descartes, nor Alexander the Great.

To the seventh: When sounds are not clearly distinguished, it must be that other well-distinguished things occupy our attention and blot them out. We must look to the organs of the body for an explanation of all lack of sensitivity and marks of imperfection in us, such as, for example, our slow progress in knowledge: for where we are passive and imperfect, we have been adapted by God, in regulating the universal harmony, to other things; and where we are active and have some perfection, other things have been adapted to us. However, we should not think of such small sounds which reach us but to which we do not pay attention as shots which miss their targets (*corps* [*sic*] = ? *coups*). Nothing misses its target, and everything that happens to us plays some part in what will happen to us.

To the eighth: There is always something in our imagination corresponding to our ideas, even those of immaterial things — consider symbols such as those in arithmetic and algebra, and also names. . . .

J3. JAQUELOT: Letter to Leibniz, 10 March 1704[16]

You have, sir, given me occasion to compare your view with that of occasional causes; and if I have understood it correctly, I find only a very small difference between them. To explain myself more clearly, I have drawn here two parallel lines which are to be joined; line A will be the soul and line C the body:

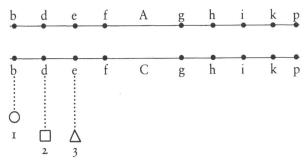

God imprinted the *ideas* marked b, d, e, f, etc. in the soul from the first, and he also imprinted physical *traces* in the body, C, in the

---

[16] From the French at G 3. 466–7.

same order: b, d, e, f. Those traces are related to objects in the universe, viz., b to object 1, d to object 2, e to object 3. In the union of the body with the soul which begins and ends at the same moment, we have something like these two parallel lines when they are joined at every point; thus b on line A corresponds to b on line C. In the body there is a physical *trace* of the circle 1, and in the soul the *idea* of that circle, and so on for the others. If that is so, then it seems to me that it necessarily follows that because he joined the *idea* of the circle, which is in the soul, to the physical *trace* of the same circle, which is in the body, God wanted the *idea* of the circle which is in the soul to correspond perfectly to the *trace* of the same circle which is in the body, in that they should begin and end at the same time. And as physical objects are not capable of acting immediately on the mind, God has to put *ideas* into it, but always in such an order that they correspond perfectly to the physical *traces*. Isn't that, sir, a proof of occasional causes? The only difference I can see is that you have all the soul's ideas put into it in advance, whereas in the system of occasional causes ideas are produced only when they are occasioned by the physical traces. To my mind the biggest problem that I have with this philosophy is that it seems to me to destroy free will entirely; and I am as certain of my liberty as I am of my existence. . . .

J4. LEIBNIZ: Letter to Jaquelot, n.d.[17]

As I have already said to you, sir,[18] I would be delighted if the authors of occasional causes have the same view as I have. We agree that the soul and the body correspond, although they perhaps do not hold that quite as generally as I. But the difference is that, according to them, things are done by miracle, inasmuch as God is constantly adjusting the soul to the body, and the body to the soul; whereas, according to me, everything which happens normally in the universe is natural, and happens as a consequence of the nature of things, so that one of these substances adjusts itself to the other by its own nature. According to the occasionalists, when God wants the body to follow the wishes of the soul, he is forced to violate the laws of corporeal nature at every moment, by changing

[17] From the French at G 3. 467–9.
[18] In J2; see also the second paragraph of the introduction.

the direction of the flow of animal spirits. I, on the other hand, think that the physical world is so skilfully made that the body, by its own laws, responds to what the soul asks; and that the same is true of the soul, which is naturally representative of the body. The physical world is like a machine which plays tunes, just as though a skilful player were playing on it.

You do not say, sir, just how my system destroys free will. Everything that happens in the soul follows from its nature, so voluntary actions are done freely, even though he who knows everything knows what it will do, and adjusts bodies to it in advance. So these free actions accord with bodily laws, because bodies are prepared for them. And although the soul's present actions are a natural and certain consequence of its preceding state, they are not a necessary consequence. It is like the way in which the knowledge of the greatest good makes us choose it, by inclining the soul but not necessitating it.

J5. JAQUELOT: Letter to Leibniz, 25 April 1704[19]

... I must tell you quite simply that your system seems to me entirely to destroy the liberty that we know and feel within ourselves. First, with regard to the soul. If the ideas that it will have in time are all as it were implicit in it from the first instant of its creation, what freedom can it have in something which already exists, and to which it has not contributed in any way? *Habuit se ut merum subjectum et mere passive.*[20] Second, if you appeal to the absolute decrees of which some theologians speak, you know very well, sir, that all the early Fathers, as well as most modern theologians, base decrees concerning that sort of thing on God's foreknowledge. Third, even if you make ideas come into being at the instant that they are actually produced, as do the philosophers who advocate occasional causes, you do not thereby any the less destroy liberty. Fourth, because, according to you, movements of the body happen necessarily, by the determination of objects; it is not in the power of man either to suspend them, alter them, or change them. For example, if the movement of my hand necessarily determines

---

[19] From the French at G 3. 469–71.
[20] 'it behaved as a pure subject and purely passively'.

me to write to you, and my soul has no control over that movement but only knowledge of it, I do not at all see how I have any liberty. And yet I feel that at every instant I have the power to stop myself and to put down my pen. Fifth, a comment, if you please, on this feeling. Is it false, or genuine? If it is true, then I have the power to stop the animal spirits which make my hand move. If it is false, how does it arise, and in what way is it false? If I am necessarily determined by this movement of spirits which it is not in my power to suspend, I have no liberty at all. Suppose I could see them arrive; it would be like watching a cannon-ball that was coming to carry me off. Isn't that contrary both to our understanding and to our experience?

Sixth, this idea that I now have that I am writing to you, was it yesterday, unknown to me, already implicit in my soul, or did it come into being only at the moment that it began to appear? You must say the first. But we obviously cannot have liberty in something that already exists.

Seventh, were these animal spirits which are now making me write already determined yesterday to do what they do today, as the water of the Spree, which yesterday was seven miles above here, was determined to flow today under the bridge at Berlin? Where would the liberty be? In short, sir, *I think therefore I am; I do what I want, therefore I am free*; to my mind these two propositions are equally clear. . . .

J6. LEIBNIZ: Letter to Jaquelot, Hanover, 28 April 1704?[21]

[1] It seems to me, sir, very easy to reply to the difficulties that you find with my theory. Far from its being inconsistent with liberty, I believe that on the contrary there is no system in which true liberty, that is to say, spontaneity with choice, or independence of the soul from everything except God, is more apparent. This kind of objection was the last thing I expected. The liberty of indetermination or perfectly balanced indifference can play no part in the matter: it is a chimerical notion, which contravenes the great principle of reason, and which I take you to reject, sir, from what I learned when I had the honour of talking to you. There is always a

greater inclination in things towards what will happen, than towards any other outcome, but it does not impose any necessity. And although this prevailing inclination has the effect of predetermining the future, as in fact everything is predetermined in this way, it does not endanger contingency in things, or liberty in minds: and that is all that pre-established harmony means.

[2] But to come to your objections. First, if the ideas that the soul will have in time are all implicit in it from the first instant of its creation, what freedom can it have in something which already exists, and to which it has not contributed in any way? *Habuit se ut merum subjectum et mere passive.* I reply: although all future things are implicit in the soul, it is not thereby any the less free; for all of the future is in God's understanding, but that doesn't take away liberty. In the second place, future things are implicit in the soul far less than they are in God, because they are in the soul clearly only in an inclining and confused fashion, and not expressly and perfectly as in the Divine ideas. And in the third place, the soul certainly did not contribute to its original constitution, but it will contribute to the actions which arise from it in the course of time. *Habuit se mere ut subjectum* in receiving its being, *sed non habebit se mere ut subjectum, imo concurret active* its actions when they happen.[22]

[3] Second, I do not remember having appealed to the theologians' absolute decrees. For I do not think that there are any decrees of God which do not have reasons for their choice, even if they are unknown to us. You add that most modern theologians base God's decrees on his foreknowledge; but as the objects of his foreknowledge also depend on him, in the end we have to come back to the choice that he makes of the best out of all possibles, a choice which is independent of his foreknowledge of what will actually happen.

[4] Third, you say, sir, that even if I made the ideas or perceptions of the soul come into being at the instant that they are produced, as do the proponents of occasional causes, I would not thereby any the less destroy liberty. Do you then think, sir, that those authors destroy it? But why would I destroy it, since what is voluntary and free in our actions always depends on choice? And although this choice has *reasons*, existing from all time, these are *inclining* reasons, not *necessitating* ones.

---

[22] 'It behaved purely as a subject in receiving its being, but it will not behave purely as a subject, but will actively engage in its actions when they happen'.

[5] Fourth, you say, sir, that according to me the movements of bodies, for example, those of my arm, happen necessarily, and it is not in my power to change them. Where, then, is liberty? *I reply* that liberty is in me, and not in the movements of bodies. However free I am, God always knew what I would choose, and was able to accommodate bodies to it in advance. Please tell me where the problem is, whatever conception of liberty you may have. You could have chosen to put your pen down. Who doubts that? But God knew that you wouldn't.

[6] Fifth, I am determined (you say, sir) by this movement of animal spirits in a way which it is not in my power to suspend. Suppose I could see them arrive; it would be like watching a cannon-ball that was coming to carry me off. *Reply*: The animal spirits do not determine you: to look and see that would be to see the impossible. Your choice and judgement determine you. And your judgement, foreseen by God, made him determine these spirits in advance to obey you at the appropriate time.

[7] Sixth, this idea (you say, sir) that I now have that I am writing to you, was it yesterday, unknown to me, already implicit in my soul? Yes. But then there is no liberty in something that already exists. *Reply*: It was not something which already existed, but something which was going to exist. The future is in the past only as an inclination in that past towards the production of the future.

[8] Seventh, finally you ask, sir, if these animal spirits which are now making you write were already determined the day before to do what they do today. Yes, they were determined; but it is not they that are making you write, although they are enabling you to.

[9] Your conclusion is that these two propositions, *I think, therefore I am*, and *I do what I want, therefore I am free*, are equally clear. Yes, sir, I whole-heartedly agree; and I add that I mean a liberty which is free not only from coercion, but also from necessity.

J7. JAQUELOT: 'A Brief System of the Soul and Freedom' (1705) (Appendix to *The Conformity of Faith with Reason, or The Defence of Religion against the Principal Difficulties Detailed in M. Bayle's Historical and Critical Dictionary*)[23]

[1] . . . Man's freedom, or the employment of his will, will be still more apparent if we consider its power over the body in free actions which are of no importance. If I consider all those bodily movements which are subject to my will, and which I can produce whenever and however I want—such as, for example, opening or closing my eyes, speaking or keeping quiet, standing up or sitting down, walking or keeping still, raising or lowering my arm, opening or closing my hand (I am assuming here that the body is in good health)—if, I say, we consider all these movements, we know in ourselves, and we feel, that the will controls them all, and directs them as it pleases—just as you can direct a stone which you hold in your hand by throwing it, if you want, and by throwing it either to the right or to the left.

[2] I accept that it is very difficult to understand how this happens. The famous M. Leibniz holds that the body is like a machine set up so as to carry out all the movements which it makes, and that the soul is like a substance which contains all the ideas which, in the course of time, will develop in an appropriate manner corresponding to the movements of the body. This means that when I want to move my arm, it comes about that my arm moves in virtue of the state of the mechanism, which is set up so as to move it at that moment. Thus the body and the soul are, in their movements, almost like two identical clocks (*pendules*, f.) which swing in parallel and exactly in time.

[3] Those who support occasional causes say that the union of the soul with the body means that, given certain movements, God forms certain ideas in the soul, and given this or that act of will, God produces this or that movement in the body. M. Leibniz is not of this opinion, because this theory involves continual miracles.

---

[23] *La Conformité de la foi avec la raison, ou défense de la religion contre les principales difficultés répandues dans le 'Dictionnaire . . .' de M. Bayle* (Amsterdam, 1705), pp. 380–90.

[4] The usual system is mid-way between these two opinions, both of which seem to have very serious problems. First, it seems that in M. Leibniz's system freedom is a *pure illusion*, since the soul and the body are directed by an effective antecedent cause to do everything that they do, whether thoughts or actions. Strictly speaking, that is nothing but the unfolding of what is encapsulated and concealed. For example, I believe that I move my arm freely, by a voluntary act. But that is not so if the machine is set up so as to move just at that instant; it is then, at most, only the willing of an effect which does indeed happen, but of which strictly speaking the will is not the cause. I think I do by my will what in fact I do not do: is that not an illusion? Because ultimately my soul was determined to that act of will, and my body to that movement.

[5] The system of occasional causes has even more difficulty, since in this system God does everything, and created things are only vain shadows, or inactive beings. What would become of virtue and vice? Should we believe that at the sight of Bathsheba God produced ideas of lust in the soul of David?[24] And that God imprinted the blasphemous ideas against the Holy Spirit in the souls of the Pharisees at the sight of the demons which J. Christ drove out of the bodies of the possessed?[25] Whatever evasions we may employ, whatever subtlety we might use, ultimately the question always comes back to that.

[6] That is why the usual system teaches that we can and must avoid these two terrible and dangerous extremes, by attributing to created things the power or faculty of acting in accordance with their natures. Would God, who gave them their being and their existence, have produced only motionless lumps, entirely incapable of action or of movement? That does not accord with reason, which teaches us that he who was able to give being was therefore also able along with it to give the faculty of movement. Being is more than action, and in good philosophy what can do the greater can also do less. The wisdom of the creator would not permit him to form created beings so imperfect that they were incapable of action. Moreover, the idea which Moses gives us of the creation and of the blessings of God teaches us that God, by his blessing, imparts the power of action; or rather, that he blesses the use which created beings make of their faculties.

[7] From that it obviously follows that since God united the soul

---

[24] 2 Sam. 11.   [25] Matt. 12. 22–37.

to the body to compose *man*, and since he also wanted the soul to direct the body in free human action, he must have conferred on the soul the power of controlling the body on those occasions.

[8] But, it will be said, it is not possible to understand how a mind can act on a body by its will. I agree; but the fact of it is none the less certain. If I suddenly want to recall the idea of an elephant I once saw, I do it straightaway. If I want to raise my hand, I raise it. Moreover, since God acts through his own will—as those of whom we are speaking will agree—why should he not have been able to confer on *my* will the power of action? It might be objected that it is because of his infinite powers that God can act through his will; I reply that God can give my will the power of action without giving it his infinite power, because my will acts immediately only on my body, and even then only in certain actions which are subject to that power, so that whatever force my will can have is infinitely removed from the infinite might of God.

[9] If we grant that, the problems we encountered with the other systems disappear in this one of their own accord. Here we find an accurate account of created beings, which fits with all that we see them do, and which is entirely in keeping with their strength and their nature. We no longer have any difficulty over its postulating free created beings capable of laws, of virtues and vices, of punishment and reward. The world is no longer a magic theatre which deceives the eyes and the mind, as we might conclude from the system of occasional causes, in which we think we see in action beings which are quite incapable of it. It is good to see principles which fit in with the feeling we have of what happens in us, when our bodies move by the operation of our will.

[10] Suppose that we are aware of a human body in a state of activity. The animal spirits in its brain can be thought of as like the water in a tank, about to form various different patterns, according as it runs through different nozzles. Now, we do not think it necessary to regard these nozzles as always open, and to think that the soul, when I want to move my arm, merely knows about and approves of the spirits which run along the arm so as to move it. Instead, we think it is more accurate, and more in keeping with what we feel and experience in ourselves, to regard the nozzles, or the valves and sluices, as being closed, so as to prevent the spirits from flowing at random, until the soul comes to apply itself to the direction of the body. Instead, we should think of the soul as the

fountain-keeper, who opens and closes the nozzles as he chooses, so as to make the water run the way he wants. In so doing, we attribute to the soul the power to open and close the valves of the brain when it wants. Would God have been unable to give it that power?

[11] I think we can also glimpse the truth of this in the convulsive movements of an arm; for how does it come about that the soul has neither the knowledge nor the approval necessary to make those movements free, if not because it knows that the control of those movements is not in its power?

[12] However that may be, we can say that this power that we attribute to the soul in its dependence on God seems to be the one and only thread which can lead us out of the labyrinth in which the other systems have involved us, and have got us lost.

[13] Moreover, as the other two theories necessarily involve the infinite power of the Creator, and since the system we are supposing is just as possible as the other two, it is even more appropriate that we should accept it, given that it fits in with the experience and that the feeling we have of what goes on in us.

[14] However, if M. Leibniz's thought and systems are correctly understood, they can be seen as not destroying freedom, because the soul has the power to take decisions, and to choose what it wants.

[15] With regard to the actions of the body over which the authority of the soul extends, the disposition of the body, which is arranged by God in such a way that its movements correspond precisely to the wishes of the soul, does not prejudice our freedom at all.

[16] To see this clearly, we can use this example: let us imagine that a skilled engineer knows what orders I want to give to my servant on a certain day of the year, and that he can make an automaton capable of performing all the movements necessary to carry out the orders that I will give on that day. It is clear that if you present me on that day with this automaton, I will order it to perform its actions with all the freedom with which I am blessed, and that the fact that its movements are determined does not in any way threaten that freedom.

[17] It is the same with the body of a man in M. Leibniz's system, which has been called the system of a *pre-established harmony*.

[18] God has made our bodies like machines which must comply

with certain wishes of our souls. Such an automaton is not at all impossible for God, who knows from all time all the decisions of my will, and who has adapted the movements of the machine to those decisions.

[19] This system is exempt from the problems which we see in the others. In the ordinary system it is incomprehensible how the will can operate on the body; and in the system of occasional causes, everything happens by miracle. God moves my arm on the occasion of my will: strictly speaking, the body does nothing, whereas in M. Leibniz's system it is genuinely active.

[20] As regards the soul, we can understand that in creating it God could have given it confused, undeveloped ideas of all the objects in the universe, and that because God created the soul and the body to be together in a perfect correspondence, these ideas develop and become distinct in proportion as those objects produce some change in the body to which it is joined.

[21] The soul then acts within itself, operating on these ideas and distinct perceptions, in order to make its judgements and form its intentions and decisions according to the choices which it makes. It gives orders, and the body follows those orders in virtue of the disposition it has received from the Creator.

[22] I therefore conclude that if it is conceivable that the soul could operate on the body by its own power, by means of some influence which can set it in motion, then we should follow the ordinary system. It is simpler and more self-contained than the others. We can even cite the example of the Creator, who created and conserves the universe by his will.

[23] But if we want to be consistent with the ideas we have of bodies and of minds, and of their respective attributes, so that we cannot allow a mind to operate on a body, nor a body on a mind, then we have to decide on the system of M. Leibniz, because the system of occasional causes is nothing but a perpetual illusion.

J8. LEIBNIZ: Letter to Jaquelot, Berlin, 4 September 1704[26]

Comment on the Appendix to M. Jaquelot's Treatise on the Conformity of Faith and Reason, which is entitled: A Brief System of the Soul and Freedom.

[26] From the French at G 6. 558–60.

[1] I did not think, sir, that I had given you any reason to talk about my theory in terms which could be harmful to me, as involving some illusion, and having dangerous consequences. I am the enemy of 'illusions'; I like to speak clearly and precisely. I defy anyone to specify one genuine characteristic of freedom which I do not explain and elucidate, and to present a system which would better satisfy all the goals of religion and morality.

[2] But according to me the soul and the body are directed (you say) by an effective antecedent cause to do everything that they do; where then is freedom? I reply that they are directed to do what they do only by their own natures—the soul freely and from choice, in accordance with real or apparent good or bad, and the body blindly, in accordance with the laws of motion.

[3] Again, you object that according to me the actions of the soul are nothing but the unfolding of what is encapsulated and concealed. But again I reply that this encapsulation should not be overstated. The encapsulation of the future is not always contrary to freedom. Isn't all of the future encapsulated in the ideas and understanding of God, and indeed in a perfectly precise manner? Yet we accept that this does not make future contingencies necessary. Now, everything that is distinct in the mind of God is confused and imperfect in our own. Thus our future actions are in us, but only as a kind of inclination, which carries no necessity with it, even though from the point of view of God it is certain.

[4] I have also pointed out to you,[27] sir, that strictly speaking it is neither the foreknowledge of God, nor his decision, that determines the sequence of things, but the *mere comprehension* of possibles in the divine understanding; or the idea of this world, seen as a possibility prior to the decision to choose and create it. It is therefore the nature of things themselves which produces their sequence, prior to all decisions; God chooses only to actualize that sequence, the possibility of which he finds ready-made. Thus all that was needed was a single decision, subsequent to that sequence, merely to establish the choice of this possible world out of an infinity of others. This possible world, therefore, which has been actualized and has come to exist, is also encapsulated, though confusedly, in each mind created in imitation of the divine understanding, where it is encapsulated distinctly. But things exist in the understanding, both of God and of all others, in a way which

[27] J6, § 2.

represents them accurately and in conformity with their natures: free ones as free, and blind, mechanical ones as mechanical. Thus this encapsulation is not harmful in any way. The sequence of things of this world is already eternally settled when considered as a pure possibility, when it is *objectum simplicis intelligentiae divinae*,[28] before any consideration of the decision which actualizes it — just as the properties of a circle and of a parabola are similarly settled. But there is this difference, that the relation between the properties and essences of geometrical figures is necessary, whereas the connection between the nature of the soul and its free actions, which is to be found in the ideas of the possibles, is contingent, although settled and certain.

[5] I believe I move my arm (you say), but that is not so if the machine is set up so as to move it at just that instant. I reply that that is so, and is not so, depending on how we understand the words, and on whether to our cost we believe more than we feel, and more than we should believe, by imagining physical influences where there are none. Do we not also believe, if not corrected by reason, that heat in water is something absolute and determinate, which everyone must feel as we do, and that the sun is only a few feet in diameter, and the heavens move, and a thousand other illusions and prejudices which come from misunderstanding our senses, and from ill-disciplined habits of mind? What truth and accuracy there is in the proposition 'I think I moved my arm' consists in this: 'I truly think that when I want my arm to be moved, it is moved' — and indeed moved by a kind of dependence which the body has on me, as a result of my nature's prevailing over it. And that is what we can, and should, call action between created things, even if it is the immediate influence of God which puts it into operation, or if such dependence comes from the connections between ideas. And in day-to-day life, what can I, or should I, ask beyond the achievement of my desires? Anything which goes beyond that is a theory or hypothesis, which is in need of proof, and in common prejudices it is *sophisma non causae ut causae*.[29] There is therefore no deception or 'illusion' here, other than what comes from our mistakes and from the hastiness of many of our judgements.

---

[28] 'an object of the pure divine understanding'.
[29] Aristotle, *De sophisticis elenchis*, 167b20–37, discusses 'the sophism of taking what is not a cause as a cause'.

[6] I shall content myself here with defending my opinion against accusations which seem to me unjust, and I do not intend here to attack your own view, which is the more commonly accepted one. I will only add, sir, that at the end you claim that your opinion is possible;[30] but that certainly cannot be accepted. The soul cannot have this immediate power of turning on the fountains of the animal spirits, and to attribute that power to it is just like attributing to matter the faculty of thinking, an opinion which you yourself deny.

J9. JAQUELOT: Letter to Leibniz, 6 September 1704[31]

[1] I will, sir, if I may, make some observations on your comments. First: When I speak of 'illusions' and of 'dangerous consequences', it is not in relation to your intentions; if something of the kind did slip out, I apologize for it. My intention was only to express the way in which I understand this system, so that, if I am mistaken, the terms 'illusions' and 'dangerous consequences' apply only to me, and to my ignorance. I call our belief that we do something an 'illusion' because strictly speaking we do nothing more than merely notice what is going on in us. And what follows from that suggestion I call 'dangerous consequences'.

[2] To justify my position, I will employ here only your own principle: out of many possible worlds which God knew '*simplici intelligentia*',[32] he chose this one, and by that choice or that decision he gave this world its reality and its existence. 'It is therefore', you say, 'the nature of things themselves which produces their sequence, prior to all decisions.'[33] Let me remark here, sir, that in my opinion we must distinguish between physical and spiritual beings. The former operate necessarily and blindly according to their nature, and certainly that nature produces the sequence of things prior to the decision as to their existence; whether a triangle exists or does not exist, its properties are still the same. But it is not the same, in my opinion, with free, intelligent spiritual beings, because they are

---

[30] J7, § 13.
[31] From the French at G 6. 561–3. Some notes which Leibniz made on this letter are signalled in the text by the superscripts A, B, C, . . . , and given in J10.
[32] 'by pure understanding'.   [33] J8, § 4.

capable of good and evil, and so can produce right or wrong actions without being necessarily determined by their natures to either the one or the other.^A

[3] I return to your world which God knows *simplici intelligentia*, and I apply it to spiritual beings. God knows *simplici intelligentia* the various decisions which Adam or David could have taken when exposed to temptation. It was possible^B that they would resist the temptation, or that they would succumb to it. Between these two intelligible worlds of spirits, which were both possible, God chose this one, and by that choice or that decision he gave to it its existence and all its reality, as he did with the physical world. Are we not then right to conclude^C that this decision, which produces reality and existence, is the effective antecedent cause of all human actions, and that as a result there is no longer any freedom? You say 'that they are directed to do what they do only by their own natures'.³⁴ ᴰ I am sorry, but their nature considered in itself, or in the world of possibles, was capable of good and of evil,^E and it was determined to evil only by the choice which God made, and by an effective decision which gave to it all the reality it possesses. If God had wanted to choose^F a soul of Adam which resisted the temptation and did its duty, he would have chosen to give reality to that soul. There, sir, you see what makes me fear there are dangerous consequences.^G You will see in the Treatise which I hope you will be good enough to read, and which I beg you not to pass on to anyone, how I see the matter: I shall say nothing of it here.

[4] In reply to what I say about our knowledge of the power we have in ourselves to move our arms when we want to, you say that we make mistakes in many other things, such as believing that heat is in water, and so on. However, not to mention that we are not mistaken about the main point, which is that the water causes the sensation we have, I must say that there is a great difference between what happens outside us, and what happens inside, in the province of our consciousness and reflection. That I should be mistaken in the judgements I make about things outside of me^H is not surprising: but that in things which I feel, which I know distinctly by reflection on myself and by continuous experience, such as the power I have of moving my arm^I when I want to; if, I say, I could be mistaken in this knowledge, I would have no

³⁴ J8, § 2.

certainty[J] that *I am because I think.* So this is not a theory which stands in need of proof, nor a sophism *a non causa ut causa.*[35] In fact, I do not see that in your system we can give any more freedom to men than to animals . . . , if we allow them the slightest consciousness, because they have complete 'spontaneity'.[K]

[5] What is the point, sir, of throwing oneself into this abyss,[L] instead of giving to created things, and in particular to free beings, the power to act within their dependence on God, and with his concourse? You say that you cannot accept that it is possible for the will to act on the body, and that it is as if one were to attribute the power of thought to matter. I do not see, sir, that it is the same thing: matter at no point connects with thought,[M] yet the will is joined to the body by its desire to move.[N] Why is it a contradiction that God should give it the ability to fulfil that desire?[O] Indeed, I cannot conceive that God should have been able to give being to created things, and yet he should not have been able to communicate to them the ability to act.[P] What would be the good of all the organs[Q] we find in animals? Is it not, after all, more in keeping with the wisdom of God to think of created things,[R] especially those which are free, as having the faculty of action, rather than thinking of them as incapable of all activity?[S] And what is more, the communication of motion from one body to another seems to me as difficult[T] as the influence of the will on the body.

J10. LEIBNIZ: Notes on Jaquelot's letter of 6 September 1704[36]

A. '. . . or the other': I quite agree. And neither are they necessarily determined in the possible world which does contain them, but which contains them as they are, that is to say, free.

B. 'It was possible': The possible world which God chose contained the whole sequence of things, both free and not free; and in it God saw Adam's not resisting temptation, because otherwise it would be a different world. He saw in it everything which, after having chosen it, he sees by his foreknowledge. God did not choose that Adam should give way to temptation, but he did choose this world, which contained, among other things, his giving way to temptation.

C. 'Are we then not right to conclude': Not at all. This possible world contains Adam's freely choosing for himself.

---

[35] See n. 29.   [36] From the French at Grua, pp. 489–91.

D. 'You say "that they are directed to do what they do only by their own natures"': Those are my words.

E. 'Their nature ... was capable of good and of evil': It was capable of both in the absolute, but in the possible world which God chose there was contained its freely deciding on evil.

F. 'If God had wanted to choose': Then he would have chosen a different world.

G. 'There, sir, you see what makes me fear there are dangerous consequences': That is because you had not paid attention to what I had said. And, moreover, you did not then know, sir, what I have now said[37] about my opinion on possible worlds, which you did not take at all as I intended it. The possible world which God chose contained, before his decision to choose it, everything that is now contained in his foreknowledge, whereas you take it that God determined by his choice something more than the existence of this particular series.

H. 'That I should be mistaken in the judgements I make about things outside of me [such as the power I have to move my arm]': The movement of your arm is outside of your soul. [See also J12, § 7.]

I. 'But ... moving my arm': It moves when you want it to; that is enough, and that is all you know. [See also J12, § 7.]

J. '... I would have no certainty': How does this follow? It is clearly not possible that you should think and not be; but it is certainly possible that you should have no physical influence over bodies. God in his omnipotence could make either my system or that of occasional causes true, but he couldn't make it true that you think without being. [See also J12, § 8.]

K. '... they have complete "spontaneity"': There are degrees of spontaneity, and in us there is choice. [See also J12, § 9.]

L. '... this abyss': I cannot understand what abyss you are thinking of. I have challenged you to show me any advantage for man with respect to freedom that I do not allow for, and you merely repeat your accusations without responding. [See also J12, § 10.]

M. '... matter at no point connects with thought': Does the soul connect with the body? [See also J12, § 12.]

[37] See J8, § 4, which replies to the pre-publication draft of the 'Brief System'.

N. '. . . the will is joined to the body by its desire to move': That is novel. Can things be joined together by desire? Not to mention the fact that there is no such desire: the soul desires that the body should move, and that is what happens. [See also J12, § 13.]

O. 'Why is it a contradiction that God should give it the ability to fulfil that desire?': There is no such desire. But I do not deny that it would be possible for God to do it by a miracle.

P. '. . . the ability to act': Have I ever said that God could not give created things the ability to act? [See also J12, § 11.]

Q. 'What would be the good of all the organs?': A curious question. What is the good of there being other created things apart from me? [See also J12, § 15.]

R. '. . . created things': Especially those which are free. [See also J12, § 16.]

S. '. . . incapable of all activity': Who ever said this? [See also J12, § 16.]

T. '. . . as difficult': There is no comparison. [See also J12, § 17.]

J11. JAQUELOT: Letter to Leibniz, 12 September 1704[38]

[1] We ask why from such and such thoughts in the soul there follows such and such a movement of the body, and vice versa.

[2] According to the system of occasional causes, the answer is that God produces those thoughts or those movements when such and such objects are present.

[3] According to the system of 'pre-established harmony', we say that God forms the soul with all its thoughts encapsulated in it, corresponding to objects and to all the movements of the body. All the movements of the body then follow one another just like the movements of a machine set up so as to produce them, so that the thoughts correspond exactly to the movements, and the movements to the thoughts.

[4] It seems to me that the difference between these two systems is very slight. To explain more clearly what I want to say, I will distinguish between the first moment of the union of the soul with

[38] From the French at G 6. 565–7.

the body and the succeeding moments in the life of the man. In the first moment we have the cause, and in the succeeding ones the effects.

[5] With regard to that first moment, we can easily see that the two systems are in agreement, because in the system of occasional causes we have to accept that there then exists a certain intention on God's part, such that on the occasion of such and such a thought he will produce a certain movement, and so on, so that in virtue of this promise, or agreement, it follows that a certain thought in the soul will coincide with a certain movement of the body. Both sides are in agreement: in the one system we say that God will produce these things, and in the other we suppose that they have already been produced but in an imperfect and undeveloped form. (And it must indeed be the case that the hatred I shall feel tomorrow for a person I love today is extremely incomplete and undeveloped; and in the same way the movements of my body which I shall need to make tomorrow when I am walking must be very different from the state my body is in today when I am sitting down or asleep.)

[16] There must therefore be some new production. What will be the cause of it? Both sides agree that it is the will of God. Will this be a new act of will, or the same act which is now coming into effect? I see no difference here except in the manner of expression, since on both sides there was established from the beginning the intention to make a certain thought always accompany a certain movement, and vice versa.

[7] For example, God made this earth to last 6,000 years. Isn't it true that every instant that it lasts is an effect of that first act of will, without there being any need to suppose another? I think the proponents of occasional causes would have no objection to their system's being explained in this kind of way. And I do not see that any more or less than that need be said according to the system of harmony. . . . And if the theory of occasional causes is sometimes presented otherwise, the difference can only be in regard to the working-out of this first act of God's will—what we ought to say about the development of our thoughts in relation to such and such movements.

[8] There are no more miracles in this than in the conservation of the universe. Let us suppose that God had encapsulated in the soul of man the thought or intention to raise five or six men from the dead. There would be no miracle in the development of that thought:

it would be like any other—the miracle would be in the bodies, which are not naturally disposed that way. Thus, so far as the ordinary actions to which bodies are disposed are concerned, no miracle is involved in the union of which man is composed, because there is no need to suppose any other act of will on God's part than the first one, which established their union under such and such conditions.

[9] In order to explain what freedom consists in, I think that, given that the soul can act within itself, and can reflect, all we need to say is that the soul takes such and such decisions in itself, since it has power over its own actions, and that God, having *foreseen* such and such decisions, has adjusted the body so as to carry them out. If we admit that, then I no longer see any difficulty for morality or religion.

J12. LEIBNIZ: Letter to Jaquelot, n.d.[39]

[1] I am astonished, sir, that you persist in interpreting my views quite differently from the way that I explained them. You claim that according to me 'we do nothing more than merely notice what is going on in us'. I don't know where you get this from. For myself, I hold that *we produce* everything that happens in us.

[2] You also want to hold me to account for views which are common to all systems, when you argue that the decision of God (in creating the world) which gives reality and existence to a possible world is the effective antecedent cause of all human actions, and that there is therefore no freedom. But you will have to address yourself to all theologians with this objection, because this decision of God's is the effective antecedent cause of actions just as much for all of them as it is for me. And all of them will answer as I do: that the creation of substances and the concurrence of God in the reality of human action, which are the effects of his decision, certainly do not amount to a *necessary determination*.

[3] I also do not understand, sir, how you can take it upon yourself to say that 'the choice which God makes to create this or

---

[39] From the French at G 6. 567–73. Leibniz notes that the letter replies to three from Jaquelot (6 (= J9), 7 and 12 (= J11) Sept. 1704). [§ 1] relates to J9, § 1; [§§ 2–9] to J9, § 3; [§§ 10–17] to J9, § 5; [§ 19] to J11. As we have omitted the second of these three letters, so we have omitted that part of Leibniz's reply which relates to it.

that being determines them to evil'. From that it would follow that according to all theologians God is the cause of sin. Have you ever seen objections which should concern me less?

[4] You also object that God, as a result of this choice, 'gives created beings all their reality'. But who can doubt that? Don't all theologians agree that realities (positive ones, that is) or perfections, which exist in both good and evil and which constitute the raw materials of sin, all come equally from God? The form (*formel* [*sic*]) of sin is a voluntary privation of the relevant perfection, and that voluntary privation comes only from us.

[5] You say that the main or most important point is that the body (for example, the hot water) causes a sensation in us, that is to say, since that is what we are talking about, by an immediate physical influence. But in saying that, aren't you taking as given exactly what is in question? Why should that chimera or false invention of the scholastics (because ordinary people will have none of it when it is explained to them) be any more important than the fancy of those same scholastics that the heat that we feel is an absolute entity, and not a phantom depending partly on our own constitution at the time?

[6] We don't make mistakes (you say again) about things which are inside us; and from that you conclude that we are not mistaken in thinking that we move our arms by an immediate physical influence. But are the arm and its movements inside us? Moreover, although we do not make mistakes about what we feel inside ourselves, we can make mistakes about what we *believe* to be inside us. We do not feel this influence, but the scholastic philosopher believed in it. Do we not sometimes think that we are awake when we are dreaming? There again, our hasty judgements mislead us with respect to what is inside us.

[7] I have (you say) continuous experience that I move my arm when I want to. But your experience teaches you only that your arm is moved when you want it to be, and nothing more. It doesn't tell you that it happens by an immediate physical influence of your soul on your arm.[40]

[8] You go on to say that if there is an error in this judgement, you will have no certainty that you are because you think. How

---

[40] Jaquelot doesn't actually say it happens by an immediate, physical influence, and in fact denies it in his letter of 7 Sept. 1704—as Leibniz recognizes in that part (omitted here) of his letter which replies to this.

does that follow? And how can you assert it without argument? Surely you must admit that my system, and also that of occasional causes, is at least possible for God, and therefore that it could be that our arms move in accordance with our will without such an influence. But it is not possible that God should bring it about that I can think without existing. So do not confuse such very different things.

[9] And how can you go so far as to say, without even offering an argument, that according to my system animals have as much freedom as men? Do I say that they choose after a process of deliberation—I who do not attribute to them anything that deserves to be called 'reason'?

[10] So do not be afraid of the 'abyss' into which you say I am throwing myself; I can see no shadow or trace of it.

[11] Have I ever denied free beings the power to act within their dependence on God? Why do you keep on ascribing to me things I have never thought of?

[12] I had said to you that it is as remote from reason to attribute to the soul an immediate physical influence on the body as to attribute to matter the faculty of thinking.[41] My reason is that the one is as incapable as the other of being explained through the modifications of the thing to which it is attributed. To answer that, you would need to show that such an influence is more comprehensible; but instead of that, you oppose the comparison on the grounds of a difference which is irrelevant, or which presupposes what is in question. Matter, you say, at no point connects with thought, but the soul is connected with the arm. I reply that anyone who maintains that there is thought in matter will at the same time maintain that matter is connected with thought, since a subject of inhesion must be connected with its attributes. And anyone who denies the influence in question will at the same time deny that the soul is connected with the arm. The fact is that it means nothing at all to talk of 'connecting' here unless you explain the metaphor; and when you have explained it, it would seem that we will end up with exactly what is in question.

[13] But (you say) the soul is connected with the body through desire. That is a wonderful thing: is desire all that is necessary for a connection? Lovers would not be sorry to hear it. Not to mention

41 J8, § 6.

the fact that the soul does not in fact have this desire to pass into the body, which the scholastics imagined when they held that a soul by itself had an urge to be inside the body.[42]

[14] I do not wish to enquire whether God in his omnipotence could give souls the ability to act by an influence on the body. It is enough for me that this could be done only by a continual miracle, since this ability or action is not rooted in the nature of the soul, as predicates or natural tendencies must be.

[15] When you ask 'what would be the good of all the organs we find in animals?', it becomes obvious that you have thought very little about the system which you are trying to refute. Remember, sir, that according to me the function of the soul is in part to express its body. Without the body, without those organs, it would not be what it is. The whole of nature is bound together by the bonds of order.

[16] It is in keeping with the wisdom of God (you add) to give created things the faculty of action. I have already told you several times that I agree, and indeed that I insist on it more than anyone else with regard to what is internal to them, which comes entirely from themselves. Souls carry out real (*physique*) immediate action within themselves, for they are always immediate causes, and often masters of their natural actions.

[17] There is no comparison between the action of one body on another and the influence of the soul on the body. There is immediate contact between bodies, and we understand how that can be, and how, since there is no penetration, their coming together must alter their movement in some way. But we see no such consequences with the soul and the body: these two do not touch, and do not interfere with one another in an immediate way which we can understand and deduce from their natures. All they can do is to be in agreement, and to depend on one another by a metaphysical influence, so to speak, in virtue of the soul's ideas; and that is contained in God's plans, which are in conformity with them. They are related through the mediation of God, not by a continual interruption of the laws of the one because of its relation to the other, but by a harmony pre-established in their natures once and for all.

---

[42] For examples, see Aquinas, *Summa Theologica*, I. 76. I. I; Eustachius, *Summa philosophica quadriparta* (Paris, 1609). For some discussion see Marleen Rozemond, *Descartes' Dualism* (Yale, forthcoming), ch. 5.

[18] All in all, I have to say that there can be neither pleasure nor profit in a correspondence in which again and again opinions are attributed to me which I do not hold, where no attention is paid to what I say, or to what is said to me; where objections are made against me about what is common to all systems; where the arguments I have presented are ignored, and objections I have refuted are repeated with no attention paid to my replies; and finally where I am charged with hateful conclusions, and no proof is ever offered that these alleged conclusions follow. . . .

[19] I have just now received your third letter,[43] about which it will be enough for now to say that if, *after having spoken otherwise* about the theory of occasional causes, you are now coming back to expressions which fit in with my own theory, and if as you say, 'the proponents of that theory would have no objection to its being explained in this kind of way',[44] then I should be delighted. But then they will also have to give up their position with regard to the most concrete point which distinguished it from my own, and instead of holding that the laws of bodies, whether concerning the quantity of movement or only (as M. Descartes thought) its direction, are changed in respect of the actions of souls, they will instead have to accept with me that they are not.

[20] As for the rest, I think that after having understood my meaning better, you will, sir, be sufficiently just not to attribute to me opinions which I deny, and which are not to be found in my writings, and that if you want to draw conclusions from my opinions, you will do so by well-formed arguments, without taking as given what you will not be granted, and without omitting what needs to be expressed. . . .

Appendix A. LEIBNIZ: Letter to Jaquelot, Berlin, 22 March 1703[45]

You are right to take up again in the letter which you have been so good as to send me, the things we discussed in our conversation yesterday. I have many things to say to make my position better understood.

(1) Firstly, matter (I mean here secondary matter, or a mass) is not a substance, but a number of substances, like a flock of sheep, or

---

[43] i.e. J11.　　　[44] J11, § 7.　　　[45] From the French at G 3. 457–8.

a lake full of fish. I count as corporeal substances only nature's machines, which have souls or something analogous; otherwise there would be no true unity.

(2) Every created substance acts and is acted on. There is nothing contradictory in that, and I believe there are no created substances which are separated from matter. The ancient philosophers and the Church Fathers gave bodies to genies and angels. Only God, who is pure action, is exempted from matter.

(3) There are two sorts of force in bodies, a primitive force which is essential to it (*entelecheia hē prōtē*[46]), and derived forces, which also depend on other bodies. And we have to realize that derivative or accidental force, which we cannot deny to moving bodies, must be a modification of primitive force, just as shape is a modification of extension. Accidental forces could have no place in a substance without essential force, because accidents are only modifications or limitations, and can never contain more perfection or reality than does the substance.

(4) Movement is not the cause, but the effect or result of force; and movement is not a being, any more than is time, since it has no coexisting parts, and so can never exist. But force subsists and can endure. And in fact it is the same quantity of derivative force that is conserved in nature, and not the same quantity of movement. Since force is present at an instant, it is by means of it that a moving body at an instant differs from a body which is at rest, or which has a lesser movement. . . .

(8) However, we are perhaps basically in agreement when you say, sir, that mind acts and matter is acted on. In all corporeal substances I recognize two primitive powers, namely entelechy or primitive active power, which is the soul in animals and mind in man, and which in general is the substantial form of the ancients; and also first matter, or primitive passive power, which produces resistance. So properly speaking it is the entelechy which acts, and matter which is acted on; but one without the other is not a complete substance.

(9) I also agree that in a certain sense the mind produces everything from its own resources; or rather, that is true of every simple substance, or unity, as I have shown elsewhere in explaining the union of the soul with the organic body. . . .

[46] 'the first actuality'.

8

Leibniz and Damaris Masham

INTRODUCTION

Damaris, Lady Masham (1658–1708), daughter of the English philosopher Francis Cudworth (1617–88), was a friend of John Locke, who lived in her house at Oates in Essex in his last years. Leibniz evidently believed[1] that Locke played some part in his correspondence with Masham, which began in late 1703, when he was told that she intended to send him a copy of her father's book, *The True Intellectual System of the Universe* (London, 1678). Leibniz wrote to her that he himself had made some small contribution to such matters, and referred her to his exchanges with Bayle (see M1). Having read the first edition of Bayle's *Dictionary* and also Leibniz's 'New System' itself, Masham, writing in English, asked for clarification about 'forms', about which, she said, she could get no clear idea from what Leibniz himself had said (M2).

In his reply (M3) Leibniz based an explanation of his system on the idea that nature is uniform, which leads him to think that there are active beings (forms, souls, minds) like ourselves everywhere in matter.

Having been at pains to understand Leibniz's theory Masham begins to suggest criticisms (M4). The first of these echoes an earlier one of Foucher.[2] Given that the body does not act on the soul, all the organization of the body 'becomes superfluous and lost labour' (M4, § 5). Then, in her next letter she raises, as did others, the question of how Leibniz's system has room for 'liberty or free agency' (M6, § 5). She does not make clear exactly what the problem as she sees it is, and, given that she says she can't understand how to defend free will anyway, it is perhaps not too unfair of Leibniz to reply that 'with regard to liberty, I do not see that there is any more difficulty about it in my system than in any other' (M7, § 9).

---

[1] Leibniz to Burnett, Hanover, 2 Aug. 1704 (G 3. 297–8).
[2] See F1, § 4.

M1. LEIBNIZ: Letter to Masham, early 1704?[3]

I understand that you are sending me a copy of the *Intellectual System* of the late M. Cudworth.[4] ... The subject-matter ... interests me greatly, for I have thought a great deal about this topic. And indeed I would claim to have discovered a new country in the intelligible world, and in this way, madam, to have added a little to the great system which your father, after passing it through the hands of the best of the ancients and moderns, and enriching it himself, has left to us. Among other things my contribution consists of a little system of pre-established harmony between substances.[5] M. Bayle speaks about this at length in the article on Rorarius in both editions of his splendid *Dictionary*, but most fully in the second edition, where he also adds some new objections which are well worth resolving.[6] I have sent him my as yet unpublished reply,[7] which, as he has acknowledged in a letter he has written to me about it,[8] has given him a deeper understanding of my view. Even in the article I have just mentioned it seems to this famous author that no one before has carried so far the idea we have of the greatness of God's perfections, and of the beauty of his creation. ...

M2. MASHAM: Letter to Leibniz, Oates, 29 March 1704[9]

... I should be glad to have a further view into the intellectual world; and would therefore willingly have right conceptions of the system you propose. To this purpose, upon the receipt of your obliging letter, I looked into the article on Rorarius in the first edition of M. Bayle's *Dictionary* (not having the second by me) and being by his quotation of you there directed to the *Journal des savants* 1695, I read what is there published of it. Perhaps my not

---

[3] From the French at G 3. 336–7.
[4] Leibniz was informed of this by Püchler, perhaps in late Dec. 1703 (see LB, p. 170). Leibniz recalls this present years later (Leibniz to Remond, 22 June 1715 (G 3. 646)).
[5] NS1.　　　　　　　　　　[6] PB1, PB4.　　　　　　　　　　[7] PB5.
[8] Bayle to Leibniz, Rotterdam, 3 Oct. 1702 (G 3. 64–5); see Chap. 5, n. 14.
[9] At G 3. 337–8. We have throughout made slight changes to Masham's punctuation and spelling.

being accustomed to such abstract speculations made me not well comprehend what you say there of 'formes', upon which I think you build your hypothesis: for (as it seems to me) you sometimes call them 'forces primitives' [primary forces], sometimes 'des âmes' [souls], sometimes 'formes constitutives des substances' [constitutive forms of substances], and sometimes substances themselves;[10] but such yet as are neither spirit, nor matter, whence I confess I have no clear idea of what you call 'formes'. . . .

I take the liberty, therefore, to request the favour of you that you will by some explication or definition of them help me to conceive what your 'formes' are; for I cannot but desire to understand a system recommended to me not only by the eminence of its author, but particularly also as tending to enlarge our idea of the divine perfections and the beauty of his works. If you please to add in short the sum of your answers to M. Bayle's objections in his second edition of his *Dictionary*, it will be an additional obligation in giving me still further light into this matter. . . .

M3. LEIBNIZ: Letter to Masham, Hanover, beginning of May 1704[11]

[1] . . . As I am all for the principle of uniformity that I believe nature observes in its fundamentals, even though it varies in its ways, degrees, and perfections, my whole theory comes down to recognizing in substances beyond our sight and observation something parallel to what we see in those which are within our range. So, taking it as now agreed that there is in us a simple being endowed with action and perception, I think that nature would show little consistency if this particle of matter which makes up the human body were the only thing endowed with something which would make it infinitely different from everything else (even in the physical world) and altogether heterogeneous as compared with all other known bodies. This leads me to think that there are such active beings everywhere in matter, and that they differ only in the manner of their perception. And since our own perceptions are

---

[10] NS1, §§ 3, 4.
[11] From the French at G 3. 338–48. Leibniz refers to this letter in one written to Sophie Charlotte on 8 May 1704, and repeats, for her benefit and at greater length, what he had said to Masham (see app. A).

sometimes accompanied by *reflection*, and sometimes not, and since reflection gives rise to *abstractions* and *universal necessary truths* (of which we see no vestige in animals, and still less in the other bodies which surround us), there is ground for thinking that this is what distinguishes this simple being which is in us and which is called the soul from those in other known bodies.

[2] Whether these principles of action and of perception are then to be called *forms, entelechies, souls,* or *minds,* and whether these terms are to be distinguished according to whatever notions one may choose to assign to them, things will not be changed in any way. You may ask what becomes of these simple beings or souls that I put in animals and other created things in so far as they are organic wholes; my reply is that they need be no less inextinguishable than ours, and that they can be neither produced nor destroyed by the forces of nature.

[3] But to extend the analogy with what we feel at *present* in our *own* bodies to the *future* and *past,* as well as to *other* bodies, I hold not only that these souls or entelechies all have with them some kind of organic body appropriate to their perceptions, but also that they always will have, and always have had, as long as they have existed: so not only the soul, but also the animal itself (or what is analogous to the soul and to the animal, so as not to argue about names) remains, and thus that generation and death can only be developments and envelopments of which nature, as is her custom, gives us several visible examples to help us to work out what she keeps hidden. And as a consequence, neither iron nor fire, nor any other violence of nature, whatever ravages they wreak on an animal's body, can ever prevent the soul from retaining a certain organic body, inasmuch as *organism,* that is to say, order and ingenuity, is something essential to matter produced and arranged by the sovereign wisdom, since products always retain some trace of their author. This leads me to think also that there are no minds entirely separate from matter (except the first and sovereign being), and that spirits (*genies*), however marvellous they may be, are always accompanied by appropriate bodies. The same must also be said of souls, even though they may be described as separate with respect to this gross body. So you see, madam, that all this is only to suppose that *things are everywhere and always just as they are in us now* (leaving the supernatural aside) except for varying degrees of

perfection; and I leave you to decide whether any more intelligible, or at least any simpler, theory could be devised.

[4] This same maxim *of not unnecessarily supposing in created things anything not corresponding to our experience* also led me to my *System of Pre-established Harmony*. For we have experience of bodies acting on one another according to mechanical laws, and of souls producing within themselves various internal actions, but we see no way of conceiving action of the soul on matter, or of matter on the soul, or anything which corresponds to it. For we cannot explain, by the example of any machine whatever, how material relationships—that is to say, mechanical laws—could produce a perception, or how perception could produce a change in the velocity or the direction of animal spirits or other bodies, of whatever subtle or gross kind. Thus the inconceivability of an alternative theory, as well as the good order of nature which is always uniform (not to mention other considerations), has led me to think that the soul and the body perfectly follow their own laws—each its own separate ones—without corporeal laws being disrupted by the soul's actions, and without bodies finding windows through which to exert their influence over souls. You will then ask how this agreement of the soul with the body comes about. The defenders of occasional causes hold that God continually adjusts the soul to the body, and the body to the soul. But since that would mean that God had to keep disturbing the natural laws of bodies, it could only involve miracles, and so is not very suitable for philosophy, which has to explain the ordinary course of nature. That is what made me think that it is infinitely more worthy of God's economy and of the uniformity and constant order of his works to conclude that from the start he created souls and bodies in such a way that each following its own laws would match up with the other. It cannot be denied that this is possible for one whose wisdom and power are infinite. In this I am doing no more than attributing to souls and bodies always and everywhere what we experience in them whenever the experience is distinct, that is to say, mechanical laws to bodies, and internal actions to souls. Everything therefore comes down to a present state combined with a tendency towards changes, changes which are brought about in the body by moving forces, and in the soul by perceptions of good and evil.

[5] The only surprising thing in this is that God's works are

infinitely more beautiful and more harmonious than had been thought. And one might say that the device used by the Epicureans against the argument based on the beauty of visible things (their claim that from an infinity of chance productions it is no wonder if some world, like our own, has come out tolerably well) is demolished, in that the perpetual correspondence of beings which have no influence on one another can only come from a common cause of their harmony. The wise M. Bayle, having considered the consequences of this theory, concluded that no one had ever given a more lofty understanding of the divine perfections, and also that God's infinite wisdom, great as it is, is not too much for producing such a pre-established harmony, the possibility of which he seemed to doubt. But I pointed out to him that men themselves construct automata which act as if they were rational, and that God (who is an infinitely greater artist, or, rather, for whom everything is art to the highest possible degree) has traced out the route for matter in order to make it act as minds demand. And that being the case, we should be no more surprised at its acting so rationally than at the way firework rockets can move along an unseen string, which makes it look as if someone were controlling them. We are responsive to God's designs only in virtue of the perfections they involve. In a similar way, bodies are subjected to souls in advance, in that they have to accommodate themselves at the appropriate time to their voluntary actions; but also in their turn souls are in their primordial nature expressive of bodies, in so far as they have to represent them through their involuntary and confused perceptions. In this way each is sometimes the original and sometimes the copy of the other, in proportion to the perfections or imperfections it contains. . . .

M4. MASHAM: Letter to Leibniz, Oates, 3 June 1704[12]

[1] . . . To a mind possessed in any measure with a due admiration of the works of God, nothing is more grateful than by further discoveries therein of his Divine perfections to be sensibly engaged to adore that being which reason pronounces ought to be the supreme object of our affections.

---

[12] At G 3. 348–52.

[2] A hypothesis thought by yourself and others conducing to such an end as this could not but excite my enquiry; and it did so the more because that in reading what you have published, it seemed to myself also you had views therein which gave a becoming idea of the wisdom of God in his works. The letter you have favoured me with confirms me in this thought. But that I may be sure of having a certain and clear knowledge of your hypothesis, permit me to tell you what I conceive it to be, in hopes you will rectify my mistakes if I am in any: which is what may easily happen to one so little conversant as I am in such speculations.

[3] You take for granted that 'there is a simple being in us endowed with action and perception'. The same, you say, 'differing only in the manner of perception, is in matter everywhere'. That the 'simple being' in us, which is called soul, is distinguished from that of beasts (and yet more from that of other bodies about us) by the 'power of abstraction' and framing thereby universal ideas. All these 'simple beings' you think have, always will have, and ever since they existed have had 'organic bodies, proportioned to their perception'. So that not only after death the soul does remain, but even the animal also. Generation and death being but a displaying or concealment of these beings to, or from, our view. The same principle of uniformity in the works of nature which has led you to believe this has, you say, led you also to your system of the 'harmony pre-established between substances', the which I thus understand.[13]

[4] Any action of the soul upon matter, or of matter upon the soul, is inconceivable: these two have their laws distinct. Bodies follow the laws of mechanism, and have a tendency to change 'suivant les forces mouvantes' [by moving forces].[14] *Souls produce in themselves internal actions*, and have a tendency to change *according to the perception that they have of Good or Ill*. Now *soul* and *body* following each their proper laws, and neither of them acting thereby upon or affecting the other, such effects are yet produced from a *harmony pre-established betwixt these substances*, as if there was a real communication between them. So that the body acting constantly by its own laws of mechanism, without receiving any variation or change therein from any action of the

---

[13] The five near-quotations (which Masham gives in English) in this section are, respectively, from M3, §§ 1, 1, 1, 3, 4.

[14] M3, § 4.

soul, does yet always correspond to the passions and perceptions which the soul hath. And the soul in like manner, though not operated upon by the motions of matter, has yet, at the same time that the body acts according to its laws of mechanism, certain perceptions or modifications which fail not to answer thereunto.

[5] This is what I conceive you to say; in which (to tell you thoughts so insignificant as mine) I see nothing peculiar, which seems not possible. I find a uniformity in it which pleases me: and the advantages proposed from this hypothesis are very desirable. But it appears not yet to me that this is more than a hypothesis; for as God's ways are not limited by our conceptions, the unintelligibleness or inconceivableness by us of any way but one does not, methinks, much induce a belief of that being the way which God has chosen to make use of. Yet such an inference as this from our ignorance I remember Father Malebranche (or some other assertor of his hypothesis)[15] would make in behalf of occasional causes; to which hypothesis, among other exceptions, I think there is one which I cannot without your help see but that yours is alike liable to, and that is from the organization of the body, wherein all that nice curiosity that is discoverable seeming useless, becomes superfluous and lost labour. To this difficulty likewise let me add that I conceive not why 'organism' should be or can be thought, as you say [it] is, 'essential to matter'.[16]

[6] But these enquiries or other that might it may be on further thoughts occur to me, are less pertinent for me to make than such a one as is more fundamental, although it does not peculiarly respect your hypothesis. Forms, explained by you to signify 'simple beings', you elsewhere call 'atomes de substance' [atoms of substance] and 'forces primitives' [primary forces], the nature whereof you in another place say you find 'to consist in force'.[17]

[7] 'Force', I presume, cannot be the essence of any substance, but is the attribute of what you call a 'form', 'soul', or 'atome de substance' [atom of substance], of the essence whereof I find no positive idea, and your negation of their having any dimensions makes their existence, I confess, inconceivable to me, as not being able to conceive an existence of that which is nowhere. If the

---

[15] See, perhaps, Malebranche, *Search*, 6. 2. 3; *Conversations on Metaphysics and Religion*, 7. 2. [16] Cf. M3, § 3.
[17] The words in quotes in this section are, respectively, from M3, § 2, NS1, §§ 11, 3, 3.

locality of these substances were accounted for by their being, as you [say] they are, always in organized bodies, then they are somewhere: but if these 'atomes de substance' [atoms of substance] are somewhere, then they must have some extension, which you deny of them; who, I think, also place the union of the soul with its respective body in nothing else but that correspondence or conformity whereby, in virtue of a 'pre-established harmony', souls and bodies acting apart, each by their own laws, the same effects are produced as if there was a real communication betwixt them. Though whether or no I perfectly comprehend your meaning in this part I am in doubt.

[8] What I have here said I think enough for me to venture to trouble you with at once: and it will perhaps be more than enough to show you that you have judged by much too favourably of my apprehension. For I remember my father as well as other assertors of unextended substance to have said: 'That it is an imposition of imagination upon their reason in those who cannot be convinced of the reality of substances unextended.'[18] . . .

M5. LEIBNIZ: Letter to Masham, Hanover, 30 June 1704[19]

[1] . . . You took the trouble, madam, to begin by briefly expounding my theory, so that I can see whether you have understood it correctly. This is a very useful procedure in this kind of discussion, and I admire the accuracy and clarity of your expression in such an abstract matter. It is such that I will be able to make use of it myself some other time when I have to explain to someone.

[2] After that you make comments on it which are certainly worthy of you, and deserve that I should try to adjust my ideas to them. You begin by praising my theory: you say that it seems plausible, that it preserves the uniformity of nature, and indeed that it contains some things which we would want.

[3] But, madam, you go on to say that it does not seem to be 'anything more than a hypothesis'[20] as yet. And though it is perhaps

[18] See Cudworth, *The True Intellectual System*, e.g. bk. 1, ch. 1, sect. 40, p. 49, and—reporting Aristotle and Porphyry—bk. 1, ch. 5, sect. 2, p. 779.
[19] From the French at G 3. 352–7.
[20] M4, § 5.

more intelligible than other theories, this doesn't mean that it is true, since '*God's ways* are not limited by our conceptions';[21] and although all ways except one seem unintelligible and inconceivable, that one way is not thereby demonstratively proved.

[4] My comments, following your order, are (1) that it seems a matter of some importance if one theory seems *possible* when all the others do not, and (2) that it is extremely *probable* that such a theory is the true one. I have always observed in astronomy and in physics that the most intelligible theories prove true in the end: for example, that of the movement of the earth to save the appearances of the stars, and that of the weight of the air to explain air pumps and other attractions which had formerly been attributed to the abhorrence of a vacuum.

[5] Furthermore, (3) since our understanding comes from God, and should be considered as a ray of that sun, we should conclude that what best conforms with our understanding (when we proceed methodically, and in accordance with the nature of the understanding itself) will conform with the divine wisdom; and that by following that method, we are following the procedure which God has given us. Also we have always found (4) that when our judgements have been made in accordance with this natural light, so to speak, they have never been contradicted by events; and the objections which the sceptics have made against this correspondence have always been taken by reasonable people as mere jokes.

[6] But, more to the point, (5) it is helpful to think of 'God's ways' as being of two kinds, one natural, the other extraordinary or miraculous. Those which are *natural* are always such that a created mind can understand them given the necessary guidance and opportunity to do so. But *miraculous* ways are beyond any created mind. Thus, magnetism is natural, being completely mechanical or explicable, although, lacking information, we are perhaps not yet ready to explain it perfectly in detail. But if someone claims that the magnet doesn't work mechanically, and acts solely by pure attraction at a distance, with no means or medium, and with no intermediary, visible or invisible, then that would be something incomprehensible to any created mind, however penetrating and informed it might be. In a word, it would be something miraculous. For the reason and order of the divine wisdom demands we make

---

[21] M4, § 5.

no needless recourse to miracles. This same consideration applies when what is in question is *the system of union between the soul and the body*. For it is no more comprehensible to say that a body acts at a distance with no means or intermediary than it is to say that substances as different as the soul and the body operate on each other immediately; for there is a greater gap between their two natures than between any two places. So the communication between these two so heterogenous substances can only be brought about by a miracle, as can the immediate communication between two distant bodies; and to try to attribute it to I know not what 'influence' of the one on the other is to disguise the miracle with meaningless words. This happens too in the case of the way of occasional causes; the only difference being that there a perpetual miracle is (whether this is admitted or not) introduced quite openly by the authors of the system, not implicitly as in the system of influence. For although this action of God, of moving the soul on the occasion of the body, and the body on the occasion of the soul, will be continual and normal, it will not therefore be any the less miraculous, since it will always be something incomprehensible to any created mind, however informed it may be, and whatever guidance God may have given it. This is all the more so, especially as this effect depends solely on the immediate operation of God, and allows of no other means or explanation, and it is admitted that God thus continually interrupts the laws of the body in order to accommodate it to the soul, and vice versa. By contrast with this, what is comprehensible is what conforms to the natural laws of things, and should be explained only by them.

[7] So (6) it seems that my theory is rather more than a theory, since it is not merely possible in itself, but is also most in conformity with God's wisdom and with the order of things. And I believe that one can say with certainty that God always acts in the way which is most in conformity with his perfections, of which wisdom is one of the greatest. And it is obvious that nothing is more excellent or better arranged than this prior agreement which God has established in natural things, and nothing shows better that it is he who has made them, for it is worthy of him to regulate everything in advance so as never later on to have to do anything contrary to his rules, which conform to the nature of things. And things could not possibly by themselves be in such perfect agreement by pre-established harmony, if they did not derive from a common cause, and if

that cause were not infinitely powerful and far-sighted, so as to be able to extend itself into all things with such precision.

[8] And what is more, (7) if one supposes that ordinary things must happen naturally and not by a miracle, it seems that we can say that, that being so, my *theory* is *proved*. For the other two theories necessarily fall back on miracles, as I have just shown in (5); and there can be no other theories than these three. For either the laws of the body and the soul are broken, or they are kept. If they are broken (which can only happen by interference from outside), then either one of these two things must act on the other, which is *the theory of influence*, which is common in the schools; or there is a third thing that acts on them (that is to say, God), as in *the theory of occasional causes*. And finally, if the laws of the soul and the body are in fact kept, and not broken, that is *the theory of pre-established harmony*, which consequently is the only natural one.

[9] (8) This preference which in the ordinary occurrences of nature should be given to the natural over the miraculous, about which I believe all philosophers so far (except some semi-fanatics, such as Fludd in his Mosaic philosophy[22]) agree; this preference, I say, is also a reason for holding that it is not matter that thinks, but a simple being which is set apart or independent, and joined to matter. It is true that the illustrious M. Locke maintained in his excellent Essay, and in writing about it against the late Bishop of Worcester, that God could give to matter the power of thinking, because he can do things beyond anything we can understand;[23] but it would then be by a continual miracle that matter thought, there being nothing in matter in itself, in extension and impenetrability, that is to say, from which thought could follow, or on which it could be founded. We can say then that *the natural immortality of the soul* is proved. One could assert its extinction only by asserting a miracle, either by attributing to matter the ability to think, *received and maintained by a miracle*, in which case the soul could perish by the cessation of the miracle; or by holding that the substance which thinks, distinct from the body, could be annihilated—which would also be a miracle, but a new miracle. Now, I say that God, in the

---

[22] Robert Fludd (1574–1637), English philosopher. His *Philosophia Mosaica* (1638) attempts to derive a complete philosophy, as revealed to Moses, from the Old Testament. In the *New Essays* (preface) Leibniz says that Fludd 'saves all the phenomena by attributing them immediately to God through miracles'.

[23] *Essay*, 4. 3. 6; *Mr. Locke's Reply to the Bishop of Worcester's Answer to his Second Letter*, in *Works* (London, 1823), iv. 460.

former case of thinking matter, would have not only to *give* matter the capacity for thought miraculously, but also to *maintain* it continuously by the same miracle, since it could have no basis there, unless God also gave matter a new nature. But if we were to say that God gave matter this new nature or basic capacity for thought, which thereafter maintained itself unaided, it would in fact be a thinking soul that he had given it, or at least something which differs from it only in name. Moreover, since this basic capacity would not really be a modification of matter (for modifications are explicable by the natures that they modify, which this force isn't), it would be independent of matter.

[10] I come next, madam, to some important problems which have occurred to you. You remark (9) that it appears that the bodily organs serve no purpose if the soul is self-sufficient. I reply that if Caesar's soul (for example) were alone in nature, the creator of things need not have given it any bodily organs. But this same creator also wanted to make an infinity of other beings, which are contained in one another's bodily organs. Our body is a kind of world full of an infinity of creatures which also deserved to exist, and if our body were not an organic whole, our microcosm or little world would not have all the perfections it should have, and the big world itself would not be as rich as it is.

[11] (10) This also is the reason why I have said that *being organic is essential* not in general to matter, but only *to matter as arranged by a sovereign wisdom*. And this also is why I define *an organism*, or natural machine, as a machine of which each part is a machine, and consequently as one such that the complexity of its construction continues to infinity, no part being so small that this does not apply, whereas by contrast, the parts of our artificial machines are not themselves machines. That is the essential difference between *nature* and *art*, which our moderns have not sufficiently considered.[24]

[12] (11) It also seems to you, madam, that force could never be the essence of any substance. Doubtless this is because you are talking about changeable forces, which is what is commonly meant. But by *primary force* I mean *a principle of action*, of which changeable forces are only modifications.

[13] (12) *The positive idea* of this simple substance or primary

[24] See NS1, § 10.

force is quite familiar, since it will always have in it a regulated sequence of perceptions, hence my analogy with our soul.

[14] (13) The question whether it is *somewhere or nowhere* is purely verbal; for its nature does not consist in extension, though it agrees with extension which it represents. So one should place the soul in the body in which is located the point of view according to which it represents the present state of the universe. To want anything more, and to tie the soul down to dimensions, is to try to think of souls as being like bodies.

[15] (14) As for complete substances which have no extension, I believe with you, madam, that there are none among created things, for souls or forms without a body would be something incomplete, especially as in my view, *the soul is never without an animal* or something analogous. And even God is only understood by us through an idea which involves a relation to *extension*, that is to say, with the continuous and systematic diversity which he has produced among simultaneously existent things. And it is also only by his effects that we come to know of his existence. But the sovereign reason then shows us that there is in him something beyond extension, and which is in fact the source of extension, as well as of the changes which take place in it. Though this will not be something we can imagine, we should not be surprised, since even mathematics presents us with an infinity of unimaginable things, witness *incommensurables*, the truth of which can none the less be demonstrated. This is why one should not reject truths on the grounds that they are beyond the reach of the imagination. It is not the imagination that should set the limits to assent, and M. Locke has clearly shown that our ideas of reflection involve something beyond sensory images.[25] . . .

M6. MASHAM: Letter to Leibniz, Oates, 8 August 1704[26]

[1] . . . Whether I have rightly represented your system, you best can tell, and what you say on that subject I am proud of; while the inferences you would draw from thence to my advantage can give me only a due acknowledgement for your wishing me so much fitter for your correspondence than I am. But however justly I may have

---

[25] *Essay*, 2. 1. 4.   [26] At G 3. 358–61.

expressed your sense so far as I endeavoured to represent it, your answers to some of my enquiries make me question whether I fully apprehended all that is included in your hypothesis. For I do not yet sufficiently see upon what you ground *organism's being essential to matter*: or indeed very well understand your meaning in these words that organism is not absolutely essential to matter but to matter 'arrangée par une sagesse souveraine' [arranged by a sovereign wisdom]. What you would build upon this forms a very transcendent conception of the Divine artifice, and such as I think could only occur to the thoughts of one possessed with the highest admiration of the wisdom of his maker; but if you infer the truth of this notion only from its being the most agreeable one that you can frame to that attribute of God, this singly seems to me not to be concluding. Since we can in my opinion only infer from thence that whatsoever God does must be according to infinite wisdom, but are not able with our short and narrow views to determine what the operations of an infinitely wise being must be.

[2] The *principle of action* called by you 'force primitive' [primary force] is you say 'a substance'; of the which I still perceive not the positive idea, *perception* being but the *action* of this substance. What you add concerning its *perceptions*, in these words, 'suivant l'analogie qu'elle doit avoir avec notre âme' [in accordance with the analogy that it has with our soul], makes me again believe that I do not fully understand your scheme, since I thought before that the soul, this 'force primitive' [primary force], or 'principle of action', had been the same thing.[27] You say 'refermer les âmes dans les dimensions c'est vouloir imaginer les âmes commes des corps' [to tie the soul down to dimensions, is to try to think of souls as being like bodies].[28] In regard to *extension*, this is true, and *extension* is to me inseparable from the notion of all substance. I am yet sensible that we ought not to reject truths because they are not imaginable by us (where there is ground to admit them). But *truth* being but the attributing certain affections conceived to belong to the subject in question, I can by no means attribute anything to a subject whereof I have no conception at all, as I am conscious to myself I have not of unextended substance. What you instance in [sic] therefore of 'lines incommensurable' [sic] [incommensurable lines] seems not to me to answer the case, for I herein do conceive the proposition, and have

[27] The phrases quoted so far in this section are from M5, §§ 12, 13.
[28] M5, § 14.

clear ideas of 'lines incommensurable', though I do not see the reason of their incommensurability; but of an *unextended substance* I have not any conception from whence I can affirm or deny anything concerning it.

[3] Why you think that there is 'no created substance complete without extension',[29] or that the soul (which you suppose a distinct substance) would without the body be a substance incomplete without extension, I understand not; but my own belief that there is no substance whatever unextended is (as I have already said), grounded upon this that I have no conception of such a thing. I cannot yet but conceive two very different substances to be in the universe, though extension alike agrees to them both. For I clearly conceive an extension without *solidity*, and a *solid extension*; to some system of which last, if it should be affirmed that God did annex *thought*, I see no absurdity in this from there being nothing in *extension* and *impenetrability* or *solidity* from whence thought can *naturally*, or by a train of causes, be derived, the which I believe to be demonstrable it cannot be. But that was never supposed by me; and my question in the case would be this: whether God could not as conceivably by us as create an unextended substance, and then unite it to an extended substance (wherein, by the way, there is, methinks, on your side two difficulties for one)—whether God, I say, could not as conceivably by us as his doing this would be, add (if he so pleased) *the power of thinking* to that substance which has *solidity*. *Solidity* and *thought* being both of them but attributes of some unknown substance, and I see not why it may not be one and the same which is the common support of both these, there appearing to me no contradiction in a coexistence of *thought* and *solidity* in the same substance. Neither can [I] apprehend it to be more inexplicable that God should give *thought* to a substance which I know not, but whereof I know some of its attributes, than to another, supposed, substance of whose very being I have no conception at all. And that any substance whatsoever should have *thought* belonging to it, or resulting from it, otherwise than as God has willed it shall have so, I cannot apprehend.

[4] That God does in framing and ordering of all his works always make use of the simple means I doubt not, this appearing to me most suitable to his wisdom. But whether or no these simple means or methods are always such as surpass not a created

intelligence I do not know, but am very apt to believe that *God's ways are past our finding out,* in this sense.

[5] I have no sooner scribbled to you these thoughts of mine, than I fear wearying you by my dullness. I shall therefore waive taking notice of anything more that has occurred to me in considering the several parts of your letter, or making any such further enquiries as perhaps, were these resolved, I might be able in some measure to clear to myself. I will, however, now mention to you one difficulty (as I conceive) in your hypothesis, which I think not that I could ever extricate it from without your assistance, and it is to me a very material one. Viz. how to reconcile your system to *liberty* or *free agency;* for though in regard of any compulsion from other causes we are according thereto *free,* yet I see not how we can be so in respect of the first mover. This I omitted taking notice of in my last, not only because I thought it too remote an enquiry for one who wanted to be enlightened concerning the very foundation you built upon, but also because I must acknowledge that I cannot make our *liberty* either with or without any hypothesis whatsoever. Though as being persuaded that I felt myself a *free agent,* and that *freedom to act* is necessary to our being accountable for our actions, I do not only conclude we are endowed therewith, but am very tenacious hereof, whence I should be sorry to find from any new hypothesis new difficulties in maintaining of this. I think not much that I need seek to justify to you the part which I own my inclination has in this opinion, since what you have said in print persuades me that you have the same belief with the same bias. . . .

M7. LEIBNIZ: Letter to Masham, Lüzenberg, near Berlin, September 1704[30]

[1] . . . When I say that being organic is essential to matter as arranged by divine wisdom, you doubt, madam, whether we can decide, by consideration of that infinite wisdom, how it will operate. I reply that in general terms we can, and can often exclude what would not be in conformity with it, but that in detail we cannot. Thus, if we suppose that there is nothing careless or crude in God's works, then atoms, for example, can have no place in them, for there is no variety or embellishment about them, a lack

[30] From the French at G3. 361–4.

which is incompatible with the divine architecture. We must guard against a clever Pyrrhonism which, disguised by false modesty, takes too far the truth that we do not properly understand God's ways. This is like those who, under the pretext that the rules of divine justice often escape us, go so far as to attribute tyrannical actions to God.

[2] Whether all entelechies should be called souls is perhaps a verbal question. It depends on how you want to define these terms.

[3] We have to accept substance without extension, for God at least could never be extended. But I believe that all created substance is accompanied by extension, and I do not recognize any which is entirely separate from matter, as I pointed out to you at the start. This is a way of avoiding a thousand difficulties, although I don't want to argue about what might be possible for God.

[4] I can well believe, madam, that you have no image of a non-extended substance; but that doesn't prevent you from having a notion of one. M. Locke was of this opinion in his Essay, and since he is living in your home, it would be a mistake for me to undertake what he could do better and more immediately. {And as you have some notion of substance and also of a non-extended thing (for example, a point), you have, despite your excessive humility, a notion of non-extended substance. It is true that we have it imperfectly, until we can demonstrate, by analysis of these two notions, whether or not they are consistent. But if our having a conception depended on our having a sufficient analysis of it, then many geometers wouldn't even have the conception of a straight line, for it must be realized that our image of it isn't the distinct idea of it, and does not suffice for demonstrating its properties. Unless we consider that carefully, we will see difficulties where there are none, and think we can't conceive what we can conceive, and can conceive what we can't. If, madam, you didn't understand the theory of the incommensurability of lines, you could have no clearer idea of it than you have of a non-extended substance, for in that case you would not be able to tell from the idea of it whether either the substance or the line was possible—that is to say, distinctly conceivable—or not. It is the understanding of possibilities, which determines the clarity of intellectual ideas.

[5] The soul never lacks a body, for the same reason that there is neither void nor atoms. An atom would be an incomplete substantial thing, and so would souls without bodies, or a body

without a soul; and extension without solidity would be the same. It would be like number without things numbered, or like duration without enduring things. These are all philosophers' incomplete notions.}

[6] I do not know, madam, how one would tell a primitive natural capacity of thought from a substantial principle of thought joined to matter.

[7] {Properly speaking, solid extension without soul is only the resultant of several substances, and not a true substance.

[8] Thus matter which thinks without a soul could only be an impossible fiction in my system, or at best a miracle. It is true to say that there is a substance which has thought and at the same time has extension, if by a substance one means the composite of a soul and a body, for example, a man; but if one means a simple substance, it is obvious that it has no extension in itself, for all extension is composite.}

[9] With regard to liberty, I do not see that there is any more difficulty about it in my system than in any other, and as M. Locke has written a quite excellent chapter on this subject, it would be impolite, madam, for me to try to improve on your ephod[31] or domestic oracle. So I will say only with regard to my system that liberty demands that we act with sponaneity and with choice, and that my system adds to our spontaneity, and does not detract from our choice. . . .

Appendix A. LEIBNIZ: Letter to Sophie Charlotte, Hanover, 8 May 1704[32]

[1] . . . An English lady called Lady Masham has made me a present of a copy of a book, by her late father, M. Cudworth. It is in folio, and entitled *The Intellectual System*. The letter of thanks I sent her for it elicited a very obliging reply in English in which she asks for some clarification of what she has seen of my ideas in M. Bayle and in the *Journal des savants*. I therefore recently had to write her a somewhat lengthy letter, in which I told her that my great principle of natural things is that of Harlequin, Emperor of the

---

[31] Jewish priestly office. [32] From the French at G 3. 343–8.
[33] The letters are M1, M2, M3. As noted at RB, p. xliv, in Fatouville's *Arlequin, empereur dans la lune* (1683), the 'repeated refrain of the final scene is that, on the Moon, everyone behaves "just like here"'.

Moon (whom I did not do the honour of citing, however), 'that all
the time and everywhere everything's the same as here'.[33] That is to
say, nature is fundamentally uniform, although there are differences
of degree and different levels of perfection. This produces a philosophy more pleasing and more intelligible than any in the world.
First I compare other created things with ourselves.

[2] There are some bodies, human bodies, for example, in which
there is some perfection. But the tiny amount of matter which
composes them would be far too privileged if it alone had an
advantage which distinguished it, completely and indeed essentially, from all the others which surround it. We must therefore
conclude that there is life and perception everywhere. But as our
own perceptions are sometimes accompanied by reflection and
sometimes not, and are sometimes more and sometimes less clear
and distinct, it is easy to see that there must be living beings whose
perception will be obscure and confused, and who even have no
reflection, which in us is the mother of the sciences. This same
uniformity of nature, which yet has its riches and its embellish-
ments, makes me think that we are not the only beings in the
universe with reflection, and that there are even some which are
wonderfully far ahead of us. And that is how we should understand
what we call spirits. Even so, fundamentally, 'they will be the same
as here', and these spirits, in my view, will also be accompanied by
organic bodies of an appropriate kind, of a subtlety and force
proportionate to the understanding and power of these sublime
minds. And in accordance with this principle there will be no
separate souls, or intelligences entirely detached from matter, except for the sovereign mind, author of them all, and of matter itself.

[3] So far I have compared created things together, and find that
ultimately they are all the same. Now let us compare their past and
future states with their present state. On this I say that from the
beginning of the world, and for all time to come, things always are
and always will be fundamentally 'the same as here', and the same
as now, not only as regards different beings, but also as regards one
being compared with itself. That is to say, each being which is
living or endowed with perception, will always remain so, and will
always retain appropriate organs. Perception, like matter, being
universal with regard to place, is also universal in time; that is to
say, each substance not only has perception and organs, but also it
will have them always. I speak here of *a substance*, not of a mere

assemblage of substances, such as a herd of animals or a pond full of fish, where it is enough that the sheep and the fish have perception and organs, even though we should realize that in the spaces between them and in the water of the pond between the fish there will be other living things, though smaller, and so on, without any empty space. For, as with matter, it is inconceivable how perception could begin naturally. With any machine that we can imagine, there is only ever the impact of bodies, size, shape, and motion, that we can understand as being produced by it—which we easily understand to be something quite other than perception. So, not being able to begin naturally, perception cannot cease naturally either. And the difference between one substance and itself cannot be greater than that between one substance and another. That is to say, the same substance can only have perception, sometimes more lively, sometimes less, and accompanied by more or less reflection.

[4] And nothing will be able to destroy all the organs of this substance. Because it is the effect and the continual emanation of a sovereign intelligence, it is of the essence of matter to be organic, and to show contrivance everywhere, although these organs and contrivances are found most often in the small parts which are invisible to us, as is easy to judge from what we do see. So here again, in the invisible just as in the visible, the maxim that it is 'the same as here' applies. From which it again follows that naturally, and speaking in metaphysical strictness, there is neither generation nor death, but only development and envelopment of the same animal. Otherwise there would be too much of a jump, and through inexplicable changes of essence nature would lose too much of its character of uniformity. Experience confirms these transformations in several animals, where nature herself gives us a small example of what is kept hidden elsewhere. Observations also lead the most industrious observers to conclude that the generation of animals is nothing but an increase combined with a transformation. This strongly indicates that death can only be the same thing in reverse, the only difference being that in the one case the change happens slowly, and in the other all at once and with some violence. Moreover, experience also shows that a very large number of tiny perceptions which are almost indistinguishable, such as follow a blow on the head, will make us dizzy, and we get in such a daze that we can and do remember so few of these perceptions that it is just as if we hadn't had any. Thus the rule of uniformity should not lead

us to think otherwise even about the death of animals, in the natural course of things, since it is easily explicable in this fashion which we already understand and have experienced, and is inexplicable in any other manner: for it is not possible to understand how the existence or action of the perceptual principle can begin or end, nor how it can be separated off. It is, moreover, easy to see that the sequence of such changes in an animal will again undoubtedly have an admirable order, and be very well adapted to their needs, since there is order and contrivance throughout. To put the idea in an approachable form, these beings can be likened to men who are trying to climb a high mountain, which is covered in vegetation, but sheer, like a rampart, and with steps or resting-places at intervals. Sometimes, after having climbed up and nearly reached a resting-place or ledge, they suddenly fall back on to one lower down, and have to try again. Nevertheless, they still manage little by little to reach one ledge after another. And often we have to take a step back before we can jump forward. But the order of providence treats beings which have reflection in a very different manner, which undoubtedly is the most appropriate, and indeed the most desirable.

[5] But, it will be asked, how can matter act on the soul or on a being with perception? And how can the soul act on matter? For we notice in ourselves that the body often obeys the wishes of the soul, and that the soul perceives the actions of bodies; and yet we have no conception of any influence between the two things. The ancient philosophers abandoned the problem in desperation, for in fact we find that they say nothing about it. The moderns have cut the Gordian knot with Alexander's sword,[34] and have introduced miracles into a natural thing, like gods in the theatre at the denouement of an opera; for they claim that at each moment God adjusts the soul to the body and the body to the soul, and binds himself to this by a pact or general volition. But that directly contravenes the principle of the uniformity of nature: bodies ordinarily go along producing their effects on one another according to intelligible mechanical laws, and then suddenly, when the soul wants to do

---

[34] Whoever could unfasten the complex knot on the yoke of the King's wagon in Gordium, Phrygia, would rule the world (it was said). According to Plutarch, e.g., Alexander the Great 'was at a loss how to proceed, and finally loosened the knot by cutting it through with his sword' (*Lives*, 'Alexander', 18; in *Plutarch's Lives*, vol. 7, trans. Bernadotte Perrin (London, 1919)).

something, a divinity arrives to disturb this order of bodies, and change their paths! Does that seem likely?

[6] Yet this is the view of Father Malebranche and the modern Cartesians, and M. Bayle, clever as he is, finds it difficult to give up, though it seems to me that I have made him waver. But what else can we do?

[7] The key to the entire mystery is there in the principle we have been using. Since we can see from machines that bodies follow laws of impact, and from the process of deliberation that the soul can follow moral laws of good and evil, let us say of other cases where we can't see what happens and which we can't untangle so well that it is just the same there, and that 'it's all the same as here'. That is to say, let us explain the things of which we have only a confused understanding in terms of those we understand distinctly: let us say that everything in bodies happens mechanically, or in accordance with laws of motion, and that everything in the soul happens morally, or in accordance with perceived good or evil. So that even in our instinctive or involuntary actions, where it seems only the body plays a part, there is in the soul a desire for good or an aversion to evil which directs it, even though our reflection is not able to pick it out in the confusion. But if the soul and the body thus each separately follows its own laws, how is it that they match up? How is it that the body obeys the soul, and that the soul is aware of the body? To explain this natural mystery, we certainly have to have recourse to God, as we should when it is a question of giving the primordial reason of the order and art in things. But this is only a once for all explanation, not at all as if he interrupted the laws of bodies to make them correspond to the soul, and vice versa. Rather, he made bodies in advance in such a way that following their laws and natural tendencies to movement, they would come to do, when the time came, what the soul asked; and he also made souls in such a way that, following the natural tendencies of their desires, they also would always come to represent the states of the body. For as movement leads matter from one configuration to another, desire moves the soul from image to image. Thus the soul is made dominant beforehand, and is obeyed by bodies in so far as its desire is accompanied by distinct perceptions, which enable it to think up suitable ways of getting what it wants; but it is made subject to the body beforehand, in so far as it tends towards confused perceptions. For we know by experience that all things tend towards change, the

body by moving force, the soul by desire, which brings it to distinct or confused perceptions according as it is more or less perfect. And we should not wonder at this primordial agreement between souls and bodies, for all bodies are arranged according to the intentions of a universal mind, and all souls are essentially representations or living mirrors of the universe, according to their own particular capacity and point of view and, as a consequence they are as enduring as the world itself. It is as if God had varied the universe as many times as there are souls, or as if he had created so many miniature universes, fundamentally in agreement, but differentiated in appearances. There is nothing so rich as this uniform simplicity accompanied by perfect order. And we can see that each separate soul will fit in perfectly well, since it is one particular expression of the universe, or like a concentration of the universe. This again shows itself in that each body, and hence also our own, is affected in some way by all the others, and as a consequence the soul also participates in it.

[8] There in a few words is the whole of my philosophy. I am sure it is very accessible, since it contains nothing which does not agree with our experience, and it is founded on two sayings, which are as commonplace as any of the Italian theatre: 'that things elsewhere are the same as they are here', and this one from Tasso: '*che per variar natura e bella.*'[35] They seem inconsistent, but can be reconciled by taking one to be about fundamentals, and the other about styles and appearances. . . .

[35] 'nature is beautiful because it changes'.

9

Leibniz and Pierre Desmaizeaux

INTRODUCTION

Pierre Desmaizeaux (1673–1745),[1] educated in Switzerland, lived in England from 1699. He wrote a 'Life' of his friend Pierre Bayle for the fifth edition of the *Dictionary* (1740), and an account of John Toland for his edition of Toland's work (London, 1726). He edited a collection of items by Locke (London, 1720), and one of some by Leibniz (including, in the second edition, the 'New System') and other people — *Recueil de diverses pièces sur la philosophie . . . par MM. Leibniz, Clarke, Newton, et autres auteurs célèbres* (Amsterdam, 1720; 2nd edn. 1740).

A few years after its publication, Desmaizeaux wrote a critique of Leibniz's 'New System', sending a copy of it to Bayle in October 1700. Bayle replied that same month, saying that he had not passed it on to Basnage for publication in the *Histoire des ouvrages des savants*, as it was too long for a journal article. He urged Desmaizeaux to lengthen it still further and to publish it on its own.[2] Desmaizeaux did not do this, and a decade later, in 1711, he wrote to Leibniz, enclosing a fragment — the whole had been lost — of his critique, and asking for copies of Bayle's criticisms of the 'New System'. Leibniz replied that same year,[3] saying that Bayle's letters to him had mostly not related to the 'New System', and that in any case he could not lay his hands on them. In their stead he enclosed his as yet unpublished reply (PB6) to what Bayle had said in the second edition of the *Dictionary* (PB4).

With an interest aroused by the reference in Bayle's correspondence (published in 1714) to Desmaizeaux's critique of Leibniz, Jean

---

[1] See Joseph Almagor, *Pierre Des Maizeaux (1673–1745). Journalist and English Correspondent for Franco-Dutch Periodicals, 1700–1720* (Amsterdam, 1989).

[2] Bayle to Desmaizeaux, 22 Oct. 1700, in *Œuvres*, iv. 793–5.

[3] Leibniz to Desmaizeaux, 8 July 1711 (published later, in 1716); see D2 below.

Masson[4] seems to have written to Desmaizeaux asking for a copy. In response, Desmaizeaux (on 29 November 1715) sent one (in the form of a letter to Jean Masson) to Masson's brother, Samuel,[5] who, as editor of the *Histoire critique de la République des lettres*, had earlier solicited articles.[6] With it he also sent a copy of Leibniz's 1711 letter to him, and of Leibniz's reply to Bayle.[7] Masson published these (i.e. D1, D2, PB6) in the volume of his journal for 1716.[8][9][10] Later that year Leibniz wrote to Samuel Masson thanking him for this.[11]

[4] 1680?–1750, tutor, in England, to Bishop Gilbert Burnet's family.
[5] ?–?1742.
[6] Samuel Masson to Desmaizeaux, May 1714 (British Library, Add. MSS 4285, fo. 156).
[7] See Samuel Masson to Desmaizeaux, 20 March 1716 (British Library, Add. MSS 4285, fos. 170–1).
[8] An editorial note to D1 reads: 'This and the following three articles cannot but please the public, and in more than one way. Leaving aside their author's merit and reputation, there is an infinity of people, people who know very little of M. the Baron de Leibniz's "New system", who would be very glad of the opportunity of learning about it here, and who would be delighted to think they were in a position to make a judgement of it.'
  The 'three articles' referred to here are art. 4 (Leibniz's PB6), art. 2 (his D2), and art. 5, an anonymous piece possibly by John Toland, 'Remarques critiques sur le système de M. Leibniz de l'harmonie préétablie . . . ; écrits par ordre de sa majesté la feue reine de Prusse' (pp. 115–33). Leibniz's letter to Masson contains some reply to this rather superficial piece of invective and also a paragraph (see app. C) of further comment on Desmaizeaux's discussion of Hippocrates.
[9] Desmaizeaux himself republished these items in the 1st edn. (1720) of his *Recueil*; see app. A.
[10] Some years later (21 Aug. 1718) Desmaizeaux also sent the fragment of his critique of Leibniz to Antonio-Schinella Conti (1677–1749). It is evident from Desmaizeaux's letter to him (app. B) that Conti, like Masson earlier, had written to Desmaizeaux because of the reference in Bayle's letters. (In the preface to the 1st edn. of his *Recueil* (see app. A) Desmaizeaux says that he sent these remarks to Conti 'who had asked me for them; the journal in which they appeared having not yet come into his hands'.) Desmaizeaux's words to Conti are much the same as those to Masson; significant differences between the first (as published as D1) and the second (in the 1st edn. of his *Recueil*—call it D1') are recorded in our notes to D1. The beginning and end of the letters are, of course, different; see app. B for D1'.
[11] See app. C.

D1. DESMAIZEAUX: 'Explanation of a Passage
in Hippocrates' Book *Diet*, and of the Opinion of
Melissus and Parmenides about the Duration
in Existence of Substances, etc. To Serve as a
Response to Part of M. Leibniz's "New System
of the Nature and the Communication of
Substances, or of Pre-established Harmony".
By M. Des Maizeaux to M. Jean Masson,
Minister of the Anglican Church, etc.'
(1700; pub. 1716)[12]

[1] It is true, sir, that about fifteen years ago, I composed some
remarks on the new system of *the nature of substances and their
communication*, proposed by the illustrious M. Leibniz in the
Journal des savants for 1695. I sent this work to M. Bayle; and the
way he speaks of it in his letters[a] has made you curious to see it. But
I cannot let you have it. This little work is lost, or at least so
completely mislaid that I could not find it when I wrote to M. Leibniz three or four years ago, to ask him to send me the letters which
he had received from M. Bayle. I could only send him a scrap,
which had somehow been preserved. Some days ago I found by
chance a rough copy of most of this fragment, and so that your
hopes will not be completely frustrated, I am going to transcribe it
here, with a few amendments. As it concerns mostly a point of
criticism, I have persuaded myself that you will read it with less
distaste than if it discussed purely metaphysical speculations, which
are often both boundless and bottomless.

[2] But before doing that, let me, sir, recall here some features of
M. Leibniz's New System, which will help you to understand what
follows.[13] 'After much meditation',[b] he says, 'I saw that it is impossible to find the principles of a real unity in matter alone, or in what

[12] 'Explication d'un passage d'Hippocrate, dans le livre de la Diète, et du
sentiment de Melisse et de Parmenide, sur la durée des substances, etc.: pour servir
de réponse à un endroit du nouveau système de M. Leibniz, de la nature et de la
communication des substances, ou l'harmonie préétablie. Par M. Des Maizeaux:
à M. Jean Masson, Ministre de l'Église Anglicane, etc.', *Histoire critique de la
République des lettres tant ancienne que moderne*, 11 (1716), art. 2, pp. 52–72
(B 159). The volume also contains a further piece by Desmaizeaux—'Nouvelle
explication du passage d'Hippocrate dont il est parlé dans le second article de ce
volume. Par M. Des Maizeaux, à M. Jean Masson' (art. 13, pp. 290–7).
[13] D1' omits ', which will help you to understand what follows'.

is only passive, since this is nothing but a collection or aggregation of parts to infinity.' This thought obliged him to have recourse to 'atoms'—not to 'atoms of matter', for, in addition[c] to being 'contrary to reason', they are 'still composed of parts'—but to 'atoms of substance', that is to say, 'real unities absolutely devoid of parts, that would be the source of actions, and the absolute first principles of things, and as it were the ultimate elements in the analysis of substances'. He thinks they 'might be called metaphysical points'; and he adds that 'they have something of the nature of life and a kind of perception, and [that] mathematical points are their point of view for expressing the universe'. He also gives them the name[d] 'substantial forms', whose 'nature consists in force, and from which follows something analogous to feeling and desire; so that they must be understood along the lines of our notion of souls'. He also calls them 'primary forces, which contain not only actuality, or the mere fulfilment of a possibility, but also an originating activity'.

[3] 'I saw', M. Leibniz continues,[e] 'that these forms and souls had to be indivisible, like our minds'; from which 'it follows that they can come into being only by creation and end only by annihilation.' 'Also',[14] he adds, 'I had to recognize that (with the exception of souls which God still intends to create specially) the constitutive forms of substances must have been created with the world and must always continue to exist.' However, he does not want to say 'they pass from body to body';[f] this would be 'metempsychosis'. He turns[g] rather to 'the transformations noted by MM. Swammerdam, Malpighi, and Leeuwenhoek, who are the best observers of our day'[15] and supposes that 'no animal or other organized substance begins when we think it does, and that its apparent generation is only a development or a kind of augmentation'. But there remained a considerable difficulty. 'What', it will be asked, 'becomes of these souls or forms on the death of the animal or the destruction of the individual organized substance?' 'There is', M. Leibniz replies, 'only one view that can be taken, which is that not only is the soul conserved, but so also is the animal itself and its organic mechanism; although the destruction of its cruder parts has made it so small as to be as little perceptible to our senses as it was before its birth.' And in fact 'no one', he adds,[h] 'can exactly tell the true time

[14] For 'Also', D1' reads: 'Thus'.
[15] Desmaizeaux quotes Leibniz's 'des plus excellents' (among the best) as 'les plus excellents' (the best).

of death, which for a long time may be taken for a mere suspension of observable actions and which ultimately is nothing more than that in the case of simple animals: witness the resuscitation of flies which have been drowned and then buried in powdered chalk. . . . It is natural, then', he concludes, 'that an animal, since it has always been living and organized should always remain so. And so, since there is therefore no new[16] birth or entirely new generation of an animal, it follows that it will have no final extinction or complete death in the strict metaphysical sense; and that consequently, instead of the transmigration of souls, there is nothing but a transformation of one and the same animal, according as its organs are differently packed up, and more or less developed.'

[4] There, sir, is a completely new system, and consequently one well worth being included with the many other discoveries with which M. Leibniz has enriched the public. However, he himself did not think so favourably of it with regard to the *inextinction* of animals; his modesty persuaded him that several ancient philosophers had had the same ideas as his on this question. 'As for the ordinary run of animals and other corporeal substances,' he says,[i] 'which up till now have been thought to suffer total extinction and whose changes depend on mechanical rules rather than on moral laws, I am pleased to see that the ancient author of the book *Diet* (which is attributed to Hippocrates) had glimpsed something of the truth, when he expressly said that animals are not born and do not die, and that the things which we suppose to come into being and to perish merely appear and disappear. This was also the opinion of Parmenides and of Melissus according to Aristotle; for these ancients are sounder than we think.'

[5] It is certain, as M. Leibniz very sensibly remarks, that 'these ancients are sounder than is supposed'. But it is no less true that what his system says about the immortality[17] of animals was not known to them. The glory of originating it is entirely his, and we should not allow him to deprive himself of a benefit so legitimately acquired, so as to give it to people who have not the slightest claim to it. You will have no doubt of this, sir, when you have seen, in the comments I have promised you,[18] these philosophers' opinion, which M. Leibniz believed was similar to his. Let us begin with the author of the book *Diet*.

[16] For 'new', D1' reads 'first'.
[17] For 'immortality', D1' reads: 'indestructibility'.
[18] D1' omits ', in the comments I have promised you,'.

[6] After a kind of introduction, he presents a general maxim—
that 'all living things are, like man, composed of two principles,
namely fire and water, which are quite different in their properties,
but which nevertheless work together'.ʲ He goes on to say that they
sustain each other by their union, and form all other beings, though
they could never produce anything separately. *Fire* gives movement,
and *water* nourishment, to everything. These two principles continually war against and dominate one other, without either ever
being able finally to vanquish or destroy the other. They also
communicate their qualities to each other. And from all of this
comes the infinite diversity which we find in all the beings of the
world. Then he presents another maxim: 'no being perishes, and
none is produced which did not already exist; they only change
form, and mix together or separate from one another.' He concludes from this that ordinary people err greatly in believing that
there are real productions and destructions. 'However,' he says,
'since men prefer to believe their eyes rather than their reason, they
imagine that a thing is produced when, by growing, it passes from
the shadows into the light' (that is to say, when from being invisible
it becomes visible), 'and they believe that it perishes, when, by
contracting, it moves out of the light into the shadows' (that is to
say, when from being visible it becomes invisible). 'As for me,' he
continues, 'I am going to prove the contrary by reason. The former
beings', (which grow) 'as well as the latter' (which contract) 'are
living', that is to say, real, actual. 'Now, a living being', (that is to
say, a substance, a reality) 'can never die, unless the whole universe
dies as well—in which case it really would die. Nor is it possible
that something which is not should be born—for there is nothing
from which it can derive its birth. But all things grow or contract,
as far as their nature permits.'[19]

[7] There, sir, is the passage from *Diet* to which M. Leibniz drew

---

[19] Citing 'ibid. v', Desmaizeaux quotes in Greek from *Diet*: 'So of all things
nothing perishes, and nothing comes into being that did not exist before. Things
change merely by mingling and being separated. But the current belief among men
is that one thing increases and comes to light from Hades, while another thing
diminishes and perishes from the light into Hades. For they trust eyes rather than
mind, though these are not competent to judge even things that are seen. But I use
mind to expound thus. For there is life in the things of the other world, as well as
in those of this. If there be life, there cannot be death, unless all things die with it.
For whither will death take place? Nor can what is not come into being. For
whence will it come? But all things increase and diminish to the greatest possible
maximum or the least possible minimum' (as trans. by W. H. S. Jones, *Regimen*, I.
iv (*Hippocrates* (London, 1923), iv. 235)).

attention. As you see, there is nothing there which gets close to what his system says about the immortality of *animals*—they are not even mentioned. The author's reasoning is general, and applies to all kinds of *beings*. He refers to them loosely as 'living beings' because ordinary people, who consider things only in terms of the closest relation they have with them, count as genuine beings only[20] plants and animals, which are 'living beings': in so far as they see things 'living'—that is to say, growing, acting, moving—they do not doubt their existence, but as soon as they 'die'—that is to say, contract or disappear—they imagine that they lose their entire existence, and return to the nothingness from which they came. In trying to combat this received opinion, our author includes, as ordinary people do, all beings in general under the name 'living being', and shows that having once existed in the world, they must always exist, albeit under different forms and modifications. In fact, the word 'zōon', which he uses, means an 'animal', as well as a 'living being'; and this indeed is how Cornarius translates it in this passage.[k] But it is so obvious that 'animals' are not in question here, that M. Dacier, a quite faithful translator of Cornarius elsewhere, has departed from him on this occasion, and has given this very good translation: 'for all beings, those which contract as well as those which grow, are living beings.' I must point out, though, that he italicized the words 'living beings' without explaining why in his notes; but whatever motive he had in this, one cannot in fairness deny that he has captured the meaning perfectly. So it seems to me that one can paraphrase the passage in question somewhat as follows: 'Ordinary people think that things which emerge for the first time[21] are created, that is to say, originate, or acquire a being they did not have—and that those which contract and disappear are annihilated—that is to say, die, perish, or lose the being they had. But will it not be agreed that things which grow, and those that contract, are (after having grown and prior to shrinking) realities, or true beings? And if so, they will perish only if the entire world perishes. For, since the world is nothing but an assemblage of particular beings, if we suppose the total destruction of each of these beings, that of the universe will have to follow. Perhaps it will be said that the world would lose nothing by that, because the things that we see come into being and grow take the place of those

---

[20] For 'count as genuine beings only', D1' reads 'pay proper attention only to the changes which happen to'.

[21] For 'emerge for the first time', D1' reads:'appear for the first time, or grow'.

which perish, in acquiring a being they did not previously have. But where could a thing which is not derive its being from? What could give it to it? It cannot be another thing which does not exist any more than it does. So will it be a thing which already exists? But where does it get what it does not have? Or if it already has it,[22] it therefore existed before becoming visible. It was therefore a real and actual being already. So it has to be admitted that there could be neither production nor destruction, properly speaking; or, if you like, neither birth nor death, in the way that ordinary people understand it. And, as a consequence, all the changes which happen in the world are only enlargements and diminutions, joinings together, turnings away, combinings and separations, modifications or ways of being.' This is how this author expresses himself in what immediately follows. For after having promised to explain for the sake of the ordinary person what he means by 'birth' and 'death', he says that he 'doesn't mean by them anything other than *combining and separating*'.[23] And he develops his thought in more detail, by remarking that there is no difference between 'birth and death; combining and separating; birth and combining; death, diminution, and separation'. And he adds that 'the relation of each part to the whole, and of the whole to each part, is the same'.[24] And what he has already said, that if a living being could die, the entire world would undergo the same fate, is founded on this.

[8] So this principle of the author of *Diet*—that in the world 'nothing is born or dies'—comes down to precisely what all the ancient philosophers unanimously maintained, namely that nothing can come from nothing, and what has once existed cannot be reduced to nothing: '... Nil posse creari | De nihilo, neque quod genitum est, ad nil revocari'.[25] Diogenes Apolloniatus also said that 'nothing can come out of what is not, nor be corrupted', or be reduced 'into what is not'.[26] And from that it necessarily follows that

[22] D1' adds: 'or if it has it within itself'.

[23] Citing 'ibid. vi', Desmaizeaux quotes in Greek from *Diet*: 'what I really mean is "mingling" and "separating"' (*Regimen*, I. iv, in *Hippocrates*, trans. Jones, iv. 235).

[24] Citing 'ibid.', Desmaizeaux quotes in Greek from *Diet*: 'the relation of the individual to all things, and that of all things to the individual [is the same thing]' (*Regimen* I. iv, in *Hippocrates*, trans. Jones, iv. 237).

[25] 'nothing can be produced from nothing, and whatever has been made cannot be brought back to nothing' (in *Lucretius, De rerum natura*, trans. and ed. W. H. D. Rouse and M. F. Smith (London, 1975)).

[26] A note at this point cites 'Diog. Laert. bk. 9, para. 57', and quotes (in Greek)

all the changes which take place in the world are only combinings and separations, augmentations and diminutions, or—in a word—mere modifications. Our author is right to say after that, 'that we should not trust our eyes about this'; for in taking them as judges here we would have to believe that what they cannot see no longer exists, and that what appears to them for the first time did not exist before.

[9] Parmenides had the same ideas. He 'distinguished two kinds of philosophy: one *popular and crude*, which considers things on the basis of how they appear to the senses; and another, *more precise and more discerning*, which considers them by reason, and as they are in themselves'.[27] Melissus was of the same mind. 'There are', says Aristotle, 'philosophers, such as Melissus, and Parmenides, who deny any kind of generation and corruption. For they say that nothing is really born or corrupted—it only seems to us to be so.'[28] Aristotle himself seems not far from this view, for he says that 'regarding substances, the generation of one is always the corruption of another; and the corruption of one is the generation of another'.[29] However, we have seen that he does not approve of Melissus and Parmenides for having 'denied any kind of generation and corruption'—though perhaps he misunderstood them. I do not know, sir, whether I dare tell you here that I am very tempted to think that these ancient philosophers were not as absurd as they are

from Diogenes: 'Nothing comes into being from what is not or passes away into what is not' (in *Diogenes Laertius: Lives of Eminent Philosophers*, trans. R. D. Hicks (London, 1925), 9. 57).

[27] A note at this point cites 'Diog. Laert. ibid. para. 22', and quotes (in Greek) from Diogenes: 'He divided his philosophy into two parts dealing the one with truth, the other with opinion. . . . He made reason the standard and pronounced sensations to be inexact' (in *Diogenes Laertius: Lives*, trans. Hicks, 9. 22).

[28] A note at this point cites 'Arist., *De caelo*, iii. 1 (bk. 1, *Opera*, p. 654. Edit. Aur[eliae] Allobr[ogum] [Geneva] 1607 in octavo), and quotes (in Greek) from *De caelo*, 3. 1, 298b15–18: 'Some of them [earlier seekers after truth] flatly denied generation and destruction, maintaining that nothing which is either comes into being or perishes; it only seems to us as if they do. Such were the followers of Melissus and Parmenides' (in *Aristotle on the Heavens*, trans. W. K. C. Guthrie (London 1939)).

[29] A note at this point cites '*Id. de Generat. et Corrupt.* bk. 1, p. 692', and quotes (in Greek) from *De generatione et corruptione*, i. 3, 319b21–3: 'in the case of substances, the coming-to-be of one thing is always a passing-away of another, and the passing-away of one thing another's coming-to-be' (in *Aristotle: On Sophistical Refutations; On Coming-to-Be and Passing-Away*, trans. E. S. Forster (London, 1955)).

made out to be, when they are supposed to have[30] denied the evidence of the senses completely and literally, and maintained *acatalepsy*',[31] the incomprehensibility of all things, and so on. It is more probable that they expressed themselves in that way only on account of popular opinion or of superficial appearances and not in a proper and metaphysical sense. But that would be the subject of a large dissertation.[32]

[10] If I wanted to pursue further the parallel between the system of the author of *Diet* and that of the[33] ancient philosophers, I would add[34] that they[35] recognize the two same principles as he does: namely, *water* and *fire*. Parmenides, in the opinion of Diogenes Laertius, attributes the generation of men to the sun, and goes on to say that this star 'is composed of cold and heat, which are', he says, 'the principles of all things'.[36] Zeno believed that 'all things derive their nature from heat and cold'.[37] Heraclitus attributed the origin of all things to *fire*. But by 'fire' he meant a warmth which was moderate, mixed with *humidity*. Lucretius did not understand this, and held it up to ridicule. 'Dicere porro Ignem res omneis esse, neque ullam | Rem veram in numero rerum constare, nisi Ignem: | Quod facit hic idem: perdelirum esse videtur, etc.'[38]

[30] For this sentence up to here, D1' reads 'And I would be glad if you would tell me, sir, whether you, who have a thorough knowledge of the different systems of ancient and modern philosophy, think that Melissus, Parmenides, Xenophanes, etc. when they'.

[31] 'Arcesilaus [*c*.315–240 BC, founder of the Middle Academy] said that there is nothing that can be known . . . : so hidden in obscurity did he believe that everything lies, nor is there anything that can be perceived or understood. . . .', (Cicero, *Academica*, I. 12. 45, in *Cicero: De natura deorum academica*, trans. H. Rackham (London, 1933)).

[32] In place of the last two sentences, D1' has 'Isn't it more likely that they only wanted to deny the ordinary person's opinion, or that they spoke only with respect to superficial appearances? Don't wait for your work on the philosophy of the ancients to be completed before telling me what you think of this.'

[33] For 'the', D1' reads 'other'.

[34] For 'add', D1' reads 'remark'.

[35] For 'they', D1' reads 'there are several of them who'.

[36] A note at this point cites 'Diog. Laert. bk. 9, paras. 21, 22', and quotes Diogenes (in Greek) from the last parts of the following: 'He held that there were two elements, fire and earth, and that the former discharged the function of a craftsman, the latter of his material. The generation of man proceeded from the sun as first cause; heat and cold, of which all things consist, surpass the sun itself' (in *Diogenes Laertius: Lives*, trans. Hicks, 9. 22).

[37] A note at this point cites 'Idem. ibid. para. 29', and quotes (in Greek) from Diogenes to the effect that 'The substance of all things came from hot and cold' (in ibid. 9. 29).

[38] A note at this point cites 'Lucret. bk. 1 [D1' adds 'vers. 690 f.']'. The text

[11] But to return to M. Leibniz: it seems to me, sir, that I have shown quite clearly that the ancient philosophers which he names had no *inkling* of anything like his theory about the *inextinction of animals* when they maintained that 'nothing is born, or dies' and that 'the things which are thought to begin and perish, only appear and disappear'. M. Leibniz appears to agree with that himself in the letter which he did me the honour of writing to me when he had seen the fragment of which I have given you a small piece. You will, without doubt, be very happy, sir, to see that letter: everything which comes from such a great man's hands is valuable; and furthermore it may help to make his *new system of the nature and the communication of substances*, or of *pre-established harmony* better understood. He was kind enough to send me, at the same time, his reply to the objections that M. Bayle had made against this system, in the second edition of his *Dictionary*,[39] and I am sending it to you, certain that you will read it with great pleasure. M. Leibniz refers to it in his careful remarks on M. (Sr. [*sic*] = ? Mr.) du Sauzet's[40] *Nouvelles littéraires*;[m] and he even implied that he would not mind if this little work were published. So, sir, you can deal with it as you see fit. I am etc.

[DESMAIZEAUX'S NOTES]

a. *M. Bayle's Selected Correspondence*, ii. 705–6; letter of 22 Oct. 1700. [*Lettres choisies . . . avec des remarques*, 3 vols. (Rotterdam, 1714)].

b. *Journal des savants*, 1695, p. 446 (Dutch edn.) [see NS1, § 3].

c. Ibid. p. 453 [see NS1, § 11].

d. p. 446 [see NS1, § 3].

e. p. 443 [*sic*] [= p. 447; see NS1, § 4].

f. p. 448 [see NS1, § 6].

g. p. 449 [see NS1, § 6].

h. p. 450 [pp. 449–50; see NS1, § 7].

i. p. 451 [see NS1, § 9].

j. 'Now all animals (*zoa*), including man, are composed of two things, different in power but working together in their use, namely fire and water', *Diet*, I. iv, p. 182 (vol. 1, Op. Hip. Ed. Vander Lind)[41] [The English for Desmaizeaux's reads: 'Further, to say that all things are fire, and that there exists no true thing in the number of things except fire, as this same man does, appears to be raving madness' (in *Lucretius*, *De rerum natura*, trans. Rouse and Smith, 1. 690).

[39] D1' diverges from here on (see app. B).

[40] Henri du Sauzet (1686–1754), who was for a time the publisher of this journal.

[41] J. Antonidae van der Linden, *Magni Hippocratis Coi opera omnia, graece et latine edita . . .*, 2 vols. (Leiden, 1665).

Greek quotation is from Jones's translation of *Regimen*, I. iv (*Hippocrates*, iv. 231).] M. Dacier[42] seems to have understood nothing of this author's philosophical system, for instead of following the original, he only translated here the Latin version of Cornarius, who supposes that 'zoa' here means 'animals'. 'All animals,' he says, 'brutes as well as men, are composed of two principles, etc.'

k. 'Animalia enim', says Cornarius,[43] 'sunt et illa et haec: et neque Animal mori possibile est, non cum omnibus: (unde enim moriatur?) neque quod non est, generari etc.'[44] This is a real farrago; besides which, instead of explaining the sense of the original 'kai gar apothaneitai',[45] he put 'unde enim moriatur?'[46] — a question which fits with neither the flow of the discourse, nor the reasoning of the author. Yet M. Dacier has followed Cornarius here, even though he had diverged from him in the preceding words. 'Car tous les Êtres', he says, 'tant ceux qui diminuent, que ceux qui croissent', are living. 'Or il n'est pas possible qu'un Être vivant meure, s'il ne meurt avec l'Univers. Car qu'est-ce qui le pourroit faire mourir?'[47] — as though the original were 'hothen gar apothaneitai'.[48] He nevertheless points out in his notes, that 'au lieu de cette interrogation, la leçon la plus commune est, "kai gar apothaneitai", et il mourra aussi';[49] but what he goes on to say shows us that he has not entirely grasped the sense of his author: 'ce qui me paroit', he says, 'remarquable; car Hippocrate diroit en termes formels, que l'Univers doit périr; à moins qu'on n'explique ce passage comme Zuingerus,[50] "car tout mourra si une partie meurt".'[51] He should have said, 'car le tout mourra, si chaque partie meurt';[52] and indeed this 'interpretation' is preferable to all the others; one can even say that it is the only reasonable one.

---

[42] A. Dacier, *Les Œuvres d'Hippocrate, traduites en François* ..., 2 vols. (Paris, 1697).

[43] J. Cornarius, *Hippocratis ... libri omnes ...* (Basle, 1538).

[44] As in n. 19, the English translation of the corresponding Loeb Greek text is: 'For there is life in the things of the other world, as well as in those of this. If there be life, there cannot be death, unless all things die with it. For whither (*poi*) will death take place? Nor can what is not come into being.'

[45] 'it will indeed die'; see Loeb text, p. 234, n. 4, for this different manuscript original.

[46] 'For whence (Greek: *hothen*) will it die?'; the corresponding Loeb Greek text (which has *poi* rather than *hothen*) translation is: 'For whither will death take place?'

[47] 'For all beings, those which contract, as well as those which grow, are living. Now, it is not possible that a living being should die, unless it dies with the whole universe. For what could make it die?'

[48] 'whence will it die?'

[49] 'instead of this question, the most common lesson is, "it will indeed die", and it will also die.'

[50] Theodor Zwinger, *Hippocratis ... viginti duo commentarii tabulis illustrati ... latina versio Jani Cornarii ... correcta ...* (Basle, 1579).

[51] '"this seems remarkable to me", he says, "for Hippocrates says explicitly that the universe must perish — unless we interpret this passage like Zuingerus, as 'for the whole dies if one part dies'."'

[52] 'for the whole dies, if each part dies'.

l. Lucretius, bk. 1 [D1' adds 'vers. 543, 544'].

m. *Nouvelles Littéraires*, 9 Nov. 1715, p. 290[53] [B 148].

D2. LEIBNIZ: 'A Letter . . . to M. Desmaizeaux, Containing some Comments on the Preceding Explanation, and on other Parts of the "System of Pre-established Harmony, etc."', Hanover, 8 July 1711[54]

[1] I am very grateful to you for the honour of your letter and for the note you sent with it. I was requested on your behalf, when I was in Berlin, to send you any letters I might have from M. Bayle. But the three or four that I had from him were related almost entirely to other writings, which meant that I did not keep them carefully, and so I could not easily find them, even though they must still be in the pile of my old papers. I remember that in one of his letters he thought that I conceived the force I had given to bodies as something which could be contained in them even when they were at rest. But I pointed out to him that according to me force is always accompanied by actual movement; somewhat as happenings in the soul are always accompanied by something corresponding to them in the body. Also, a momentary state of a moving body—which cannot involve movement, since that requires time—still contains force.

[2] However, in order to go some way towards satisfying your request, sir, I am sending you my *Reply* to what M. Bayle included about my system in the second edition of his *Dictionary*, in the article on 'Rorarius'. Perhaps M. Bayle has replied to it in some supplement to his *Dictionary*, or somewhere else as yet unpublished. For he told me, I seem to remember, that he wanted to think about it. But as neither this reply of mine nor his response has yet appeared, I am sending you what I have written pretty much as I sent it to M. Bayle. I say 'pretty much as', for on rereading it I changed it a little. I would be glad to learn your view of it, if you

[53] See Ch. 5, n. 17.

[54] 'Lettre de M. Leibniz à M. Des Maizeaux, contenant quelques éclaircissemens sur l'explication précédente, et sur d'autres endroits du système de l'harmonie préétablie, etc.', *Histoire critique de la République des lettres*, vol. 11, 1716 (art. 3, pp. 72–8) (B 160; R 192). Desmaizeaux reprints this (= D2') at *Recueil*, 1st edn., ii. 382–8.

would be so good as to compare it with M. Bayle's above-mentioned piece. I would be delighted to have your views on my last book too.ᵃ

[3] I come now to the fragment from your reflections on my *New System*, which were sent to M. Bayle; I wish I had seen them all. I do not refuse to *men* the privilege I allow to *animals*. Accordingly, I believe that human souls have pre-existed, not as rational souls, but only as sensitive souls, which rose to this higher level—that is to say, to reason—only when the men that they were to animate were conceived.

[4] I grant an existence as old as the world, not only to the souls of animals, but generally to all *monads*, or simple substances, from which compound phenomena result. And I hold that each soul, or monad, is always accompanied by an organic body, though one which is in perpetual change—so much so that the body is never the same, even though both the soul and the animal are. These rules also hold of the human body; but obviously in a more excellent manner than with the other animals which are known to us, since man must remain not only an animal, but also a person and citizen of the city of God—the most perfect state possible, under[55] the most perfect monarch.

[5] You say, sir, in your fragment, that you don't really understand 'what are the other corporeal substances, besides animals, in whose complete extinction we have until now believed'. But if there are living organic bodies in nature other than those of animals (and there certainly appear to be, for plants seem to provide an example), these bodies too will have their simple substances, or *monads*, which give them life—that is to say, perception and appetite, although that perception certainly does not have to be sensation. It would appear that there are infinite degrees of perception, and hence of *living things*. But these living things will be for ever indestructible, not only in respect of the simple substance, but also because it will always retain some organic body.

[6] As for the ancients, I admit that their usual views do not get so far as mine about the *inextinction* of animals. Their *indestructibility* ordinarily extends only as far as matter, or as far as atoms at the very most; and so it can be said that according to the theory of those who admit neither atoms nor entelechies, no substance is conserved. However, in all the variety of ancient thought there may

---

[55] Dɪ' omits '—the most perfect state possible, under'.

have been some whose opinions get close to mine. Plato believed that though material things were in perpetual flux, true substances continued to exist. He seems to have meant only souls, but perhaps Democritus, atomist though he was, still conserved animals, for he taught that there is revival, since Pliny says of him: *reviviscendi promissa Democrito vanitas, que ipse non revixit.*[56] We know almost nothing about this great man, except what was used by Epicurus, who was not always capable of taking the best. Perhaps Parmenides, who (according to Plato) taught that all was one, had views close to those of Spinoza, and so it should not be so surprising if some should have got close to mine. And although the conservation of the animal is supported by the microscope, minute bodies had been recognized before its invention; and so minute animals could also easily have been predicted, just as Democritus predicted stars in the Milky Way which were undetectable before the invention of the telescope. The mere conservation of matter or of elements does not seem sufficient to explain the author of *Diet*, since he expressly says that 'nothing living dies', and, generally, that 'no true being' (no substance) 'is either born or perishes'. If he only meant the conservation of matter, would he speak of it in this way? At the least, it must be admitted that in that case his words fit my system better than his.

[7] As for the rest, sir, you are right in this extract to attribute to me a 'remnant of Cartesianism'; for I agree that I accept part of the doctrine of the Cartesians. But my view on the commerce between the soul and the body has foundations which were generally accepted before the advent of Cartesianism. . . .

[DESMAIZEAUX'S NOTE]

a. *Theodicy.*

Appendix A. DESMAIZEAUX: Preface (dated 27 October 1719)
to *Recueil* (1720)

M. Leibniz sent me this reply [PB6] in 1711; and some time afterwards, as he had indicated that he would be happy if it were

---

[56] 'simils et de adservandis Democriti vanitas, qui non revixit ipse': 'Similar also is the vanity about preserving men's bodies, and about Democritus's promise of our coming to life again—who did not come to life again himself!' (Pliny, *Natural History*, bk. 7, ch. 25 (in *Pliny: Natural History*, 10 vols., trans. H. Rackham (London, 1942), ii. 635); see also text at Ch. 2, n. 39).

made public,[a] it was published in volume 11 of the *Histoire critique de la République des lettres*, preceded by some *Remarks* on a passage in the system of *pre-established harmony*, which I had sent to M. Leibniz [D1], and by the letter which he then wrote to me [D2]. I had made several other remarks on this new system, but they had been lost, and I was able to send M. Leibniz only this fragment, in which I consider whether he was right to say that his hypothesis about the *inextinction* or *indestructibility* of animals was familiar to Melissus, to Parmenides, and to the author of the book *Diet.*[b]

M. Leibniz died before the volume of the *Histoire critique de la République des lettres* which contained his reply to M. Bayle could reach him. It appears that in order to make this piece of work better known he would, if he had lived longer, have had it put in the French journals as well—as was his practice with several other pieces. Yet even that might not have made it known to everyone who has M. Bayle's *Dictionary*, because it is the usual fate of pieces published in journals to be soon forgotten, or to be read by only a small number of people. In only a few years, it is as if they are buried there. So convinced was M. Leibniz of this that he hoped that several small writings of his which were scattered through the journals would be made up into a collection. 'If some publisher', he says in one of his letters to M. Remond, written from Vienna,[57] 'wanted to put together what there is of mine in the different journals, he could make a small volume out of them. When I get back to Hanover,' he adds, 'I will tell you where they all are.' He himself took the trouble of collecting together those pieces which concerned his *system of pre-established harmony*, and of sending them to M. Remond. 'I am sending you', he says to him in another letter,[58] 'a small discourse on my philosophy which I have produced here for M. the Prince Eugène of Savoy.[59] I thought that this small work would help towards making my thoughts better understood, by putting it together with what I have published in the journals of Leipzig, Paris, and Holland.'[60] So I think that in reprinting here his

[57] As a footnote at this point reminds us, Desmaizeaux printed this letter (Leibniz to Remond, Vienna, 10 Jan. 1714) in his *Recueil*, ii. 129–36; 2nd edn., 130–7 (see also G 3. 605–7).
[58] Desmaizeaux printed a version of this letter (Leibniz to Remond, Vienna, 26 Aug. 1714) too, in *Recueil*, ii. 155–8; 2nd edn, 144–7 (see also G 3. 624).
[59] 'Principles of Nature and Grace' (R 335).
[60] If Desmaizeaux's words here imply that in Aug. 1714 Leibniz sent Remond

reply to M. Bayle I am conforming to M. Leibniz's wishes. I have accompanied it by the *Remarks* which I made on the passage in his system of *pre-established harmony*, of which I have spoken [D1]. These *Remarks* are just as I sent them to M. the Abbé Conti, who had asked me for them [D1'], the journal in which they appeared having not yet come into his hands. I have also included the letter which M. Leibniz wrote to me after receiving them [D2]. It contains an explanation of some passages in his *new system of pre-established harmony*.

[DESMAIZEAUX'S NOTES]

a. See *Nouvelles Littéraires*, 2 (9 Nov. 1715), p. 290.
b. It is commonly believed that this book was written by Hippocrates, but the critics do not agree.

not only a manuscript copy of the 'Principles of Nature and Grace' but also 'pieces which concerned his *system of pre-established harmony*', they are wrong. Not only had Leibniz not yet returned to Hanover then, but also, even after he had returned, Remond still pressed him to fulfil his promise—having warned him he would do so (Remond to Leibniz, 5 May 1714: 'When you return to Hanover I shall not fail to make you remember your promise' (G 3. 618)). It is true that by the time of receiving the copy of the 'Principles' Remond appeared to have read some of the articles Leibniz must have had in mind (Remond to Leibniz, Paris, 12 Oct. 1714: 'I confess to you that after having read some of what you have communicated to the public about your philosophical system, I thought I had a fair idea of it. The excellent writing which you honoured me by sending . . . has confirmed me in that' (G 3. 629)). But on 9 Jan. 1715, when Leibniz was back in Hanover, Remond still asked for 'the list, which you promised me you would give me as soon as you returned to Hanover, of all your works whether they are printed separately or scattered in different journals' (G 3. 633). Though (see n. 62) Leibniz did send Remond various things (which Desmaizeaux later published), there is no evidence that, in Desmaizeaux's words, Leibniz 'took the trouble of collecting himself those pieces which concerned his *system of pre-established harmony*, and of sending them to M. Remond'.

Has Desmaizeaux perhaps misunderstood what Leibniz meant when, in sending the 'Principles of Nature and of Grace' to Remond (Aug. 1714; see n. 59), he says: 'I thought that this small work would help towards making my thoughts better understood by putting it together with (*en y joignant*) what I have published in the journals'? Perhaps he has taken Leibniz to mean '*and I am hereby putting with it* what I have published in the journals', rather than '*when it is taken in conjunction with* what I have published in the journals'.

Appendix B. DESMAIZEAUX: 'Letter to M. l'Abbé Conti,
Containing the Explanation of a Passage from Hippocrates' (1718;
pub. 1720)[61]

Kensington, 21 August 1718

Sir, I have read with much pleasure the manuscript pieces of
M. Leibniz which you kindly sent me.[62] Without doubt they deserve
to be given to the public; and I shall certainly add them to the other
writings of this great man, which I am going to have printed in
Holland. The public will be indebted to you for it. . . .

With regard to the remarks on M. Leibniz's *New System of the
Nature and the Communication of Substances*, which I wrote in
1700, and which you ask me for, sir, I will give you the same reply
as I gave, three years ago, to M. Masson,[a] who, like you, read what
M. Bayle said about them in one of his letters[b] and was curious to
see them. I told him that this little work had been lost, or at least
so completely mislaid that I could not find it when I wrote to
M. Leibniz in 1711, to ask him to send me the letters which he had
received from M. Bayle; and that I had been able to send him only a
fragment, of which I had no copy. However, having afterwards by
chance retrieved some of this fragment, I sent it to M. Masson,
having rewritten it a little; and he printed it in his brother's journal.[c]

---

[61] 'Lettre de M. Des Maizeaux à M. l'Abbé Conti, contenant l'explication
d'un passage d'Hippocrate . . .', in Desmaizeaux, *Recueil* (1720), ii. 362–81; 2nd
edn., 457–77.
[62] Which manuscript pieces of Leibniz were these, which Desmaizeaux said he
would print with other Leibniz writings in his forthcoming *Recueil*? In the course
of discussing the *Recueil*'s contents, Desmaizeaux refers in the preface to 'several
Letters and Fragments of M. Leibniz' (pp. lxvi–lxvii; 2nd edn., p. lxxxix). The
letters, he says, 'are nearly all written to M. Remond, to whom M. Leibniz sent at
the same time the articles which make up the *Fragments*. I give them here after the
originals which M. l'Abbé Conti had the kindness to send me from Paris. I have
put with them two or three pieces of M. Leibniz which have already appeared but
which have become quite rare, and into which in addition there had crept many
faults, which I have corrected.'
Apart from a letter to him from Leibniz, Conti presumably got what he sent to
Desmaizeaux from Nicolas Remond (through whom Conti and Leibniz first came
into contact; see the Leibniz–Remond correspondence from 5 May 1714 in G 3.
615 ff.). At any rate, Remond was in possession of manuscripts of some of what
first appeared in the *Recueil*—having got them from Leibniz (see e.g. Leibniz to
Remond, 11 Feb., 22 June 1715 (G 3. 637, 645)), or (in one case) from Pierre
Coste (Remond to Leibniz, 4 Sept. 1715 (G 3. 650)). The pieces which 'have
already appeared' are PB6, D1/D1', and D2. As for the 'many faults which had
crept in' to these, the main differences between the texts we have translated and
Desmaizeaux's are noted in the relevant places.

This piece concerns the similarity that M. Leibniz thought he saw between his theory about the *inextinction* and *indestructibility* of animals and the opinion of some ancient philosophers. Since you have not seen it, sir, you will perhaps not object if I add it here. . . .[63] As M. Leibniz had indicated some time afterwards that he would not mind if this little work were made public,[d] it was published in M. Masson's journal, together with the letter of which I spoke.[e] You will find it attached to this letter. Apart from the explanations which related to M. Bayle's objections, this *Reply* contains many things that you will read with pleasure. You know that M. Leibniz had the knack of always enlivening his material by some curious and interesting point. I am with perfect devotion, sir, your etc.

[DESMAIZEAUX'S NOTES]

a. M. Jean Masson, so well known for his profound knowledge of chronology, antiquities, and coins.
b. *M. Bayle's Letters*, letter of 22 Oct. 1700 (iii. 801).
c. *Histoire critique de la République des lettres tant ancienne que moderne*, xi. 52 f.
d. See M. Du Sauzet's *Nouvelles Littéraires*, 2 (9 Nov. 1715), p. 290.
e. *Histoire critique de la République des lettres*, xi. 72, 78.

Appendix C. LEIBNIZ: Letter to Samuel Masson, 21 August 1716[64]

I am grateful to you, sir, as well as to M. Desmaizeaux, for the publication, in volume 11 of your journal, of several articles pertaining to my system. His learned reflections on the passage from the author 'of the book *Diet* attributed to Hippocrates' are worthy of being preserved. When he denied a true generation and a true destruction, perhaps this ancient author had the atoms of Democritus in mind, for they were supposed to persist for ever. But perhaps also the words 'A living being cannot die, unless the whole universe also dies (or perishes)' mean something more. For when they are taken literally, I can think of no better way to express my view. I do not know if it is likely that by the word 'zōon', or 'living being', the author meant all reality, as for example an atom

[63] From here on, until its own ending (see n. 40), the letter is identical with D1 from § 2 to near the end of § 11.
[64] From the French at G 6. 624-9.

according to those who believe in them. In fact, according to me, everything that one can truly call 'a substance' is a living being; so the author would also agree with me about this, it seems, if by 'zōon' he meant all true substances. But I do not want to enter into an argument about that with M. Desmaizeaux; and given that they do not go into detail, it would seem difficult fully to decipher the views of the ancients. It is worth while to consider them nevertheless, and to observe the intimations of the truth when it first began to show itself to men.

Leibniz and René Joseph de Tournemine

INTRODUCTION

René Joseph de Tournemine (1661–1739) was the founding editor, in 1701, of the Jesuit journal *Mémoires pour l'histoire des sciences et des beaux arts*, otherwise known, from its place of publication, as the *Mémoires de Trévoux*.[1] In 1703 he published in it his own 'Conjectures on the Union of the Soul and Body' (T1), in which he supported Leibniz's 'New System' account of the union against that of the occasionalists. His one caution was that Leibniz's pre-established harmony did not sufficiently account for the *intimacy* between soul and body.

Though it was not published until 1708, Leibniz had composed and sent off a reply (T2) to Tournemine's 'Conjectures' by early 1706.[2] In it he conceded that Tournemine's one worry was indeed just as applicable to his system as to that of the occasionalists. He added, however, that he had attempted to give only a non-miraculous, natural explanation of the perceived relation between soul and body, and had not attempted to say anything further than that in explanation of the metaphysical union of the mind with the body and their 'presence' to each other. In response (T3), Tournemine found Leibniz's concession very important: it showed that more work needed to be done.

---

[1] There was also a Protestant version of the *Mémoires*, a 'Seconde Edition, augmentée de diverses Remarques, et de plusieurs Articles nouveaux', published in Amsterdam. So it can happen that the same article has two different sets of publication details (as e.g. in n. 3), and that the Amsterdam edn. can have an article that was never in the corresponding Trévoux edn. (as e.g. in Ch. 5, n. 114).

[2] See Leibniz to de Volder, 19 Jan. 1706 (G 2. 281), to des Bosses, 2 Feb. 1706 (G 2. 296), 14 Feb. 1706 (G 2. 301), 3 Sept. 1708 (G 2. 354); and, for all of this, Donald Rutherford, 'Metaphysics: The Late Period', in N. Jolley (ed.), *The Cambridge Companion to Leibniz* (Cambridge, 1995), p. 173, n. 88.

T1. DE TOURNEMINE: 'Conjectures on the Union of the Soul and the Body, by Father Tournemine' (*Mémoires de Trévoux*, May 1703)[3]

[1] You[4] ask me, sir, to explain to you clearly what the union of the soul and the body consists in. . . . Most university philosophers would reply to your question that the soul and the body are united because a certain thing unites them. If you ask them what this thing is, they will solemnly tell you that it is an *entity*, whose distinctive quality is to unite; that it is neither body nor mind, and that although it is indivisible, it is partly corporeal and partly spiritual. If you don't understand that, so much the worse for you: you don't have a mind which is suited to speculative studies. Others will reply to you more briefly that the soul and the body are united because they unite themselves—there is a nice neat answer for you.

[2] But your curiosity goes further. You want to know what [the] union of the soul and the body consists in, what it is that makes them unite. The Cartesians, who have greatly refined the philosophy of the universities, will perhaps satisfy your curiosity. The soul and the body, they will tell you, are united because to each change in the body there corresponds a change in the soul, and in the same way to each change in the soul there corresponds a change in the body. But you will say that the mutual interchange of passions, of feelings, and of movements is a consequence, an effect, of the union of the soul and the body; and that you are asking for its proximate cause, for what creates that union. You are not easily satisfied! However, those Cartesians who aren't content to stay on the surface of a problem, and who enquire into everything, will know perfectly well how to reply: the soul and the body are united because God willed it, and set up a law about it. This reply is very devout: I don't know whether you will find it sufficiently philosophical. You are doubtless aware that everything happens because God wills it, but would like to know how what God has resolved to do takes place. Well, the Cartesians will again attempt to satisfy you. They will tell you that the soul and the body are united

---

[3] 'Conjectures sur l'union de l'âme et du corps. Par le P. Tournemine', *Mémoires pour l'histoire des sciences et des beaux arts*, May 1703, art. 91, pp. 864–75; June 1703, art. 106, pp. 1063–5; Amsterdam edn., art. 16, vol. 7, Mar. 1704, pp. 231–9 (B 71).

[4] We have been unable to determine to whom Tournemine is referring here.

because God, in consequence of a law which he has laid down for himself, doesn't produce any change in the soul without producing one in the body, and that he doesn't produce any movement in the body without producing a change in the soul. For God, according to them, is the immediate originator of all movements. You know about what the Cartesians call 'occasional causes': you remember that it isn't the cannon-ball which knocks down the wall, but God who knocks it down on the occasion of the ball. If this reply doesn't satisfy you, you can look for another: the Cartesians have nothing further to say to you.

[3] The famous M. Leibniz, that universal mind who has written on all branches of learning, and who has excelled in them all and cast new light on everything he has considered, has brought out the absurdity of the Cartesian view by the simile of two clocks, the motions of which are perfectly matched. If the whole secret of this correspondence consisted in the continuous involvement of the clock-maker, adjusting the springs of these two clocks at the same time and in the same way, then the agreement between the two machines would be no great achievement, and would show no great skill on the part of the workman. What M. Leibniz has come up with on the union of the soul and the body shows much more imagination, and is much more worthy of God. He suggests that God, perceiving through the clarity of his infinite knowledge everything that will happen to the animated body in all the situations it will ever be in, was careful to create for every body a soul which, from within itself and its own nature, passes through all the same changes as the body, and which at every moment has the disposition and the feelings which correspond exactly to the current state of the body—and all without the body's operating on the soul, which is impossible, and without God's being obliged at every moment to raise the weight of the clock, which is ridiculous. Once again, this idea is excellent and splendid; but its splendour and its excellence have concealed its weakness from its ingenious creator.

[4] He makes against the Cartesians an objection which entirely destroys their theory of the union of the soul and the body. Neither the law which God lays down for himself to act in parallel on the soul and on the body, nor the correspondence between the changes in the one and the changes in the other, can produce any genuine union between the soul and the body. There is, if you like, a perfect correspondence; but there is no real connection, any more than

there would be between the two clocks we have just discussed. There is no answer to this objection; but unfortunately, it destroys M. Leibniz's theory as well as that of the Cartesians. For after all, *correspondence*, or *harmony*, does not make a *union*, or essential connection. Whatever parallels we imagine between two clocks, even if the relation between them were perfectly exact, we could never say that these clocks were united just because the movements of the one correspond to the movements of the other with perfect symmetry.

[5] We must therefore go further to find a principle which will explain clearly the union of the soul with the body. We need to find a principle which will show that there is not only harmony and correspondence between these two substances, but also a connection, or essential dependence; not merely a virtual or apparent union which depends on some arbitrary law, but one which is actual and real: a union which is not superficial but intrinsic; a union of possession and of right, not merely of occupancy and custom. We need a principle which will show that the soul and the body are united in a different way from the citizens of the same town, from the workman and the tool he uses, or from a space and the body that fills it. In a word, we need a principle which shows that there is between a certain body and a certain soul a connection so natural, so essential and so necessary, that no soul other than mine could animate my body, and no body except mine could be animated by my soul. It is on that basis that I am going to offer you my conjectures. . . .

T2. LEIBNIZ: Extract from 'Comment on an article in the *Mémoires de Trévoux* for March 1704' (1708)[5]

[1] The Reverend Father Tournemine has spoken of me so kindly in one of his *Conjectures*, which the *Mémoires de Trévoux* have brought to us, and which are ingenious as usual, that it would be

---

[5] 'Remarque de Monsieur de Leibniz sur un endroit des *Mémoires de Trévoux* de mois de mars 1704', *Mémoires pour l'histoire des sciences et des beaux arts*, Mar. 1708, vol. 21, art. 35, pp. 492–6 (B 100; R 175). T1, which first appeared in the Trévoux edn. of the *Mémoires* for May and June of 1703, came out in the Amsterdam edn. for Mar. 1704 (see n. 3).

wrong of me to complain that he attributes to me an objection against the Cartesians of which I have no memory, and which could quite obviously be turned back against me. However, I do declare that if I ever made this objection, I renounce it from now on. I would have made this declaration earlier, if I had not seen this article in the *Mémoires* so late.

[2] I have to admit that I would be greatly mistaken if I objected against the Cartesians that the agreement which, according to them, God maintains immediately between the soul and the body, does not create a genuine unity, because most certainly my *pre-established harmony* could not do it any better.

[3] My aim was to explain naturally what they explain by perpetual miracles, and in doing so I attempted only to give an explanation of the phenomena, that is to say, of the relation we perceive between the soul and the body.

[4] But since this metaphysical union, which is added on to that, is not a phenomenon, and as we have not even been given any intelligible notion of it, I have not taken it upon myself to look for an explanation of it.

[5] However, I do not deny that there may be something of this kind; it would be something like presence,[6] which is also something whose notion has not been explained as it is applied to incorporeal things, and is distinguished from the *relations of harmony* which go along with it. These relations, too, are phenomena which serve to indicate the location of the incorporeal thing.

[6] When we see that there is union and presence in material things, we think there must be something somehow analogous in immaterial things; but since there is nothing more that we can understand about these things, we have only obscure notions of them.

[7] It is the same with mysteries, where again we try to elevate what we understand in the normal course of created things into something more sublime which would correspond to them with respect to nature or the divine power; but we cannot understand in such things anything sufficiently distinct to be suitable for making a fully intelligible definition.

[8] And that is the reason why we can never perfectly explain such mysteries, or fully understand them, here on earth. There is

[6] Leibniz discusses the notion of 'presence' further in correspondence with des Bosses (G 2. 389 ff.).

more to them than mere words, but there is no way we can come to a precise explanation of them. . . .

T3. DE TOURNEMINE: 'Father Tournemine's Reply' (*Mémoires de Trévoux*, March 1708)[7]

[1] . . . With regard to the objection against the Cartesians which he [Leibniz] disowns, I agree that it is clumsy; yet my memory still tells me that I read this objection some years ago in one of the articles with which M. Leibniz has illumined the journal of Paris.[8] Nevertheless, it is quite irrelevant to my system *of the union of the soul with the body* whether M. Leibniz put forward this objection against the Cartesians or not. But I regard his acknowledgement that his *pre-established harmony* is not enough to make a real union between the body and soul as very important.

[2] This union is not, as he claims, a metaphysical idea. The body is really, physically united to the soul, more united than are two perfectly identical clocks. The relation between the movements of the body and the thoughts and feelings of the soul can only ever be seen as a consequence of that union; and although M. Leibniz explains this relation more successfully than the Cartesians, he doesn't at all explain that union, which I attempted to explain by the conjectures of which he did not disapprove.[9] Nevertheless, I do not claim to have hit the target—I have given only conjectures, and not proofs—but I do claim that those who undertake only to give an account of the relation of the movements of the body to the sensations of the soul have not yet entered the competition for which the prize is on offer. . . .

---

[7] 'Réponse du P. Tournemine', *Mémoires pour l'histoire des sciences et des beaux arts*, Mar. 1708, vol. 21, art. 35, pp. 496–8.

[8] In his initial 'New System' article in the *Journal des savants* ('the journal of Paris') Leibniz *does* say as much as that his own system does enable us to 'understand how the soul has its seat in the body by an immediate presence, which is as close as could be' (NS1, § 14), but he does not go so far as to say that the system of occasional causes does not.

[9] i.e. in T1.

INDEX

Académie Royale des Sciences 1 n. 1, 3, 15 n. 44, 28, 39 n. 15, 40 n. 17, 136

Academy/Academics 32, 37, 44, 48, 50 n. 42, 51, 55, 85, 120, 235 n. 31

acatalepsy 235

Acta eruditorum 1, 171

activity, *see* substances as active

Adam 87, 146, 191, 192

agreements, theory of 19, 62 n. 13, 143
  see also concomitance, theory of; correspondence, system of; pre-established harmony theory of

Aiton, E. 10 n. 21, 28 n. 75, 29 n. 78, 66 n. 34, 124 nn. 123, 124

Albert the Great 12, 24

Alexander the Great 176, 223

Almagor, J. 226 n. 1

America 159

analysis 55, 219

angels 82, 84, 94, 109, 114, 122 n. 115, 170, 201

animals 23, 109, 139, 198, 199
  as machines 11, 42, 46, 48, 54, 68, 72–3, 88–9, 99–100, 112, 113, 129, 158
  no birth and death of 14–15, 25, 72–3, 229–30, 231–6, 239, 241, 244
  subject to moral laws 42, 46
  see also souls, animal

animal spirits 51, 179–80, 182, 185–6, 190, 206

Anteus 120–1

apperception 77–8

Aquinas, T. 12 nn. 27, 29, 21, 23, 94, 119, 170 n. 66, 199 n. 42

Arcesilaus 235 n. 31

archees 22

Aristotle 11, 12, 14 n. 17, 15, 21, 23, 24, 31, 55, 68, 84, 85, 111, 127,

170 n. 66, 189 n. 29, 210 n. 18, 230, 234
  see also Scholastic philosophy Schools

Arnauld, A. 2, 3, 7, 10 n. 20, 12 n. 29, 27, 38, 57, 64, 65, 111 n. 68, 116, 125 n. 129, 156

astronomy 20, 47, 211

atoms (and atomism) 11, 12, 14, 16, 23, 24, 36, 66, 85–6, 90–1, 101–2, 108, 109, 112, 114–15, 218, 219, 240, 244
  declination of 90, 112
  material 114, 229, 239, 240, 244
  mathematical 41–2, 45–6, 123, 229
  substantial (formal, metaphysical) 114, 209, 210, 229

Augustine 44, 55, 121, 167

automata 83–4, 89, 90, 92, 93, 95, 96, 97–100, 104, 108–10, 112–13, 144, 158–9, 167–8, 186–7, 207
  bodies as mechanical 13, 53, 99–100, 104, 112, 113, 144, 148, 158, 167, 179, 183–7, 188–9, 190, 206, 224, 230
  souls as spiritual 13, 15, 18–19, 25, 26, 36, 53, 75, 104, 112, 116, 144, 158, 167, 188–9, 190, 206, 208, 224, 230

Baconthorpe, John of 12, 24

Barber, W. H. 1

Bathsheba 184

Bayle, P. 4, 5, 29, 65, 68–132, 134, 135, 137 n. 20, 153, 156, 158, 161, 167, 168, 169, 171, 175–6, 183, 202, 203–4, 207, 220, 224, 226–7, 228, 236, 238, 239, 241, 242, 243

Beauval, H. B. de 3 n. 10, 4, 29 n. 84, 61–7, 68–9, 86 n. 36, 137 n. 20, 226

Berlin 171
Bernier, N. 56, 67, 74
Bernoulli, J. 66 n. 34, 70, 124 n. 123,
    126, 130
Bignon, J.-P. 28, 136
Bodemann, E. 9
body
    action of one on another 192, 199
    action on mind, *see* union of, and
        interaction between, body and
        mind
    nature of 32, 4; *see also* extension
Boineburg, Baron von 3
Borelli, G. A. 170 n. 66
Bossuet, J.-B. 3, 7–9, 10 n. 21,
    21 n. 56, 27, 30 n. 85, 35–6, 38,
    61
Bourignon, A. 125 n. 126
brachistrochrone 66 n. 34
Brown, S. 9 n. 17, 39 n. 13
Brunswick:
    Countess Sophie of 4
    Duke Ernst August of 4
    Duke Johann Friedrich of 3–4
Burnet, Bishop G. 227 n. 4
Burnett, T. 202 n. 1

Cabbalism 85
Caesar, J. 88–91, 98, 102, 112, 214
Carneades 120
Cartesians 2, 3, 27–8, 29, 40, 42, 43,
    49, 58, 67, 74, 81–2, 85, 86, 87,
    89, 92, 94, 99, 100, 107, 112,
    113, 135, 145, 158, 159, 164,
    224, 240, 247, 248, 250, 251
    see also Descartes
Catelan, F. 28
characteristic, universal 126
Cicero 31, 112, 120 n. 110, 128,
    235 n. 31
clocks 42
    analogy of the two 43, 62–3, 73–4,
        76, 82–3, 144, 174, 183, 248–9,
        251
cohesion 66–7
colours 105, 117 n. 97, 141
conatus 33, 39, 101
concomitance, theory of 3, 38, 40,
    42–4, 47, 48, 53, 54, 58, 60
    see also agreements, theory of;
        correspondence, system of; pre-
        estabished harmony, theory of

of direction 51–2, 58, 59, 65, 113,
    200
of force 28, 33, 58, 65
of matter 240
of motion 27–8, 33, 51, 58, 59, 67,
    200
church reunification 7, 29 n. 83
Conti, A.-S. 227 n. 10, 242, 243–4
contingency 3, 25, 26
continuity 59, 66, 122–3, 222
    see also uniformity of nature
continuum, composition of 11, 45
    see also atoms, mathematical
Copernicus 47, 49, 157
Cordemoy, G. de 16, 23
Cornarius 232, 237
correspondence, system of 26
    see also agreements, theory of;
        concomitance, theory of; pre-
        established harmony, theory of
Costabel, P. 28 n. 75
Coste, P. 135 n. 12, 243 n. 62
Cousin 8–9, 35, 38, 40, 58, 59, 127,
    135
created things:
    perfection/imperfection of 15, 26,
        106, 118, 149, 154, 157, 161,
        163, 176, 177, 184, 207, 221
    power of 38, 161, 163–4, 169, 184,
        192, 194, 201
Cudworth, F. 5, 202, 203, 210 n. 18,
    220

Dacier, A. 232, 237
David 184, 191
declination, *see* atoms, declination of
Democritus 14, 16, 85, 90, 99, 129,
    240, 244
Des Billettes, G. F. 3 n. 8, 39 n. 15,
    55–6
Des Bosses, B. 246 n. 2, 250 n. 6
Descartes, R. 1, 7, 8, 16, 17, 23, 30,
    32, 45, 51, 58, 65, 68, 157,
    170 n. 66, 174 n. 14, 176, 200
    his notion of material substance 1,
        2, 7, 16, 23, 27, 30–3, 45 n. 34,
        52, 55, 64, 66, 164; *see also*
        extension
    see also Cartesians
Desgabet, R. 37, 53
desire 102, 106, 194, 198–9, 224
Desmaizeaux, P. 5, 65 n. 31, 71, 226–
    45

Index